WHERE DO IDEAS COME FROM?

I0239860

WHERE DO IDEAS COME FROM?

The Hidden Dimension of Creative Thinking

ITZHAK BAR YONA

LINDISFARNE BOOKS
2010

2010

Lindisfarne Books
an imprint of Anthropsophic Press/SteinerBooks
610 Main Street, Great Barrington, MA 01230
www.steinerbooks.org

Copyright © 2010 by Itzhak Bar Yona. All rights reserved.
No part of this publication may be reproduced, stored in a retrieval system, or transmitted, in any form or by any means, electronic, mechanical, photocopying, recording, or otherwise, without the prior written permission of the publisher.

Translated from Hebrew by Boaz Yachin; revised by Nicky Brown
Some quotations of translated material have been revised.

Design: William Jens Jensen; cover based on original Hebrew edition
Cover image: Layers of Earth's atmosphere as the Sun sets:
by the STS-127 crew on the space shuttle Endeavour (NASA); the inset image: Otto "Glider King" Lilienthal (1848–1896) flying one of his gliders.

Library of Congress Cataloging-in-Publication Data

Yona, Itzhak Bar, 1945–

Where do ideas come from? : the hidden dimension of creative thinking / Itzhak Bar Yona.

p. cm.

Includes bibliographical references.

ISBN 978-1-58420-081-9

1. Creative thinking. I. Title.

BF408.Y656 2010

153.3'5—dc22

2010034878

Contents

Acknowledgments

I wish to offer gratitude to Pol and Noël Pilven, my spiritual teachers in the Fourth Way initiative school; and to Georg Kühlewind, whose insights are woven into the book wherever higher thinking is at stake. I also wish to thank those who worked so hard to see this book through to publication: thanks to Boaz Yachin for his translation from the original Hebrew; to Nicky Brown for her editorial skills in smoothing out the English text; and to the many others without whom publication could not have been realized.

Itzhak Bar Yona

There is a true self working in the background of esoteric reality. Once, when my presence on Earth was still new and young, it used to visit, pausing for a glance and fading out again, leaving an unforgettable trace.

It did so numerous times and still does, not yet situated in the forefront.

My life is woven with unseen threads of mysterious appearing and disappearing: Where does it lead? What is its sense?

The call was heard; internal response made its way to my external existence, and I still did not know where I was going and why.

Sure of my serious intentions I made some efforts: changing my pattern of habits, trying to be present as frequently as I could—and imagined I had made some progress…

Silently whispering from behind, an unspoken Word, so patient, so compassionate, caressed my childish attempts and pushed its way farther, downstream into my body and feelings, infusing an ignorant land with life and hope.

So sweet its murmur, so effective Thy Work; will I ever give up my cravings for personal efforts and apparent achievements?

—I.B.

Introduction

"The beginning of Science is the examination of the truths of the world-force that underlie its apparent workings such as our senses represent them to be; the beginning of philosophy is the examination of principles of things which the senses mistranslate to us; the beginning of spiritual knowledge is the refusal to accept the limitations of the sense-life or to take the visible and sensible as anything more than a phenomenon of the Reality."

—Sri Aurobindo, *The Synthesis of Yoga*

In the late seventies, as I was taking the first steps in my career as a professional inventor, I attended a meeting with my patent attorney and his assistant in which they were arguing about the nature of my first invention. One of them took the position that my idea did not comply with the official demand for the "inventive step" needed for obtaining a patent, while the other claimed that, if such stringent criteria were applied to all inventors' ideas, true innovations would number only in the teens rather than in the thousands of ideas and applications constantly brought forward.

What essentially is an "inventive step" or "inventive novelty"? Is it possible to create anything truly new? After all, most inventors' ideas derive from principles that are already present in nature. The question at the heart of this discussion stayed with me as a seed that gradually grew through the years. Years later, I began to examine this question more fully—what is inventive novelty? At that time, my life was moving in two parallel planes. On the professional level, inventions had become the foremost source of my income and occupied the greater part of my days. At the same time, I was also growing more aware of a path of inner development, one that allowed me to consider the essential questions of existence and to question the meaning of my own life. It is commonly believed that these areas of activity—one scientific and technical and the other spiritual—are completely separate from one another. Yet, I have observed that mutual fertilization of ideas between these two distinct areas takes place naturally and unintentionally. The act of creating in my daily work caused me to become conscious of the activity of creative thinking itself. I began to see how ideas spring forth and how they develop, from their first prototypical application to their physical manifestations. At the same time, the more sensitive tools of awareness that I acquired from my esoteric studies fostered penetrating observation at the moments of creation that were occurring in my professional life. Gradually, I came to understand the conditions that encourage creative activity; which aspects of creative thinking work and which do not, and when one needs an unusual solution to solve a problem. The more I became aware, the larger my circle of observation grew.

I began to realize that investigating the nature of creative thinking could be just as fascinating as my work with the manifestations of that thinking, and I started to look for written material to expand my understanding of the questions at the heart of this subject. I read the life stories of inventors, scientists, and artists, and browsed through material about the development of the creative faculties, yet ended up with nothing deeper than what simple observation reveals.

One of the things I observed is that new ideas flash through us like bolts of lightning; yet as swiftly as they appear, they quickly retreat to a hidden plane of reality not easily accessible to our limited day-to-day awareness. I wondered why this flash of creativity is so short. Why does it disappear so quickly, leaving one feeling surprised and almost powerless? Is it possible for the idea to remain for just another second so that we may hold this power and channel it as we wish?

I also noticed that, shortly after these flashes of inspiration, I tended to be impressed with the resulting idea. I was immediately drawn into thinking about how the idea could be grasped, practically applied, and used to lead to further developments. My attention was clearly given to the fruits of creative thinking, *the results,* rather than to the *process* of creative activity.

This important realization led me to begin nurturing an inner stance opposite to my automatic inclination. I consciously chose to search for a more stable point of view from which I could observe occurrences without being caught up in the urge to apply the ideas immediately.

My efforts began to bear fruit once I started to realize the complexity of the problem I had set for myself. To acquire the inner view I desired, it was not enough simply to make an inner decision; I realized that it would require years of nurturing my inner capacity for observation and would include a complete transformation of all my soul's faculties. I decided that, in order to follow this path, I would use esoteric methods such as those of the Fourth Way school founded by G. I. Gurdjieff, and later the writings of Rudolf Steiner and Sri Aurobindo (see appendix 2).

The path of inner initiation offered by these esoteric teachings is complex. Although the shroud of secrecy that blanketed these paths throughout history has been removed somewhat in the twentieth century, according to my limited experience, few people who read and study these doctrines seem to understand them completely. Why is this? The knowledge enshrined in these doctrines and other esoteric schools is not simply theoretical; rather, it must be practiced if one is to reach a deeper understanding. Those who benefit from the fruits of these esoteric paths find that they have not only gained new knowledge and understanding, but also, and most important, new powers of observation that can shine a brighter light on those questions at the heart of one's inquiry into self-knowledge.

This book is the result of my personal research. However, if I had relied only upon my own powers, the research could not have borne worthy fruit, and this book might never have been published. The reader should, therefore, not be surprised to find the names of humanity's great spiritual teachers and their findings throughout the following chapters. Where my own research is concerned, I have described things simply as they appeared in my own direct experience. When I felt that comments and clarifications from the teachings of the great masters were needed, I tried to quote them verbatim, because it is impossible to discuss creativity without relying on the deep insights found in the unique literature of esoteric philosophy.

This book is intended, first and foremost, for those interested in creativity. Human creative powers are found in all areas of human activity—art, technology, science, and social relations. For example, teachers in our school systems need creativity just as much as artists or inventors do. The proponents of the modern education system prefer that teachers focus on the acquisition of knowledge and skills more than on nurturing creativity because they fail to understand the essence of the creative impulse and the promise it holds. Similarly, when engineers and developers of modern technology focus on innovation itself while completely ignoring themselves as creative human beings, we see the results of the cultural phenomenon of a society that worships the products of technological innovation and neglects the creative ability of human beings. The eventual losers from this kind of thinking are not just the researchers but also the research itself, the engineers and the products they create, and teachers and their pupils. By focusing on the result rather than the process, we devalue not only the creator but also limit the possibilities of what the end result may be.

Therefore, one of the purposes of this work is to probe the deep mystery of human creative drive in relation to two connected questions: How is human creativity intertwined with nature's own creative impulse? And, what is the significance of humanity's personal powers?

The language of this book (which often draws its concepts from deeper knowledge of esoteric philosophy and is somewhat different from the language of technology and the natural sciences) should not discourage the reader who is unfamiliar with its vocabulary. I grew up with a passion and admiration for science and technological innovation, and it is now the focus of my professional life. Therefore, the contents in this book do not ignore this conceptual world. However, to complete the picture of my search into the heart of the meaning of creative thinking I needed new concepts and these have come from my esoteric studies. I have tried to present them in a way that would be accessible to a reader encountering such concepts for the first time. This book then is not meant for the scientific community alone. On the other end of the spectrum, the search for spiritual meaning is very popular these days, and some people believe (mistakenly, in my opinion) that withdrawal from the complexities of everyday life is a necessary condition for creating a meaningful spiritual life, and that transformation of the soul's life is impossible without abstaining from everything smacking of materialism. Some of the chapters in this book focus on such idealism. I have also included clarifications of technical concepts and supplementary appendixes at the end of the book.

This book is organized into three parts. The first raises theoretical questions about human creativity—the place human innovation holds in the universal perspective—and asks whether human beings are capable of creating anything truly new. Further, what is the relationship between the powers of destruction and those of creation in the overall process of evolution? What is the relationship between madness and genius? Between suffering and creativity?

The second part of the book offers practical examples from the inventor's professional world so that the reader can have an idea of how an inventor approaches problems and devises creative solutions. This section also offers suggestions for ways to nurture creative powers. The practices included are meant to exercise the power of imagination by strengthening visual memory, breaking habits of thinking, and more. As the book progressed I realized that I would need to go into the realm of esoteric practice, since developing the creative impulse has much to do with freeing ourselves from the patterns of thought and behavior that constrain the creative power of one's soul, and keep it in a depressed state. In this sense, there is no difference between those who wish to walk the path of esoteric initiation and those who wish to develop their creative skills. I have personally tried every exercise in this book. They are presented here with the sincere wish that the reader may share some of the blessings I have been fortunate enough to enjoy.

In the third part of the book, I present practical examples from my professional world as an inventor, so that the reader can gain some idea of how I approach problems and creative solutions in my work.

I began writing this book by asking questions without knowing where they would lead me. Although I already understood some of these questions from prior reflection and involvement, other answers and the new questions they raised appeared during the process of writing. In this sense, literary activity, which for me is a novelty, became in itself a fine example of creative activity in which pleasure and difficulty walk hand in hand.

Out of deep respect for the teachers of humanity—spiritual messengers whose great contribution to human advancement is rarely understood—I decided to begin each chapter with a quote from their teachings. Readers are encouraged to read them, to the best of their ability, in a meditative state and to allow them to have their blessed effect. Only in this way can one perceive their deepest dimension, which lies beyond the words.

Dear reader, the attention that you are about to give my book is a genuine reality for me and I greatly cherish it; my thanks are yours in advance, as well as my blessing.

PART ONE

CREATIVITY AS A UNIVERSAL FORCE

Chapter 1

Is There Anything Really New?

"Every man should know and believe, that there is a first, primordial and eternal being, and it was He who invented and invents anything in reality, and He is God, praise unto Him."

—Rabbi Haim Luzzatto, *The Way of God*

"There is no new thing under the sun" (Ecclesiastes 1:9). What a deep and mysterious claim! Understood simply, this phrase seems to indicate the complete negation of any chance of renewal. Indeed, there are many examples from nature to prove this point. Thousands of years before the invention of paper, wasps were building their nests according to the same principles by which paper is made in modern industry (fig. 1). Nor can human beings claim credit for first inventing the wheel as an efficient means of transportation. A certain species of beetle (*Scatabaeus Sacer,* fig. 2) packs food into giant balls in order to move them from one place to another. Or, in the case of our body, if we observe the *inner structure of the elbow*[1] (fig. 3), we find in the history of architecture that reinforced concrete structures (fig. 4) used in the beginning of the twentieth century have only begun to approximate the skeleton's *constructive efficiency.*[2] In the construction of buildings

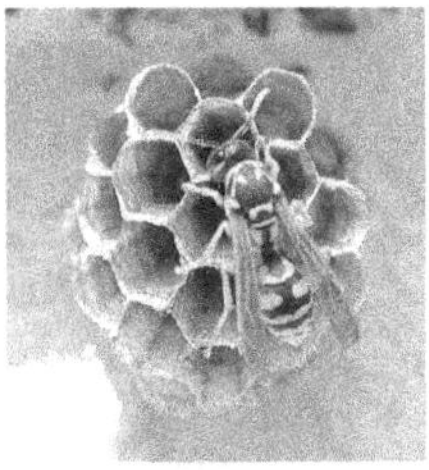

1

2

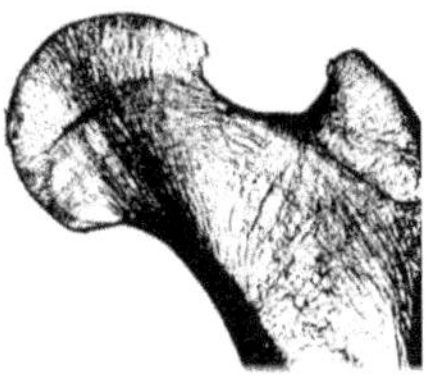

3

1 This is the sinovial joint connecting the arm and forearm.

2 Constructive efficiency is determined by the ratio between the quantity of matter and the desired constructive result. In the structure shown in fig. 4, the constructive result is the size of span that the structure can bear without using additional pillars. Instead of spreading the effort all over the ceiling (fig. 5), it was concentrated on the ribs only, and the superfluous mass was removed. This created a lighter ceiling over a larger span. In the bone's inner structure, force is concentrated on inner ribs, while the bone's inner space remains void. This allows for lighter bones, while maintaining their strength and ability to support the body.

4

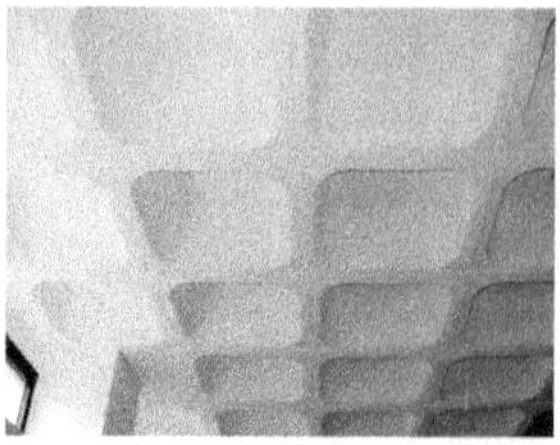
5

6

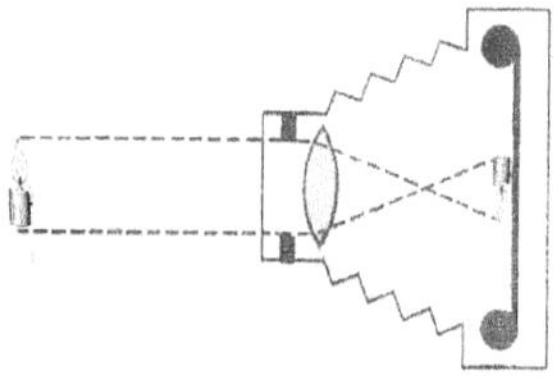
7

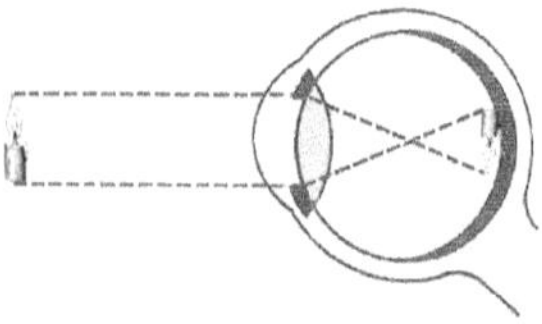
8

this is accomplished using reinforcement ribs made of pre-stressed concrete so that a larger span can be created using a minimum of material.

Further examples of the point made in Ecclesiastes that there is nothing new under the sun point to inventors like Samuel Brown, the engineer who first developed the principle of a bridge hanging on steel cables. He was reportedly inspired after watching a spider spin its web[3] in the corner of his room. Leonardo da Vinci is said to have borrowed the idea for tanks from observing the defensive nature of turtle shells.

Our most complex cameras still utilize the principle of *camera obscura* (fig. 7), borrowed from the mechanics of the human eye (fig. 8). Halfway through the twentieth century, jet engines (fig. 9) have only recently replaced the older propellers in fighter plane, while squid (fig. 10) have long propelled themselves through water using exactly the same principle, ejecting strong jets of water to their rear. And what about radar? Bats and dolphins have always used sound to identify external objects with great accuracy.

In addition to engineering principles, nature's wisdom exceeds that of human beings in the field of medicine as well. Animals, for example, use antiseptics in original ways. Starlings have a habit of searching for anthills and then brushing the ants between their feathers. These ants are in fact miniature laboratories of formic acid, which has antiseptic and pain-subduing qualities. The starlings use this in reaction to the ticks that reside in their feathers.

Not only starlings use antiseptics. A phenomenon observed among capuchin monkeys is that

3 The cobwebs of spiders are incredibly strong (fig. 6). Though made of organic materials, they are stronger than steel cables of the same diameter. Recently, a fabric manufactured from cobwebs showed exceptional strength. This unusual fact remains unexplained.

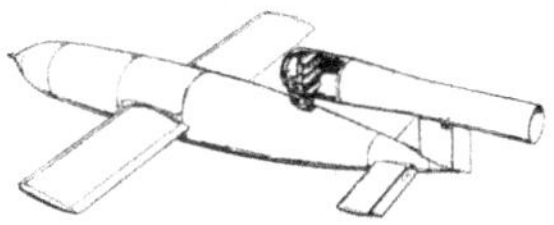
9

10

they pick branches and whip themselves like ascetics. Although monkeys are known to be imitators, it is highly improbable that they learned this habit from observing some human martyr monks. Furthermore, they are particular about the plants they use. Peppers are their favorites because of the concentrated juices they release when thrashed.

Among indigenous people, the Navajo have a custom of inhaling the vapors of the Usha plant to cure inflammations and diseases. When asked where they received this knowledge, they said they learned it from the bears that, when injured, pick Usha leaves and rub them against their wounds.

Monkeys also preceded humans in the use of antiseptics. In the Amazon rain forest, monkeys are often infected with parasites that cause diarrhea and vomiting. They have been observed swallowing as many as a hundred leaves at a time, folding each three or four times. Their stomach cannot handle the condensed mass and the hairy clump of leaves is pushed like a piston along their guts, pulling with it the parasites caught in the hairs.

Given all these examples, is it possible that humanity has exhausted the pool of ideas offered by nature? With the most recent developments in modern technology, partially based on ideas borrowed from the animal and plant kingdoms, it would seem that the answer is "no." For example, when bees or ants swarm, self-interest disappears while the whole community's interest takes precedence; a single ant may sacrifice its life to save the swarm, and when it can no longer fulfill that function, another ant takes its place, keeping the system whole. Military strategists today are already developing such a technique, called "ant-swarm technology," for the battlefield of the future. This technology is based on an array of small robots that, communicating by radio, can carry out missions that a single unit could not normally accomplish. Flying vessels less than two inches long are also being developed to carry out assault or surveillance missions behind enemy lines, not unlike a swarm of bees. The world of insects has a constant appeal to designers, inspiring countless inventions of which, unfortunately, only a small part are used to good ends. Either way, we are again confronted with this question as we begin: Is there anything new under the sun? Is our creative force limited to more sophisticated uses of principles already found in nature, or do we have the ability to bring something truly new to light? Before we can discuss this question thoroughly, we will examine the very nature of the way human beings think. We will examine the creative forces that abound in the world of concepts and observe some aspects of their usefulness and limitations. Later, I will present some practical examples that will demonstrate what is described theoretically in this section.

CHAPTER 2

CREATIVE THINKING

"An opening into this higher mind is usually accompanied by silence of the ordinary mental thought. Our thoughts are not really created within ourselves independently in the small narrow thinking machine we call our mind; in fact, they come to us from a vast mental space or ether, as mind-waves or waves of mind-force that carry a significance which takes shape in our personal mind or as thought-formations ready-made, which we adopt and call ours. Our outer mind is blind to this Nature; but by the awakening of the inner mind we can become aware of it."

—SRI AUROBINDO, *The Synthesis of Yoga*

What a complex world is constituted by human thinking activity! It includes simple associative activity; the ability to make analyses within the world of concepts; to gather several concepts into a new whole; or to construct a logical structure of deductions or to reach insights. And while some of those insights derive from our synthesis of the concepts we know, there are some that surprisingly draw only to a limited degree upon this structure of deductions.

Human intelligence is a riddle whose limits grow broader and deeper with the growth of human civilization. The boundaries of scientific thought, which we once believed to be clear and well defined, now seem to have been shaken. For example, scientists at the forefront of scientific research are beginning to recognize the limitations of human thought and our inability to completely penetrate the riddle of our existence, the puzzle of the boundaries of knowledge, or the very secret of life itself. Research into thought itself cannot deduce the origin of thought or its connection with the laws it observes in nature, with the principles of mathematics, or even with the world of art. The best example of this concept is to consider the difference between the functions of a computer and the way in which thinking human beings operate.

The creative element of thought is still a mystery. If the process of our thinking is merely a logical process wherein facts are gathered and conclusions reached, the process of creativity would be simple, and, in fact, we would not be able to point out any significant difference between human thought and the output of a computer. But things are not that simple. Unlike computers, we can create results that do not derive directly from the database of any given problem. The fact that we can recognize and define a problem reflects an intelligence that is not limited to the mechanical level. Our mental considerations can include shades of will and emotion, aspects of our thinking that are not mechanical, and it is not always possible for us to tell where thought ends and emotional intelligence begins. No computer is able to use will and emotion, no matter the level and degree of sophistication of its calculating power.

The truth is that human thinking activity does not rely solely on the computation ability of neurons, as some believe, but rather on multidimensional planes in which our emotional life and our will have an organic role. Furthermore, our intelligence could not exist as it does now without the power of imagination, which is a unique component of our being. Imagination has an important role in many functions of our intellect—in creating concepts and mental images; in creating analogies intertwined in the world of phenomena; in inspiring technological and artistic creation; and in higher revelations, such as the prophetic visions found in the holy scriptures. Our reasoning world is complex and bountiful in colors and dimensions; it seems we will never be able to understand it fully.

The complexity of human wisdom and the mystery that so inspires our awe should not lead us to let the mystery slide beyond our grasp. In conjunction with the mystery of human consciousness, there is an inner impulse that calls on us to observe the patterns of thought —its many different hues and shades, the laws it follows—and to pursue the subject of our present discussion, creative thinking.

How can we investigate the nature of thought if thought itself is the instrument of our investigation? Is it possible to lift our mind out of its own thought activity, as though pulling ourselves along by the top of our own head? This would be impossible if our mental capacity were limited simply to the brain's activity, as some researchers in the natural sciences seem to believe. Thinking activity, as observation reveals, is not limited to the physical apparatus inside one's skull. Indeed, even a superficial examination shows that thinking activity transcends the physical.

How can we believe that thinking is limited to the brain's activity when we consider the moments of inspiration described by talented artists? What are those flashes of enlightenment that strike great inventors and scientists, making them aware of something they had not seen before? Did this intelligent process take place inside their skulls? We are, indeed, inclined to frown and knot our brows when trying to solve an urgent problem, sensing that the effort has something to do with the head area. Yet in moments of inspiration, we are surprised to discover that this understanding finds its way to our mind with no effort at all, coming not from our head but from some mysterious reality that is not limited to the physical body.

In this example, direct experience of intuition already points to an area of thinking activity that does not necessarily have to do with the brain. We can add another experience to this example—the special moments we experience in the deep peace of nature or, more surprising, amid social turmoil as we suddenly become aware of our presence in the moment, feeling a sensation of quiet, searching alertness and self-awareness. Such moments bring about deep, penetrating soul-searching. When these moments occur, we sometimes see a broad panorama of our past life and, at other times, a clear, unprejudiced awareness of the present situation. This new vision is directed by its own volition and without need for our consent, obeying a law we do not understand, as if it abides by a different set of rules.

Through such experiences, we become aware of a unique quality of our intelligence—the ability of our own activity to divide itself into two distinct parts: routine, constant thinking that organizes and executes, and, beside it, an observing or witnessing activity, broader than the first. This latter activity envelops and contains the first one within a greater field of consciousness. It is this special ability of our intelligence to witness that allows us to research the patterns of thought, their various aspects, and the fields in which they operate. At the same time, it is this ability that allows us to discover a new, deeper mystery that we did not have access to before. We may therefore turn to the field of our thinking world and take a closer look at every aspect of it without destroying the sense of the greater mystery that vibrates within us.

The area of activity that we can immediately observe is associative thinking, which runs on ceaselessly, beyond our control, with no intention or aim. It is a stream of mental activity giving rise to emotional reactions that create further associations, and so on. Can this activity even be called thinking? The chain of automatic activity seems to be set in patterns that are associatively connected to each other through links that have been embedded in us over the years. As soon as we encounter a new stimulus, a conditioned response arises, at times a memory, at times a tendency to connect the stimulus with similar experiences. An urge to act may arise, or a desire for more stimuli. This process goes on and on throughout our waking life. In this case, it is hard to discern the touch of awareness or a guiding hand as part of our thinking process. The word *thinking* seems insufficient to describe this activity in our life, and if we spend the majority of our time in this type of thinking we must accept the proposition that most of our waking life is occupied more by daydreaming than by active initiative.

Nonetheless, reason arises at once from its reverie when presented with a problem or task. Confronting a problem—not necessarily a complicated "Sherlock Holmes" kind of problem, but even a simple situation that requires more than inattentive daydreaming—we immediately find the power to focus our thought more intensely. In other words, we perceive the structure that arises from the problem's data and deduce the required course of action. Analytic and deductive thought cannot happen in a completely mechanical fashion; they require active involvement by a thinking subject who recruits them to carry out the task. Yet, not even this would be possible were it not for the cohesive world of concepts—the paradigms we operate from that are based on solid inner laws.

We shall discuss this world of concepts in more depth later. However, for now we can say that this conceptual world, the world of our paradigms, appears whole and unified in us as adults. The process of its crystallization was completed in our childhood, and by the time we are adults our inner world contains a complex pattern of "finished" concepts. Since this part of our childhood is no longer as vivid in our consciousness as it once was, it is difficult for us to examine, years later, how this finished world of concepts developed and became a basis of our thought world. Because of this "finished" quality of mental concepts, we tend to associate them with the brain's activity, sometimes called the human mind. In other words, we do not actively think about it consciously.

We shall now consider those flashes of inspiration that seem to come from another world and last but a fraction of a second, yet provide fresh insights and dramatically affect our lives. Such flashes come with no warning, and they are so brief that we regard them at times with awe and at other times with disbelief. We perceive them as something less personal than the usual course of our associative thoughts. Are we right to be surprised by this gift from a reality unknown to our normal consciousness? Experts in the field of inventive thinking, such as Peretz Manor, regard these flashes as "an unreliable phenomenon, upon which no solid conclusions may be based."[1]

1 See, for example, an overview of Systematic Inventive Thinking (SIT) on the Internet at www.sitsite.com. SIT is based on the work of Genrich Altschuller.

We shall return to this subject later when discussing different approaches to the world of creative thinking, comparing the approach common in the natural sciences with that found in the sources of esoteric knowledge.

I have used the word *gift* to describe these flashes of thinking, since they truly radiate from a source of intelligence not at our command—that is, not from the persona we know in our daily lives as the thinking subject, the one who dictates what and when to think. The reality from which these flashes of thinking come is not limited to the narrow area of our external being; instead it coincides with a plane of wisdom that is truly universal.

Essential understandings do not always reveal themselves through flashes of inspiration. At times, they seem to arise from the inner depths of one's soul. Though the way they materialize in our awareness may differ, in both cases we experience a sensation of intimate connection to a higher plane, one beyond the scope of subjective human consciousness. Why is it so seldom that this plane's activity reaches our awareness? Could it be that this plane awakes to life only occasionally, while at other times is in retreat? Or does it always exist, whereas it is our awareness that habitually hides behind walls of forgetfulness?

We will return to these questions when we discuss the hierarchic structure that typifies our reasoning activity as thinking beings. This will make it easier for us to characterize the field of human creativity and its limits; and to understand how this creativity relates to universal creative reality in which we are the Maker's agents, placed on earthly planes to fulfill a meaningful task. For the purposes of this discussion, the word *intuition* will be used to describe the penetration of universal wisdom into the boundaries of individual consciousness, even though normally the use of this word in spiritual sciences denotes a higher level of consciousness.

What is the source of the term *spiritual science?* Science is precise and logical. Its findings can be measured or weighed and the data is accessible to anyone who performs the experiment under exactly the same conditions. What does this have to do with mystical revelations, which few people are privileged to experience and which cannot be repeated in a verifiable way? If this wisdom is indeed esoteric (hidden and secret), how can we trust the findings that are either encoded or sometimes given by hints? If such knowledge is truly meant for the betterment of humankind, why is it hidden?

These are important questions indeed, and we must treat them with respect. Rudolf Steiner, who coined the term *spiritual science,* considered the knowledge he brought humanity to be of a vast array in which regularity and scientific precision are no less prevalent than in the natural sciences.

Gurdjieff, founder of the Fourth Way school, presented a conceptual world that is adopted mostly from materialistic conceptions. His hydrogen table, the reverberation levels of materials, the law of the octave and other laws are phrased with scientific precision in the spirit of the age. Yet, is this enough to justify the term *science?*

Esoteric knowledge is mostly unique, in that it is received through tools of perception different from those we use in daily life. The expanded awareness developed through esoteric practice can interrelate with planes of existence not accessible to daily awareness. Does this indicate that such experiments have a vague, mystical character? It is, in fact, quite the contrary; such experiments are based on thinking that acts at higher levels of awareness and is incredibly lucid and sober, more so than the rational thinking we use to solve daily problems. The spiritual researcher finds facts through direct experience whose validity is greater than that derived from sensory-based thinking.

The natural sciences strive for objectivity; an experiment's reliability and credibility will be enhanced the more researchers can separate themselves from the objects they observe. An experiment in which the researcher is involved emotionally or otherwise is considered unreliable. Moreover, while this criterion has admittedly lessened since the birth of quantum mechanics and since the observer has become part of the game, the spirit of this attitude is still deeply entrenched within the minds of researchers of the macrocosmic world.

In spiritual-scientific research, on the other hand, there is no separation between researcher and research matter. The researcher, the laboratory, and the facts under investigation are one united field, lit by divine consciousness. The subjective boundaries of the researcher gradually melt away, and the planes of existence revealed are not something separate but a continuum, a unitary whole of which the researcher is also a part.

Spiritual science does not reject the demand by science for repetition and for the findings to be identical through additional inquiries conducted under the same conditions. The main difficulty arises in bringing the conventional researcher into the same condition in which the spiritual researcher made the original findings, since this condition is about the transformation of one's entire being. Clearly, one who remains within ordinary, limited consciousness cannot verify the findings of suprasensory spiritual science; yet those who read the unique literature of this tradition can feel an inner sense of credibility. Many people report a sense that the inner knowledge found in esoteric literature existed within their souls well before reading the texts. According to their testimony, the knowledge and the expression of that knowledge simply awakened what had always been waiting within the depths of their soul.

Esoteric knowledge, or at least a great part of it, is not hidden at all. According to modern spiritual messengers, the period when this divine knowledge was kept secret has come to an end. If this knowledge is not easily available to modern readers, it is not because it has been withheld intentionally, but because it requires an effort to reach the inner depth of such wisdom. Among other things, esoteric material is meant to transform the reader's thinking. It is not aimed toward an intellect that packs in organized bundles of lifeless information; it is itself a means to stimulate hidden skills that students do not yet have at their disposal. In Gurdjieff's writings, information is not given in a way that is accessible to ordinary thinking and is often intentionally coded; yet students should find the key to understanding within their own experience when the moment is right. Until then, they are asked only to exercise their intellectual muscles as much as possible through experiment and error until they can reach the depth of knowledge.

I have tried to characterize briefly the relation between esoteric knowledge and the knowledge available to the natural sciences of today. One detects a tone of criticism toward the scientific research within this book whenever I compare these two ways of knowing; perhaps such skepticism is useful if it is framed properly.

There is no doubt that Western scientific research is guided by a deep impulse to understand the world and ourselves within it, and there is still good reason to observe research methods—that is, the tools and systems used in the various scientific disciplines. As noted, spiritual research deals with observing the reality underpinning the phenomenal world directly, and meditative research enables the researcher to make an immediate investigation of reality through direct contact. One experiences things and knows them. In the Hassidic path of initiation, there is a saying: "I knew him; I became him," indicating the special nature of divine knowledge. One does not acquire such knowledge without becoming one with the object of inquiry, becoming part of it. There is a rule within the divine path of inquiry that, in order to know the object of inquiry, one must vibrate at the same frequency that it does. This experience includes all of the soul's faculties, rather than just *thinking* as a separate faculty; and, when it is revealed, it requires no circumstantial evidence, since it qualifies itself.

As it advances toward an understanding of the secrets of the universe, natural-scientific research sets a careful foot down, pulls it back, and then sets it down again on a different spot. It sends a probing ray of light into a hidden world that refuses to yield its secrets. Spiritual science goes toward the light itself. The ray of light sent back from an unknown existence supports our own progress as researchers, calling on us to reveal our oneness with the universe. Natural scientists, seeking to know the secrets of the universe, base their investigation on sensory information, while moving gradually by theorizing and testing those theories and by developing and using various tools of measurement. Because normal awareness relies on sensory input, its database is limited to the physical world; each theory that scientists raise is vulnerable to the next.

It is a fact that quantum mechanics is not accepted by many modern physicists, despite its great reliability in predicting experimental results on a microscopic scale. In fact, even some of its developers think it is far from ideal for describing the workings of the universe. The scientific community is sharply divided over most theories that try to "understand God's thoughts," as scientists call it. The timeless debate between Niels Bohr, with his theory of probability, and Albert Einstein's rejection of it is just one well-known example of the arguments that can arise between two leading scientists when one claims to hold the theory that unlocks our understanding of all reality, and the other dismisses it as just so much nonsense. Einstein's oft-quoted comment was "I, at any rate, am convinced that He [God] does not throw dice." Regardless of which one is right, the very fact that such sharp debates can occur between scientists at the forefront of their field tells us something about the nature of the theories and the way they are developed.

What, then, are the conclusions of scientists at the forefront when it comes to the secrets of the universe? I am no expert in modern astrophysics, but from my reading of relevant materials I can identify a thinking process something as follows. First, it is assumed that light behaves at least partly according to the rules of wave theory. Accordingly, we can assume that the Doppler effect, relating to the change in frequency of moving bodies should apply to light, as well. When we examine the spectrum of the light that comes to us across space, physicists find that there are patterns in it that are similar to the elements of our own planet, except that there is a shift toward red. According to the theories, when light reaches us, it is slightly different in the case of a moving source than if the distance between its source and us were to remain unchanged. This matter of color then becomes one of the tools for calculating the speed at which light sources move away from us, and this leads to hypotheses about the possible expansion of the universe, its age, and its birth from a single point in the so-called Big Bang. Though this may be a somewhat simplified description of conjunctures and may not be entirely accurate, it does reflect the scientific way of thinking and allows us to see the weaknesses that accumulate at every junction on the path of theories and deductions, until the theory at the end of this process looks like it, too, is headed toward a big bang.

Scientific research makes liberal use of mathematical equations provided by talented mathematicians; nevertheless, it seems that a considerable number of the cosmological theories presented recently derive solely from an analysis of mathematical equations that handle gravity, bent space, and the relativity of time and space.

It is true that many of the phenomena of the material world can be expressed properly and accurately through mathematics; this is convincingly authenticated by the numerous achievements of modern technology. Yet the world is more than just mineral masses coming together on microscopic or galactic scales. Mathematical equations cannot describe the life forces that resonate in the great creation we find every morning when we open our eyes. The deep mystery of consciousness cannot be explained through complex calculations of nervous systems, nor can the origin of our emotional life be understood through chemical analysis of glandular excretions and reactions.

Physicists search for a simple, elegant model that can be expressed through simple equations to explain the infinite variety we see around us. Albert Einstein best expressed this attitude when he said, "All physical theories, their mathematical expressions apart, ought to lend themselves to so simple a description that even a child could understand them." Still, scientific theories chase one another, at one point describing reality using atomic theory, then using quantum mechanics. At another point invoking deterministic Newtonian laws, then by applying statistical principles under uncertainty principles. At yet another point employing relativity theory, and then using the new string theory. The "theory of everything" that everyone looks for—that is, the theory that would bind all universal laws into a single, cohesive rule—does not seem to lie at the doorstep of scientific research. Is it not strange that spiritual messengers discovered such a unified theory thousands of years before modern physics?

For example, "$E = mc^2$" expresses the idea that energy and physical matter are initially the same entity. The ancient text of the Upanishads expressed this idea almost five thousand years ago. Heisenberg's findings about how the electron sometimes appears as a wave and sometimes as a massive particle strictly corresponds to the ancient teaching of the Fourth Way, which describes the universe as a mass of vibrating entities, self-transforming from one plane of existence to another that is higher or lower.

Using the materialistic approach, scientists have tried to understand the secrets of the universe through thorough investigation of the presumed universal building blocks. Scientists believe that by discovering the fundamental building block they can assemble a perfect model of all reality. Spiritual science presents the opposite approach; it starts with overall unity and then descends to the investigation of details derived from that unity. According to spiritual science, it is impossible to understand the details when they are disconnected from their original unity.

This essential characterization leads us to another deep, essential difference between the two fields of research. The natural sciences look for regularity in a one-dimensional environment perceived through the senses. In spiritual science, we discover the existence of additional planes of existence that mutually permeate one another. According to esoteric wisdom, reality spreads not just through the infinite spaces of the visible dimension, but also, and even more, into the depths of a vertical dimension—a Jacob's ladder whose base is in the world of the senses while its top rises into the world of spirit. According to this approach, the materialized world is no more than a coalescing, or condensation, of the spiritual essence of its existence; this essence vitalizes the world toward a broader evolution of its hidden possibilities.

Until the appearance of the strange phenomena in subatomic research that led to the creation of quantum mechanics, five classic qualities were required of scientific method: visibility, causality, locality, self-identity, and objectivity. Because scientific investigation is essentially one-dimensional—that is, ignoring the existence of higher planes of activity not revealed to the senses—the foundations of modern physical research were shaken by the appearance of strange phenomena, since subatomic phenomena completely contradicted the classic assumptions. It was discovered that reality's tiny building blocks behave at times as particles and at other times as waves, and, further, that two particles fired at the same target each influences the behavior of the other. It was also discovered that the behavior of a single particle cannot be predicted; only the whole can be predicted, and then only statistically. Even more shocking, it was also found that the observing researcher influences the very results of the experiment.

One by one, the classic criteria were contradicted; causality was shaken, locality dropped, and even self-identity was lost forever.

Spiritual science, on the other hand, never recognized those five standards. It was never based on the demand for visibility or sensory perception.

Spiritual science does not seek the self-identity of objects in the sensory world; it finds causes in a higher world, where self-identity can be found if it exists. For example, regarding the behavior of schools of fish, beehives, or flocks of birds, it is noted that they respond to the demands of the moment as one body. Spiritual science does not view a single fish as having self-identity; it points toward a kind of "group self" that determines the school's behavior from a higher plane of existence.

The latest subatomic research, which reveals that a beam of electrons influences the behavior of a single electron, would not have surprised researchers had they been familiar with the principles of spiritual science. The mysterious appearance and disappearance of particles would not be seen as such if researchers had been familiar with the ancient esoteric idea that passage between different planes of existence is possible. In fact, esoteric wisdom has long been familiar with the principles evoked in Albert Einstein's revolutionary statement about the duality of matter and energy.

Reality's quantum behavior is a new discovery for the natural sciences, yet it stands at the center of esoteric traditions such as Kabbalah and the cosmology of the Fourth Way. The discontinuous nature of processes is a profound principle that is broadly discussed in theories that identify cosmic vibration as the originator of universal order, while phrasing its laws through concepts. This is a field of infinite depth that could expand greatly and enrich scientific research, if only natural scientists had ears to hear.

Is spiritual science interested only in matters of the spirit? Does it consider higher worlds to be its sole area of interest? Not at all; spiritual science also involves itself with the physical reality revealed to our senses. Yet, in doing so, it does not limit itself to the strictly material aspect but examines the whole—the physical object and its roots, which lie in etheric or spiritual planes. This is why it can also shine new light into some shadowy corners in areas being studied by physics and medicine. For example:

- According to current scientific research, the heart, a highly efficient "pump" that works constantly through our decades of existence, makes blood flow through our highly-branched blood system. A simple pressure analysis shows that no mechanical pump could push liquid through such a complex system, which includes tens of kilometers of microscopic capillaries; any planner who specializes in liquid mechanics will attest to this. Dr. Rudolf Steiner pointed to a sheath of etheric forces as being responsible for making the blood flow through the thousands of minute capillaries in our body. This miraculous sheath of unseen forces bolsters our body in its struggle against the forces that threaten its regular activity and, as noted, it also has to do with the functions of memory and thinking.

- Our motions are governed by a double nervous system: the proprioceptive system, which provides the brain with spatial information about our organs; and the motor system, which transfers the brain's orders, to the muscles that move our organs. Schematically, this is how science sees the functioning of the nervous system. Anthroposophic science claims that the nervous system does not send orders to the organs at all; rather, it sends spatial and sensory information from the organs to the entity that makes them work. The nervous system is first and foremost an aid to human consciousness, providing an overall picture of the moving organ. The motivating force is supplied by our will forces, which, despite their great importance, are not at all known to science because mechanistic and analytical tools are used to research them.
- Thinking occurs in the brain. Electric currents run through nerve cells, process the information received by the brain, and allow it to create thoughts. This is how most brain research theories see things. Sri Aurobindo's Integral Yoga or Steiner's spiritual science see the brain as an aid, a reflecting tool for human consciousness. The brain does not create insights and thoughts. Human thinking acts in the subtler layers, which thread the human body, and are constantly moving around and inside it. Deep thoughts and creative intuitions come from the intelligent spaces of universal reality.

Spiritual science has much to tell the thirsty human soul, even in the fields of physiology and medicine. Its tools of research go to hidden areas where even the most powerful microscopes are useless.

The evolution and history of humankind are fascinating fields for science, which investigates them using archaeological means and historic documents. The age of artifacts is discovered through various methods, such as examining radioactive elements and mathematically calculating the loss of radiating mass. Spiritual science derives its findings from a historical document not created by humans at all. According to the spiritual messengers, reality is imbued with "etheric" substance, which like a cosmic memory preserves a record of everything that happens on our planet, including the changes in the planet itself. Spiritual messengers point to this great cosmic ether as a source for the tremendous information it gives us about human history, human evolution, and the evolution of the planet. Humanity's prehistoric way of life before the invention of reading and writing is described in amazing detail in the writings of spiritual messengers; they describe the ancient civilization of the Rishis, which left no physical traces; the civilization of Atlantis that preceded us and was lost in the sea; and even more ancient civilizations, such as the Lemurian period, which left only old folk tales to attest to its existence.

If these lines make some readers smile, such skepticism can be attributed to the enormous gap between the findings of spiritual science and the scientific world of concepts on which we were raised and in which our education is so firmly rooted. If criticism here is aimed at the attitude of the scientific establishment, it is directed only at its stubborn refusal to draw on the ideas of spiritual science revealed to Western culture since the beginning of the twentieth century. Yet, esoteric wisdom enters human consciousness even without our awareness. Some inspired scientists have been exposed to divine knowledge, which until recently was limited to narrow circles of the ancient mysteries and the schools of the esoteric path. Meetings and fruitful conversations took place between David Bohm and Jiddu Krishnamurti, between Einstein and Rabindranath Tagore. Evidence of those conversations can be found in Einstein's many sayings in favor of the existence of divinity, and in Bohm's holistic approach to the many pieces of the puzzle of reality that modern physics investigates.

Esoteric knowledge is destined to give humanity back the inner warmth and the sense of existential meaning it has lost. In ancient times the cultural split was not as deep as it is today. Scientists of the past were priests, neophytes, and Rishis who held all-encompassing knowledge about the nature of our being and our soul. The sharp dichotomy between science, religion, and philosophy would not have been possible in the past. The goals of modern civilization should include a unified human knowledge with a wide perspective, presenting scientific research, the humanities, and art as part of an overall cultural mosaic, imbued by the light of the spirit.

It seems, then, that human intelligence actively operates between two poles—a mental pole relying on the physical brain and the intuitive pole deriving from universal intelligence that uses the individual as a channel of expression. What happens between those two poles that seem so distant from each other? It is human reasoning that is capable of moving back and forth between the two different planes of thought, enriching the world of mental concepts with the fragrance of greater cosmic consciousness, which pulls the whole of reality and the human being into a single continuum.

Like creators in other areas, inventors discover the objects that they manifest in the earthly world, defining them through an array of concepts and logical connections. Inventors are inclined to search for the solution on this level; when no solution is found, the problem's data is metamorphosed to a higher level, where thinking is no longer concerned with the concrete forms that compose the problem, but rather with a special category of archetypal principles, of which the given problem is a specific example. At the level of the archetypal principle, thinking parallels the intuitive plane, and can therefore transport the problem's data to this superior plane, where it is further processed. The results of this process will strike the inventor as a flash of enlightenment at a time when least expected, perhaps while one is taking a walk or lying in bed.

It is this power of active reasoning that pulls the two planes, the mental and intuitive, into a mutually inspiring encounter that creates new solutions in the earthly plane of defined concrete shapes and forms. Active creative reasoning is valuable because it can merge with a multidimensional cosmic intelligence to inspire creativity in the earthly realm of matter and power.

Nature's abundant creation realizes a world that is rich with shapes and colors. Thanks to the unique process I have outlined, human beings can continue the general universal process of creation and imbue it with a new quality, bringing it to new planes beyond the reach of nature's creativity. Later we shall again examine the relationship between human creation and general creation from the special viewpoint of the conceptual world.

Chapter 3

The World of Concepts

"Concepts and ideas arise through thinking. Words cannot say what a concept is. Words can only make us notice that we have concepts. When we see a tree, our thinking reacts to our observation, a conceptual counterpart joins the object, and we consider the object and the conceptual counterpart as belonging together. When the object disappears from our field of observation, only the conceptual counterpart remains. The latter is the concept of the object. The wider our experiences extend, the greater the sum of our concepts. But the concepts by no means stand apart from one another. They combine into a lawful whole."

—Rudolf Steiner, *Intuitive Thinking as a Spiritual Path*

The human world of ideas is perceived by many to be a unique creation of the human mind. Yet this seemingly reasonable opinion is challenged when the internal regulation of this system of thinking is examined and unexplained parallels are found to exist between this supposedly abstract world of thinking and the world of phenomena revealed by our senses.

1

2

The most fascinating example is what is commonly known as the *Golden Mean,* an irrational number that holds a unique position in the world of phenomena. This special proportion, found in nature, can be seen in the arrangement of leaves around the stalk in some plants, in the spiral shape of a sunflower (fig. 1)[1] or daisy, a nautilus shell (fig. 2), the

1 Examining the arrangement of the poppy blossom, we find that it maintains the same regularity as the nautilus shell. The creature living in the shell has no notion of geometry, of course; it changes its house every year, moving from the old chamber to a larger one, according to its rate of growth. Since this rate is linear, cells relate to one another in a geometric progression that can be shown graphically.

3

4

5

whorl of a hurricane (fig. 3), or the structure of the galaxy Messier 81 (fig. 4). These proportions are paralleled in the field of mathematics—in a Fibonacci series; in the logarithmic spiral based on the genomic growth of the Golden Mean; in the geometric shapes of a pentagon or a star contained in a circle. This mysterious factor is the number called *phi* (not to be confused with *pi*, which has to do with the ratio of the circle's diameter to its radius). This magical number is found using the equation $X^2-X-1=0$. Solving this equation results in two possible approximate values: 1.61803398875 and 0.618. Both represent the numeric proportions of the Golden Mean.

In geometry, if you divide a given segment into two parts, A and B, the whole segment should relate to A in the same way that A relates to B. Once it is calculated we find that this ratio is equal to approximately 1.618. We can also construct a rectangle whose sides relate to each other in the magic ratio *phi*. We find this ratio in architecture and art from the ancient periods of our history, and recognize that it creates a feeling of harmony or a sense of inner beauty. These facts hint that what lies behind this number is not mere coincidence, but an expression of an inner regularity underlying the structures seen in nature that at the same time lies at the base of the consciousness of the human being.

Using the proportions of the Golden Mean, we can geometrically build the spiral found in the shell of the nautilus crab, in the spiral structure of the Andromeda galaxy, and in other spiral phenomena. Gyorgy Doczi's original work, *The Power of Limits,* presents a wonderful analytical description of geometric laws underlying the forms and shapes we encounter in nature, as do the works of those inspired by him—Mario Livio (*The Golden Ratio*) and others.

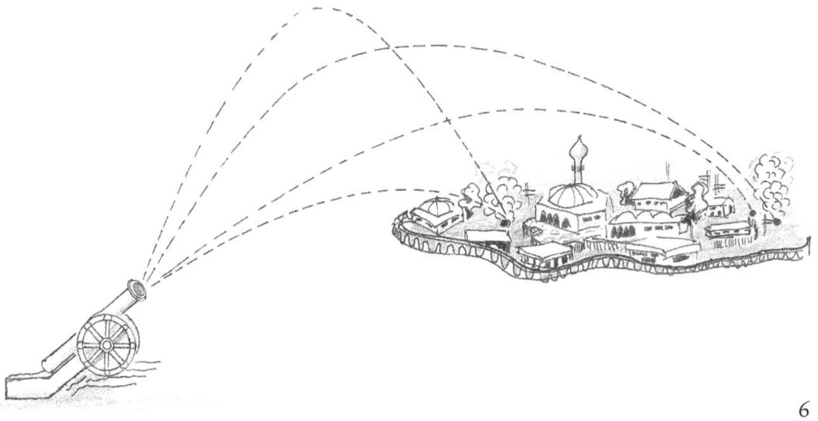

6

Another example can be found in precise geometric laws that are manifested in the world of mineral crystals, a world that we conceive as unanimated. In quartz crystals such as (fig. 5), dioptase, aragonite, or rhodochrosite, we can see highly polished planar areas so precise that they appear as though designed and constructed by human machinery.

This thought-provoking parallel between the world of phenomena and the world of mathematics, which is part of the world of concepts and ideas, can also be seen in the laws of symmetry, in parabolic trajectories of projectiles[2] (fig. 6), and in many other natural phenomena. Granted, the human world of concepts, of which mathematics is a part, is a creation of the human mind, so how do we explain the presence of natural laws that do not originate with thinking human beings?

There must be a bridge between the world of human thinking and that of natural phenomena, since natural laws are not compatible with the common opinion that concepts are a coincidental creation of the thinking human being. How are concepts created? It is commonly believed that a person looks at a series of objects and recognizes a common attribute. We see a tree trunk dividing into many branches and the branches dividing into long, thin, green leaves, and we name the whole thing a "pine tree." The concept *pine tree* arises from the particular shape of the tree as perceived by the human organ of sight. Had no one been there to see the tree and notice its particular shape, the concept *pine tree* would not exist. Similarly, scientists have

2 Those unfamiliar with the laws of physics should consider the trajectory of a projectile or stone thrown from a distance. Different initial velocities or angles will create different trajectories, yet we are able to describe all of them with mathematic formulae sharing certain characteristics. This family of formulae is called "parabolic" in descriptive geometry.

classified species in the Darwinist system of evolution, in which different types are classified according to external characteristics such as the number of their vertebrae, jaw structure, and so on.

In the beginning of the twentieth century, two authors—Rudolf Steiner (*Truth and Science* and *Intuitive Thinking as a Spiritual Path: A Philosophy of Freedom*) and Sri Aurobindo (*The Synthesis of Yoga* and *The Life Divine*) presented new approaches to the study of human consciousness, overturning the existing worldview and providing a new basis for the development of human consciousness. Through their individual esoteric studies, these great men realized a supreme reality—the "World of Ideas," the "World of Intelligence," and "Divine Gnosis"—a creative, intelligent basis of existence that creates all that we later perceive as the multifarious phenomena of nature. They described the genealogy of the species as a gradual evolution out of this archetypal world. This supreme world was known and described by the Rishis, ancient teachers of humanity in the Vedas and the Upanishads, and by Plato and Pythagoras. These different cultures include inspiring descriptions of this creative world that are not part of our limited modern awareness. Academic institutions have a regrettable tendency to teach Plato's ideas intellectually rather than presenting the spiritual aspects of his philosophy. In many cases, Plato's world of ideas is described as an abstract world of thought rather than the real, intensive, creative world such as that described by modern spiritual science. The mission of the great teachers, then, was to bring a new form of science with a holistic view that includes the spiritual aspects of consciousness. The parameters of Western thought in the centuries following the appearance of these teachers are now enlarged by that holistic perspective.

According to these esoteric teachings, the world of ideas is an effective, intelligent world that integrates the universal law. Material reality perceived by our senses is only a gradual condensation, or realization, of this supreme impulse. We should not be surprised to find the same laws that govern thought merged and integrated in material reality. The ability of human thinking to recognize the inner regularity of outside objects is possible only because supreme thinking is the basis both of our thoughts and of the objects we perceive. This idea may be difficult to accept for those accustomed to conceiving of thinking as a subjective human act. Yet throughout all ages, teachers of humanity have always testified that essential thinking is "a living being." For those willing, it will not be difficult to accept the testimony given by initiates of spiritual science, who tell us that what we usually regard as reasoning or thinking activity is only a shadow, a lower level of a living essence that is not fully revealed to our senses and that operates from higher planes of reality.

According to Steiner, when we examine any object, our senses reveal only part of it—the side that presents itself to our senses—textures, surface colors, or emitted sounds. These partial impressions are complemented by thinking, since the object is composed essentially of supreme thinking itself, condensed into a material form. This is something we may see by looking at a stone that has been thrown. Observing its flight through the air, we see not only the stone, but also its trajectory, which we call a "parabola." The trajectory is an integral part of the phenomenon of a thrown stone. Yet, while we perceive the stone itself with our organs of sight, the particular form of its trajectory can be perceived only through thinking. Thinking is therefore a special sense that recognizes and can define the intelligent aspect of the phenomenal world, even when not naming it.

If we could face reality without our thinking faculty, our world of impressions would be chaotic and inexplicable. For example, we see a round red surface and name it an apple. The information about the shape and color was provided by our senses, yet recognizing the input and organizing it into meaningful patterns is done not by the senses but by our thinking, which "sees" in the apple something essential to it, no less than its shape or color. A simple experiment may help us see that this is not some contrived theory but something that continuously happens in our process of perception, without our awareness. Go out into an open field, relax, and close your eyes; try to forget where you are and just wait for a few minutes. Then, open your eyes suddenly to what is in front of you. In this way we can see that there is a brief gap between the moment when objects enter our awareness and the moment when they are organized into meaningful shapes. Impressions do not enter our awareness perfectly arranged and ordered; rather, they are perceived as spots of light and color. It is our thinking that organizes the spots of light into the patterns of images and concepts that are stored in our memory. This process is lightning fast, yet in that split second before the impressions are organized into shapes, it is possible to notice the role of our thinking faculty.

We see now that the description of the concept-creating process just described in regard to the pine tree was not completely accurate. This process would be better described this way: when we look at a group of trees and find something essential that is fundamental to them all, it is not just internal resemblance that creates this understanding, but also an inner intuition that these trees are part of a whole, one that materialized out of a real world of ideas and is expressed in great variety in a group of pine trees. This way of thinking is difficult to accept because our conceptual world is already fully developed. Nevertheless, remembering childhood and the way these concepts gradually evolved into a meaningful whole, it will be easier for us to understand this epistemology, even though we lack the ability to directly perceive the aforementioned world of archetypes.

I still recall an exciting childhood experience that is compatible with this understanding. I was very young, and we were going on a trip to the mountains of Galilee. As the bus meandered up the mountainside, I saw a lake in which two finger-sized boats were sailing. Those are nutshells, I thought to myself, and those are midgets rowing them, the ones I heard about in the bedtime stories. This vision was so captivating that I can still recall it vividly, as if it happened just the other day. I cannot say when I first understood the laws of perspective, but it was only later that I realized that those were human beings rowing real boats in the Sea of Galilee.

If we accept that the world of archetypes is an intelligent world to which our thinking is connected and whose laws it obeys, and that the world of phenomena gradually evolves from this intelligent world, it will not be hard to understand the amazing correlation between the shapes formed in nature and the world of concepts that we have created. Both come from the same divine source.

The process of creating concepts and their inner meaning is a broad and important subject that forms a great part of epistemology, a discipline taught both in academic institutions and in schools based in spiritual science. Here, I have described it only briefly in order to lay the ground for the description of the process in which inventions originate. In the next chapter we will examine the particular way in which the inventor utilizes the world of concepts in the process of invention. We will see how ideas, processed at a suprasensory level, are realized on earthly planes and try to characterize the creative freedom the inventor has in the process. In this way, we will examine the question posed at the beginning of this book: Can human beings invent something truly new?

CHAPTER 4

CONCEPTS IN THE CREATIVE PROCESS

"The human mind is never quite sure of its intuitions until they have been viewed and confirmed by the judgment of the rational intelligence: it is there that it feels most well founded and secure. Man surmounting reason to organize his thought and life by the intuitive mind would be already surpassing his characteristic humanity and on the way to development of supermanhood."
—SRI AUROBINDO, *The Synthesis of Yoga*

In the previous chapter, we discussed the assertion of spiritual science that the human world of concepts is no random human creation, but stems from recognition of a particular and essential characteristic of a given object, something fundamental to the object's particular nature. Human conceptual language is therefore based primarily not on the ability to form words and vowels, but on the ability of a person of any background, to look at an object and recognize the essential characteristic that sets it apart from another object. This recognition comes not from a difference in the outward appearance of objects but rather it comes from an intuitive understanding of their archetypal source.

For example, when someone points at a passing cloud and cries "That!"—whether spoken out loud or expressed by pointing, the concept *cloud,* of what a cloud is, already exists in that person's mind. When two people who do not speak the same language are in an open field together and one of them points toward the Sun or a cloud, the other knows what is meant, even when nothing is said. Pointing at the cloud, human thinking separates the object from the unity in which sensory perception found it. In order to create a means of communication, one first has to create conceptual separateness in the unified whole of the surrounding.

According to spiritual science, the world of phenomena—indeed, all of reality—is part of a unified world that constantly metamorphoses according to supreme, intelligent laws. This unity of the higher planes of reality is described in both ancient and modern esoteric literature. It is a world of conscious essences metamorphosing from one level to another, one role to another, always moving, always serving an ever-higher force. The world of phenomena that we perceive is seen as one of separate objects; yet, while we cannot observe directly the unity of the phenomenal world with its underlying spiritual basis, it is easy to see that it contains no clear borders. A fish in water is surrounded by it and to some extent saturated by it; water, on the other hand, is saturated with air, which is in turn taken in by living beings that breathe it. Are not water and air—entering the fish's body through its gills and later flowing through its respiratory system, blood system and metabolic system—actually part of the fish? Conceptually, they are not; yet, in effect, they certainly are.

It is possible, then, to see the conceptual world and the thinking associated with it as an intermediary world standing between perceived reality and human intelligence, which has no form. These two planes provide for the world of human concepts—the world of phenomena with its many shapes, and the world of human reasoning that recognizes the original archetypes that underlie it. Although the world of concepts also includes concepts related to our inner life, for the purposes of this discussion we will consider only outer impressions, as they are the main component in our conceptual world. These two sources, outer phenomena and inner reasoning, provide the consistency in our conceptual world; although people from different cultures employ different sounds to describe the same objects, the inner logic of language maintains a high level of cohesion throughout human tongues. Had languages not obeyed a logical set of rules derived from the very essence of the human being, there would be no way to make translations from one language to another.

Considering our use of language, we should note the fundamental difference between a small child, still in the process of developing concepts, and an adult, who has developed the use of those concepts toward new fields. The way infants learn to connect heard words with concepts may be described as follows: when a mother opens her arms to her son and calls, "Come to mommy, sweetheart," he "reads" the mother's intention for him to go to her. He does not know the verb *come,* the preposition *to,* or the pronoun *me*. He senses what the mother expresses and affectionately complies. Only later do children learn to distinguish directions such as "come," "go," or "to me," or to understand "there," "home," and other terms for places. What seems surprising about all this is children's ability to understand what mothers expect of them without the relevant vocabulary.

We must deduce that infants are exceptionally sensitive and able to "read" their mother's intentions directly, with no need for words. This ability to read other people implies that our cognitive faculties have never been limited to our thinking organ, but rather apply naturally to the world of emotion as well the kind of subtle intuition that fades away as we mature. As adults, we tend to understand others' intentions by using the intellectual world of concepts, using our concepts as a means of guessing the speaker's inner position. We have developed a diverse and sophisticated world of concepts, yet in the process we have lost a great deal of our sensitivity and our ability to recognize directly subtle shades developing in another person's soul.

As we continue to examine the inventor's process of creating work and the central role that the world of concepts has in that process, we will take a deeper look at the world of concepts and the way they are created. One useful approach is to examine objects made by human beings. Since we create these objects, it is easier for us to recognize the essential characteristics of their components than those of the creations made by God.

We may ask, What is a table? An immediate reply would be, "A four-legged object used to eat meals upon." What if we throw a piece of cloth over a rock to eat picnic food? Is that a kind of table? Or, imagine that, while negotiating, we say to the other representative, "Bring your client to the table." What kind of table are we talking about? Clearly, the concept of a "table" does not describe the object's material characteristics, and perhaps not even its geometric shape. The main purpose of this concept of table and what a table is seems to be that, in terms of the concept of table, it is the functionality, its service or purpose, that counts.

Consider a simple paper clip, one you can find in any office. There are dozens of different types of paper clips. They can be made of plastic, metal, punched tin, bent wire, or plastic injected into a mold. Which of these is the most exemplary representative of the paper clip family? All of them together, and not a single one. The best way to represent the concept of a paper clip would be to imagine—without words or shapes—the idea of the paper clip as a minimalist means to hold several papers together. This is the very idea that once existed in the thoughts of the inventor who made the first paper clip. We have said already that the idea born in the inventor's thoughts is not an abstraction, but that the idea itself is an intelligent being that can be seen and perceived, though of course only by those who have acquired the relevant tools.

Let us consider another product of our civilization, the sewing needle. We have already learned that the material qualities of a sewing needle are not the essential characteristics. The shape does have an important role, and we could admittedly define a needle as a sharp wire topped by a loop.

But can we find a more creative way of understanding the idea behind the metallic needle? When we examine its field of activity, we see immediately that the needle has no independent existence. Its existence is connected to the thread that it pulls. Which, then, is more important, the thread or the needle? Though most would perceive the needle as having greater value, the needle, in fact, serves the thread, and not the other way around. With poetic imagination, the needle then appears to act as a pioneer, since it is the needle that leads the way for the thread through terrain that it could not cross on its own. The concept of a needle is more about this act of serving the thread than it is about the material of which it is made. Clearly, then, refined conceptual thinking requires a measure of artistic imagination. Anyone who lacks this subtle sense cannot discover the beauty of human creation or its essence.

Having witnessed the functional essence of concepts connected with objects created by human beings, let us consider a subtler aspect of their essence. Closing our eyes for a moment, we will reflect on the word *to*. The word is immediately felt to contain an inner movement. As soon as we use this word with intent, something is moved in the intimate depths of our soul. In our daily lives, where we often identify with the content of our speech and pay no attention to our inner selves, this sensation goes unnoticed. Yet developing self-awareness brings this inner motion to our attention. For example, the words *inward* and *outward* have a cadence in our souls that sounds in a direction that is in tune with the words' meaning. In our daily life, this world of inner movements escapes our attention, because we are usually completely caught up in identifying with outer events. Nevertheless, right schooling brings about a subtle field of self-consciousness that is sensitive enough to perceive delicate inner movements whenever we talk, listen, or do anything externally.

Words that do not denote a direction in space such as those in the previous paragraph also affect us this way. Think of the words *despite* and *nonetheless,* which also create a resonance in the soul of one who expresses them with intent. A sort of mimicry occurs in our soul. A certain resonance accompanies the pronunciation of words and transforms the dry concept into a living movement with experiential meaning for those involved. The more we become aware of the occurrence of this inner motion during the expression of the speaker's emotions and ideas, the richer and livelier their conversation becomes and the deeper the effect their words have on us. The acquisition of self-knowledge involves the development of exceptional sensitivity to the inner movement that arises inwardly when we speak to others.

Readers are encouraged to inspect their own inner mimicry by silently imagining some concept, preferably with eyes closed. Doing this, one examines the effects that this has in the soul—where it reverberates, and in what way. It must be emphasized here that such a task is not easy to accomplish. Our awareness is drawn to external sounds and figures and tends to ignore the inner play taking place in our soul. Extensive sensitivity, enveloped by an enhanced field of consciousness, reveals the fantastic inner movements taking place when we manifest or perceive anything new.

The element of motion exists in more than prepositions and adjectives. Looking at concepts we have already examined, like the paper clip or a needle and thread, we can sense an element of motion there, too. Our language is alive and breathing to the extent that our concepts are in constant inner movement. Lacking this inner element leaves our soul in a static position in which creativity is adversely affected.

Let's look more deeply into the world of concepts and heighten our sensitivity to its contents. Try finding the common denominator in the following: our circulatory system (fig. 1), our nervous system (fig. 2), a tree (fig. 3), a flash of lightning (fig. 4), a river delta (fig. 5), a military unit, the solar system, and even higher systems. The answer is hierarchy. Everything named here obeys this principle. It is important to note that, while the hierarchic principle is expressed in external forms, the archetype itself lacks form.

When Moses ordered his people into formation, appointing commanders over units of hundreds and of thousands, was it a new principle he had invented? Did he create a hierarchical system that had never existed before? The truth is that hierarchy is a universal principle; it lived in Moses' mind as it lives in cosmic systems or in the circulatory system. We could say that when Moses instituted this basic principle in human society, he extended universal principles into new fields, thus fulfilling the mythological role of the human being as

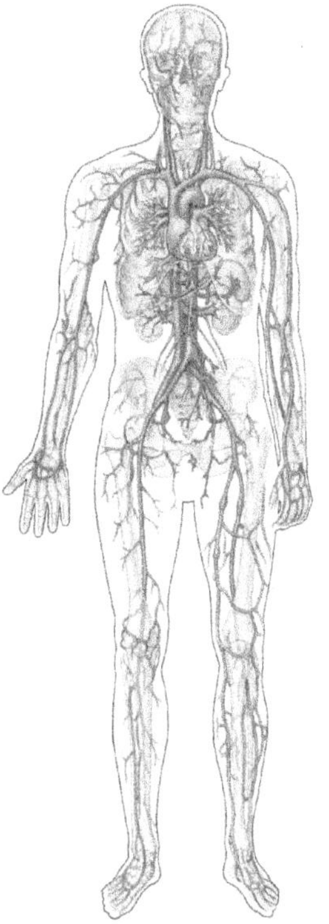

1

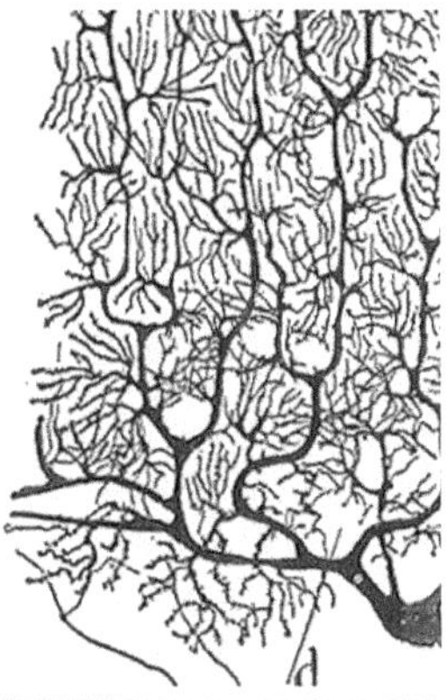

2

3

4

5

God's agent in the lower planes. I invite you to close your eyes for a few moments and try to imagine this archetypal principle as vividly as possible.

Just as the concept *hierarchy* nests in all levels of creation and takes form in the world of human reasoning through inner laws, so, too, do concepts such as *order, equality, autonomy,* and thousands of others. Things become even subtler when we turn to the world of concepts connected with our internal world. Surprisingly, those very concepts are mentioned in Rudolf Steiner's lecture series of 1911, *Evolution in the Aspect of Realities,* in which he discusses the creation of the existential basis of the universe. According to spiritual science, reality is not based on cold, blind particles such as atoms, neutrons, and quarks, as assumed in the natural sciences. Underlying what we perceive as material reality are the moral powers of divine, creative leadership. Gradually, we come to see that our world of concepts is not a random creation of our brains, but something universal that is expressed in us as human beings and in the reality in which we live. For those who grew up with a materialistic education, the ideas of spiritual science may be hard to digest, and many tend at first to reject them as unacceptable and unreasonable. Yet those who would delve into these ideas with an open mind and let their world of concepts be influenced by them will gradually find new depths that cannot be reached by scientific theories of the natural sciences. As one who comes from a scientific and a technological background, I can personally attest to this fact.

However, let us turn again to the world of concepts and examine another type of concept, a type that human language has not yet been able to name but exists in the inventor's reasoning world. Every concept is based essentially on some understanding, yet some insights cannot be reduced to one word or definition. Consequently, we often tend to ignore their existence, all the while making much unconscious use of them. Inventors are intuitively connected with this pool of insights and make intensive use of them as they transpose or adapt them from one field of activity to another.

For example, after World War II a senior supervisor in a Scandinavian municipality developed complete paralysis of his speech faculty. Medication failed to help, and he was taken to a renowned psychotherapist, famous for his creative approaches to healing. The therapist tried several methods and was frustrated to see that the man, who had spoken before and throughout the war, would still not speak a single word. As he learned more about the patient, he came to discover a dark side to the man's past. During the war, he had cooperated with the Nazis and caused several innocent people to die. Toward the end of the last therapeutic session, the therapist said to his client, "Look, if you had cooperated with me you would already be cured. But you prefer to cooperate with the evil in this world. With your own mouth, you brought about the death of innocent people. You scum! No punishment is painful enough to erase the pain that you brought to those people and their families." He kept on and on, criticizing and cursing the patient, until the man collapsed and cried, "I could not refuse! My whole standing in the community was threatened! I am a victim of a harsh reality, not the hideous criminal you think I am." Several moments of profound silence passed; both men stared at each other with tears in their eyes.

In Eastern martial arts, such as ju-jitsu, two opponents try to unbalance each other. Often, the smaller fighter can be seen throwing a much heavier opponent. How? The answer lies in a change in the fighter's attitude. When the larger fighter attacks the smaller one with all available power, the smaller fighter does not try to counter, but uses the opponent's force to pull the other in the direction of the charge. With little effort, the attacker is unbalanced through the momentum of the charge.

An inner similarity can be seen in these two examples, both of which use the same principle. In the first case, the principle is psychological; in the second, physical. Inventors may be unable to verbalize the archetypal principle behind these examples, but they can easily use it to their purposes, changing and adapting them to fit particular situations. What enables this amazing human capability to perceive the common denominator in apparently two different phenomena is a great mystery. Nevertheless, it points to the universal, all-abiding laws at the basis of existence.

The next example is not about a human physical or psychological system, but a mechanical one. It is another example in which someone, in this case an outsider, realized that the developers of a mechanical system would not reach their desired goal by working in the usual way, but should instead focus their efforts in another direction. In one of the development teams in a new innovative project, the mechanical chassis started developing a vibration that grew stronger with time. The development team worked very hard at calibrating the system's engines so that no eccentric forces would develop, yet even after all of the system had been balanced and recalibrated, the vibrations did not subside. A guest from a parallel development crew, invited as an outside observer, suggested that the team stop the attempts to improve the balance and instead disrupt it. To the team's surprise, once the system had been disassembled and its parts tuned out of balance, the system's gentle vibration did not grow beyond an acceptable level. The observer's advice to the development team was based on the understanding that the chassis locomotion system created vibrations at a frequency approaching the system's natural frequency. By intentionally disrupting the delicate balance in the locomotion system, the developers created contradicting vibrations, thus preventing the development of a linear vibration at a frequency equal to the system's natural resonance.

An element called the object's self-resonance exists in every oscillating system. A simplified example is that of a girl on a swing (fig. 6) gently pushed by her father each time she reaches the full height of her backward motion. The little additions of thrust that her father provides add up to a constantly growing amplitude of the swing and the girl sitting on it. If she were pushed at the wrong times, perhaps when the swing had not yet reached the height of its motion, the amplitude would not have increased appropriately. The self-resonance of the girl on the swing is determined by her weight and the length of the swing's rope. Likewise, every system or element thereof contains

6

natural resonance as an integral characteristic, which can be empowered or restrained according to need.

There are several cases in the history of great bridges in which stable bridges, built according to all known criteria and incorporating the appropriate safety standards, collapsed as a result of wind constantly hitting the bridge at the same amplitude as its natural resonance (see next page, figs. 7 and 8). It is well known that infantry platoons, which often march at a steady pace, are ordered to break into a casual walk when crossing a lightweight bridge. This is a traditional safety measure intended to prevent the bridge from oscillating at its self-resonance and going out of balance.

We have observed a psychologist, a martial artist, and an engineer's use the same "archetypal insight" in completely different fields. Human thinking can recognize the similarities in different situations by going beyond prescribed thinking and utilizing an ideal plane where abstract principles have actual, though formless, existence. I have mentioned this ideal plane several times already, claiming it is not merely a plane of abstract activity, but rather a being that obeys the basic, intelligent law of reality, the very intelligence at the basis of all creation. This principle enables the inventor to act sometimes like a "thief," not in the sense of stealing others' ideas, but by being able to recognize an archetypal principle in one field and apply it in another.

Let us consider another archetypal principle that is not conceptually defined in daily language, although it is used in many areas of daily life. At Passover, it is said of the Jewish people that the more they are tormented, the more they grow and prosper. The more they are afflicted, the more they multiplied and spread abroad. This may be interpreted as pertaining to the growth of an enslaved population, but it is interesting to consider the spiritual implication of the phrase. The harsh conditions of their existence bred inner strength in the Hebrews in Egypt, which prepared them for their future role as humanity's vanguard in the transition to monotheism. We can think of other situations, too, in which this inner principle holds true; the best known expression of this is Nietzsche's dictum, "What does not kill me only serves to make me stronger."

Anyone who tastes a wild apple grown in nature without irrigation or fertilizers knows that it tastes much sweeter than apples grown in an orchard. Consider how architects apply this principle for their aims. Hard structures are designed to withstand any possible assault by an outside force, such as winds, for example. A general external force can create focused local force that would decimate a limited area of the building's infrastructure and thereby topple the whole building. That is why a hard structure must include

7

8

Tacoma Narrows Bridge was nicknamed "Galloping Gertie" owing to vertical movement of the deck during windy conditions. The bridge collapsed into Puget Sound November 7, 1940, during high wind conditions.

its own counterforces in every part. To solve this problem, engineers have created a whole family of structures capable of arousing counterforces in a more sophisticated manner than do hard structures. These are called "dynamic structures," characterized by the unique ability to mobilize counterforces from all parts of the structure, not just from the area suffering the assault. Furthermore, the building's flexible constructive shell provides for resistance that grows in proportion to the growth of forces that have the potential to unbalance the structure.

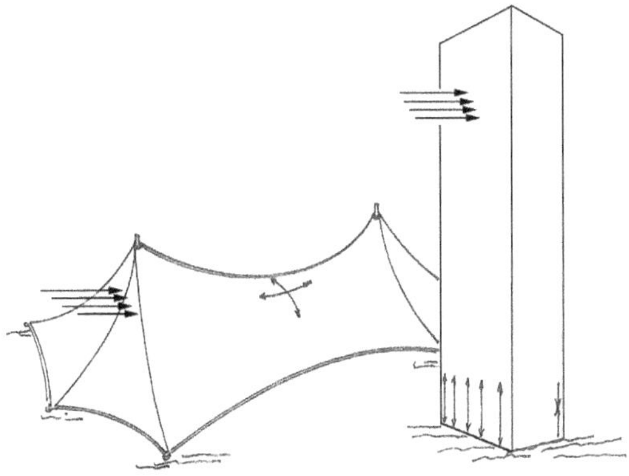

9

This type of structure can be seen on the left in the drawing (fig. 9). The structure is called a hyperbolic paraboloid, and its shell[1] has two curves, like a saddle. Unlike a simple rigid structure, the whole saddle-like shell bends when even a single, locally focused force is brought to bear on it. The radius of the curve in critical areas is diminished and the structure's overall resistance to the transformation of its shape grows as the assaulting forces grow. In other words, the more it is afflicted, the more it multiplies and spreads. It is quite amazing that human beings have learned to use a principle of nature in such sophisticated fashion.

The enormous importance of this archetypal principle becomes clearer when we consider how creation grows constantly more complex, owing to the play of counterforces within it. Any single thing that grows stronger naturally does so only because of the beneficial influence of its encounter with opposing forces. Creation stories about Iblis, God's beloved son who was sent away to serve as a counterforce to creative forces; the power of *Sitra Achra* in Hebrew myths; the characters of Lucifer and Ahriman in modern spiritual science; all these are not merely popular figments of imagination, as some Western intellectuals seem to believe. Rather, they are picturesque expressions of an actual,

1 Double-curved shells are unique in not containing bending forces at any point. For example, in a flat ceiling, collapse is prevented by the fact that at every point there are balancing pairs of pulling and pressing forces. These ceilings may be functionally useful, but their constructive efficiency is inferior. The bent surface's geometry is typified by the possibility to draw two opposite arches through every point; the forces, working at opposite directions, balance every point through pulling forces alone.

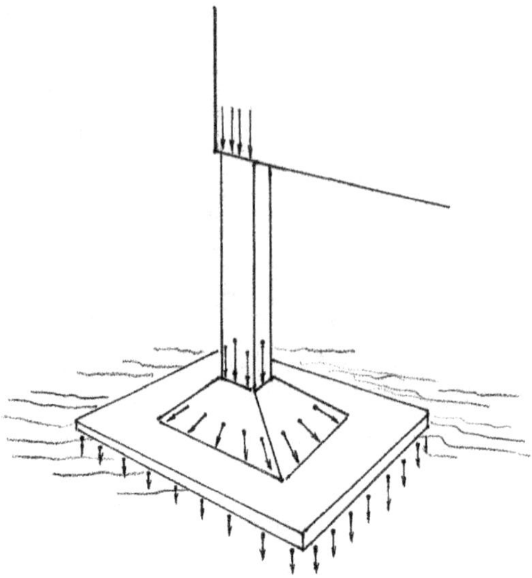

10

universal intelligent reality that has created counterforces within and for itself, making it able to grow and develop. The interested reader can consider these ideas as a hint at the guidelines and exercises for the improvement of the capacity of creative thinking to be presented in later chapters.

However, this illustration does not tell the whole story. Inventors do not just mechanically copy principles from one area to another; they may also reverse the principle's focus of activity according to their need. Imagine we are slicing cheese with a knife. What is actually happening as far as the inner forces of the activity are concerned? We transfer force from our arm to the knife handle and from there to the sharp edge, where contact occurs between the blade and the surface of the cheese. Since the cheese cannot mobilize sufficient counterforces in the limited area in which pressure is applied, the forces connecting the different parts of the cheese are severed and a passage is made for the blade. We can see, then, that when we want to achieve a penetration effect, we gather a large yet dispersed quantity of force and concentrate it on a limited surface.

On the other hand, this very principle could be used in reverse. Instead of concentrating dispersed force on a limited area, we could disperse concentrated force over a large area. One possible use for this principle would be the process of building a structure's foundation (fig. 10) in soft ground. Builders would cast a broad concrete base, preferably shaped somewhat like a pyramid, and once the concrete has dried, cast the pillar on which the structure itself will be built. Thus, the concentrated force of the pillar is dispersed over the entire area of the concrete pyramid and the soft ground can withstand the dispersed load.

By carefully observing the entire process of a given activity and observing the principle that operates in the specific objects involved, the inventor acquires a specific skill. This skill is based on using the reservoir of archetypal means that is stored in our consciousness through learned observation and is ready for use in case of need. An experienced inventor's skill is measured by the size of this inner reservoir and the ability to "intuit" an archetypal principle at the right time and place. This is what inventors often refer to as "experience," not usually giving this intelligent content the central role it deserves in their creative work.

What, then, is creative thinking? What differentiates an inventive engineer's work from that of an executive engineer whose work it is to apply an idea rather than produce it? The habitual tendency to create definitions for creative thinking is a sin against human creation's natural inclination to be free of the yoke of the mind, the yoke of definitions. Definitions serve us in the fields of logic, of law, and of scientific order, but do not help us reach a new understanding, and in fact usually narrow our understandings rather than broaden them. However, we can examine the characteristics of creative thinking—observing its play through its field of activity—and compare it with its complementary partner, logical thinking, whose clearest expressions are analysis and deductive thinking, or a combination of both.

Whereas analysis and deductive thinking are best at processing given materials and reaching a conclusion, creative thinking can rise above the data circle and surprise us with a solution that has no apparent connection with this data. Some problems we encounter may contain sufficient data for their solution from the beginning; these can be solved with several analytical and deductive steps. Electronic computers are a clear example of systematic problem-solving using processes of analysis and deduction. This is demonstrated in the following example:

> Problem: Which animal's name has three characters and obeys the following criteria?
>
> 1. It has two letters in common with *cat.*
> 2. It does not contain the letters *b* or *i.*
>
> Solution: we can try combinations—eat, fat, cot, rat, and so on—each time methodically adding a different letter of the alphabet and trying the few possible variations in character order.

Finally, the only answer that satisfies all demands will be "rat." That is our solution. This sort of problem requires no creativity at all; simple computer software could easily solve it. In this example and in general, the computations of electronic computers, based on analysis and deduction from a predefined data pool, take place on only one plane. Human beings also analyze and deduce, but unlike computers we operate on more than one plane. Our data pool is endless, starting with our own personal knowledge and understanding and expanding to range over cosmic intelligence, since this intelligence fills the cosmos and penetrates human consciousness.

Developing their consciousness, practitioners of the various spiritual disciplines find deep and vast knowledge within their soul, and they experience the sensation that this knowledge is something to be remembered rather than discovered for the first time. They find their normal consciousness artificially limited by an inner apparatus of forgetfulness, yet feel that when cracks appear in the walls of forgetfulness, the road to vast knowledge is opened—to knowledge that is not only subjective but also merged with the universal intelligence of reality.

The extent of the data pool is not the only difference between human thinking and that of a computer. Another difference is that human beings think with more than the head. Mental activity, which regrettably typifies most of modern materialistic scientific thinking, can indeed be characterized this way, and in this sense resembles that of a computer; yet human reasoning also includes and merges the functions of will and emotion, which artificial intelligence lacks completely.

For example, given a digital camera and the appropriate software, a computer is able to recognize a human profile after the person's characteristics have been registered in the computer's memory bank. The recognition process is carried out completely mechanically, comparing the formal characteristics of the object with those stored in its memory. Despite the amazing speed with which it performs its calculations, the computer is no match for a little boy with fewer than twenty friends. The boy will recognize any of his friends from a distance, from up close, and from every possible direction, whether they are running or standing still, whether they are awake or asleep—and all this takes less than a tenth of a second. How does he do it?

If our memory were to act only mechanically, comparing items of data one by one, this task would be impossible, even for experienced adults. Our memory, however, involves the soul with its emotional intelligence—something a computer's mechanism completely lacks. Once a memory portrait of a relative is imprinted on our soul, sensations, emotions, and images are associatively linked to it and these live within us, even when the imprinting object is absent. Every time we remember this person, emotional experiences identified with them arise; one such emotional flash is enough to confirm to the child that it is indeed this person and no other he perceives. At times we try to remember a certain event and fail. We run a series of events through our imagination, rejecting one after another for not arousing the emotion that was part of the original, and we keep trying. Finally, we feel something "click," a sense of things falling into place, as the right event is remembered. The image, with its shape and all its colors, the experience of disappointment or satisfaction connected with it—in short, the whole experience—locks into place in perfect array. How different, indeed, is our recollection activity from that of a computer.

Where a solution in the context of inventions is concerned, the differences between artificial intelligence and human intelligence are even more apparent. One difference is that the inventive solution is not sought within the given data circle. It almost always contains an element of surprise, a need to rise above the circle of given data. The following story humorously expresses the surprising aspect of innovative technological solutions.

One day, when the limitations of borders and customs were just a bother to cunning merchants, a biker arrived at the border between Mexico and the United States with two large, apparently full sacks tied to his back. When the customs officer inquired about the content of the sacks he said, "Sand. They're full of sand." The officer grinned mischievously and poked the bags. Feeling nothing but sand, he allowed the rider to enter the United States.

A month went by and the rider appeared again, riding an expensive Harley-Davidson and carrying the same two sacks. This time the officer was not so easy with him and ordered him to empty the sacks for a thorough inspection. Again he was unable find anything out of place in the unusual cargo. After a while, these encounters became routine, and the inspector had to live with the frustration of being unable to stop the smuggling that he was sure was occurring.

The years went by and the officer retired. After a time, he started missing his old workplace and decided to pay a visit to his remaining friends at the border station. To his great surprise he found the inspector on duty dealing with the very same unusual biker, and eventually letting him pass.

As the biker started pulling away from the station he heard footfalls and bellowing behind him. It was the old customs officer, panting and excited, who said, "Look, my friend, I'm retired, I'm not on duty anymore, I promise not to tell anyone. I've thought about you night and day, I've become nervous. My health has been damaged. Please have mercy and tell me—what in God's name are you smuggling?"

"Bikes," said the man, smiling, and rode on his way.

In every joke there's a surprise; that's why analytic thinking is powerless where humor is concerned.

In this chapter we examined the inventor's ability to move from one field of thinking to another while maintaining the principle shared by both. But what is it that lets inventors see two different systems as expressions of the very same thing? This question leads us to the investigation of another ability, linked to and merged with thinking—the amazing power of imagination.

Chapter 5

Intelligence and Creativity

"All Nature is simply, then, the Seer-Will, the Knowledge-Force of the Conscious-Being at work to evolve in force and form all the inevitable truth of the Idea into which it has originally thrown itself."

—Sri Aurobindo, *The Life Divine*

When presented with a simple yet surprising idea, people I speak with often say, "How come I never thought of that? Inventors must be especially gifted with intelligence." What is intelligence? What is that mysterious intelligent element expressed in so many different ways at all levels of existence—the spiral structure of a plant, the complex structure of the femur, the surprising behavior of animals, or the special creative faculties of the human species? How can we characterize this intelligence and how can we measure it?

In the early twentieth century, the first attempts were made to treat human intelligence as a measurable quality. Western culture, charmed with the ability of modern science to measure and weigh anything, tried to address the question of intelligence with similar "measurement and weighing" tools. The French psychologist Alfred Binet was the first to create a system of questionnaires meant to quantify a person's intelligence faculty in relation to age. The idea of precisely monitoring intelligence created great enthusiasm and became an important yardstick for the acceptance of students in school, employees in workplaces, and so on.

With time, the enthusiasm that first welcomed the popular "intelligence quotient," or IQ, tests began to erode as their reliability increasingly came under attack. The careers of gifted students did not always take off as the writers of IQ tests anticipated, while brilliant individuals who would eventually leave their mark on the scientific and technological world sprang from the sector that received comparatively moderate grades. The renowned inventor, Thomas Alva Edison, had difficulties with relatively simple algebra. It is easy to see that intelligence tests are problematic as a reliable measurement of human intelligence in all its variety.

At the time when Edison already had a successful industrial company, he once asked his assistants to measure the volume of a new light bulb going through the first development stages in the labs. After several hours of waiting for the results, he went back to his assistants and found them working meticulously but unsuccessfully on a complex series of integrals. With typical impatience, Edison grabbed the empty tube, dipped it into a pail full of water, and measured the water volume in a calibrated beaker.

The question of the validity of intelligence tests obviously raises another question: How is creative intelligence measured? Almost everyone understands the important contribution that memory, visual imagination, and analytical thinking make to a test subject's intelligence capacity, yet how do we measure a factor whose very essence is surprise itself?

Debates about the existence of any coherence in what we call "human intelligence capacity" have gradually increased. Is intelligence an overall phenomenon that merges many different abilities? Or do we have several intelligences—a multiplicity of skills united in a single human being?

David Perkins and Howard Gardner are considered world-class researchers of creative thinking, and are therefore proper representatives of the scientific approach that dominates Western culture today. In their books *Archimedes' Bathtub* and *Art, Mind and Brain: A Cognitive Approach to Creativity,* they express the idea of multiple intelligences: linguistic intelligence, interpersonal intelligence, spatial intelligence, musical intelligence, and so on. Surprisingly, neither book yielded any expression of the deep vertical dimension of thinking—that is, the fact that it has an internal hierarchy. David Perkins often speaks of a "cognitive click," yet it seemed that even here he did not notice that the surprising cognitive moments do not occur on the shallow, horizontal plane of thinking, but are rather an expression of an intuitive stream of thinking that springs from the deep foundation of one's soul. An approach that claims that intelligences work in their own separate ways based upon their own biological basis and cannot see that our physical body does not create intelligence but serves as an aide to its expression, cannot be the basis of an all-encompassing cognitive theory, since it treads only the horizontal planes of intelligent expressions and does not see their roots.

One of the clearest examples of this dilemma is a book that became a bestseller, *Emotional Intelligence.* Daniel Goleman's book created a sharp turn in the research on human intelligence, which is now alive with discussions of several different kinds of intelligence that brain research experts locate in different centers under the scalp.

The common scientific approach identifies human intelligence with the brain's activity. This, indeed, is the direct sentiment of our modern culture—we think that our processes of reasoning, judgment, and decision-making all take place somewhere in our skull. According to this line of reasoning, locating the precise centers of the brain's activity and comparing them to patterns of thought and behavior should shed more light on the mystery of "human intelligence." This approach to the research of phenomena is comparable with the dominant scientific approach at the turn of the twentieth century, which held that in order to understand the whole of reality, the basic building blocks of reality must be recognized and understood.

This common assumption that the whole universe is merely a combination of basic elements gradually declined. Exceptional physicists such as Richard Feynman began to notice that the cosmos has an essence that is more than the sum of its components. This approach takes modern physics closer to the approach of spiritual science, which sees the spirit as the very foundation of reality, a foundation that is the source of the infinite variation found in the world of sensory phenomena.

To understand the unique character of the intelligence that talented creators possess, it would be best if, in the spirit of spiritual science, we examine universal intelligence as a whole before examining the particular intelligence of a certain inventor or creator in one field or another. Deep meditative observation brings an observer's developing awareness to a different sense of existence than what we experience in ordinary life. When the process of association calms down, alert thinking discovers another existence, a quiet dimension that exists in the background of the associative process of thought. The soul becomes interested in the new dimension and the attention usually given to mental images and inner chatter is gradually shifted to the quiet background. This infinite silence is found not to be inert, but rather an intensive life vibration. Quite a few years of practice are usually needed before these planes of existence begin to surrender their secrets, revealing a boundless universal reality to our consciousness. Meanwhile, human beings are indeed separated from their surroundings in the physical plane, whereas personal intelligence in the world of silence is established firmly in a more universal intelligence.

This new inner discovery changes the human feeling of a personal, separate existence to a sense of something larger than the personal self. We continue to feel the associative flow in our minds, yet no longer consider it actual thinking. Pure thinking is revealed in a boundless space in which individuals are rooted and nourished by it to the extent that they are inwardly open.

This inner openness is not reached easily, but once achieved through proper practice it reveals thinking to be a multifaceted force belonging to all reality. When genuine thinking occurs, individuals become a kind of vessel with a unique character, expressing aspects of the intelligent activity that exists at the base of reality rather than feeling that they are original creators of their own thoughts. Even those whose present situation in life does not yet allow them to become aware of this hidden aspect of intelligence can realize that it exists when they can recognize the supreme intelligence in the plant and animal kingdoms and in various natural phenomena. We are filled with a sense of humility when human evolution is no longer attributed to mechanistic development according to the Darwinist principles, but is seen in the perspective of a supreme wisdom, higher than our own, that is present at the base of all processes.

The intelligence for which we have been given responsibility includes a limited field of intelligent judgments in the fields of science and technology and, naturally, in daily life. Yet the intelligence that oversees our rhythms like blood circulation or the breath cycle, our metabolic balance, the growth and orderly operation of our organs—this intelligence is supreme, and its complex field of activity is not given to human intelligence. Imagine if we should be given direct control of our metabolism; what would happen then? What would happen if our breathing rhythms were under our sole control?

We are thus called upon to consider our powers of intelligence in a different light, no longer as a collection of separate computations or the electrical activity of neurons in our central nervous system, but as a semi-autonomous participation in an intelligent universal reality expressed in the simplest of animals and reaching the highest levels of reality.

Meditative observation reveals another secret—the original unity of the intelligent soul's faculties: mind, emotion, and will. We often alternate between emotional and logical expressions, with one or the other taking the lead as needed. We tend to see each as "king of the hill" when it dominates and try to cultivate each separately. Yet meditative experience, when sufficiently intense, reveals harmony as the desired soul condition and that the use of the soul's faculties should be in balance. One-dimensional activity of the soul has many concrete implications in our life, including, for example, patterns of stereotypical perception, whose varied expressions are found in our private life, including a sentimental approach that may cloud one's judgment or obsessive desires that can divert us from the appropriate path. Balanced functioning of our soul's faculties cannot lead to extremism. The soul is full of emotionally charged intelligence; thinking lights one side of the problem, while compassion lights the other.

There are those who see the activity of cold logic as the worthy pinnacle of our sober life; they consider emotions to be a disruptive influence upon making intelligent decisions. Yet this faulty conclusion is not based on experiencing the harmonious activity of the soul but rather on chaotic activity, on moments when emotional impulses flood awareness and prevent clear perception. In true harmonious activity, each of the soul's faculties participates according to its relevant ability to contribute, and only to the needed extent. One faculty does not usurp the other's place; they mutually support, stimulate, and balance each other, acting essentially as aspects of a unified whole. Balanced intelligence—thinking charged with compassion and will—reveals life in its profound dimensions. The routine superficiality of life is now replaced with a vertical dimension that reveals itself to wakeful intelligence; superficial, one-dimensional intelligence is replaced with a broader, deeper intelligence. This is not a theoretical ideal, but an existential experience that may reveal itself, if only for brief moments. Once revealed, the experience provides a new perspective on our unused potential, while at the same time making it clear that we are far from its worthy fulfillment.

We have observed two important fundamental principles of human intelligence. First, human intelligence flows from the ocean of universal intelligence. Second, human intelligence (at least, that which has not yet deteriorated through the process of fragmentation) is essentially a unified whole. The soul's faculties of thought, emotion, and will are inseparably linked.

We shall now add a third principle, which is connected with the hierarchical nature of intelligence. This principle is also revealed when the field of inner awareness is expanded during meditative practice. A subtle alchemy releases thinking from its identification with the world of associations and inner images, bodily sensations, and gross desires and begins to live on an independent plane, free of the weight of these distractions. It now becomes more dynamic and capable of perceiving the human world of concepts as hierarchical and multidimensional. This aspect was described in the previous chapter about the world of concepts; now it is revealed as a direct experience of the capability of free thinking to move vertically over more than a single plane, uniting several concepts into a single higher idea, or of developing separate forms from a general archetypal idea in order to apply them as tools of material essence.

Considering all of this, we can better understand the nature of the intelligence that inventors might use in their work. This intelligence is composed of

- the ability to observe a series of familiar patterns as though presented to the inventor for the first time;
- the ability to observe physical objects and identify the essential idea behind each one;
- an appreciation for the inner beauty of principles, ideas, and ideals living in the background of the phenomenal world (this aspect is the contribution of compassionate attention supporting thinking activity);
- the ability to recognize the common factor in a series of patterns or connected ideas and realize what is faulty or missing;
- the ability to position several archetypal principles within the soul and wait for the result of their encounter (this is where the contribution of imagination takes place);
- the ability to move vertically over hierarchic planes, uniting different ideas into a central one, or to develop several different ideas out of a central archetype, so that they can be realized in physical tools and objects;
- and the ability to form a question and turn it inward, to a higher plane of intelligence, and patiently wait for an answer in the form of new intuition.

Let us look at an inventor's actions in dealing with the need for an innovative solution. We cannot trace the different directions of thinking activity, of course, because they are not linear and consistent, but zigzag with lightning speed. However, it is the very elusive nature of this particular intelligence that makes it interesting to observe the hidden segments of its activity through a magnifying glass. The reader is requested, therefore, to pay no attention to the order in which different stages are described but to focus instead on their substance.

In instances when a problem does not present itself directly, the inventor needs to show initiative to recognize its nature, regarding the array of data and calling the parts by name: "This is a wheel; that is a lever; the other is an engine." Whereas we know the elementary components, arduous thinking never takes the objects before it for granted. "This is a wheel," says lightning-quick thinking, Yes, but what is a wheel? What is a lever? What is their inner essence beyond the concrete shape? What geometric and functional possibilities do they offer?

Therefore, thinking quickly moves to examine the relationship among the various elements: "What inner regularity exists between a revolving wheel and the lever that moves it? What geometric idea describes the relationship between a line and a circle, between a lever and a wheel?" Those who work in a specialized field may smile when reading this, thinking, "If I did that while I was working, I'd be a philosopher, not a transport-system designer." This claim should be taken seriously, because we do not need to reconstruct our concept of a circle every time we encounter it; we pull it out of our world of concepts. Still, it seems that, even in the process of drawing on prepared concepts, there is a very quick intuitive phase when some of the data are (or need to be) reexamined. This tendency to reexamine our conceptual world may at times slow one's progress, but it allows us to reach solutions that are less and less routine. Indeed, a certain degree of abrupt forgetfulness can be useful when a genuinely original approach to a problem is required.

At this point, the designer calls on analytical thinking. This kind of thinking is expressed by the mental activity of gathering data and grouping the various components into logical patterns. This makes it easier for higher intelligent thinking to understand the roots of the problem. It is worth remembering that analytical thinking activity is never independent; a more intelligent thinking supervises it, as if from above. It is this intelligence that directs our analytical thinking, enjoys the fruit of its actions, and eventually sends it on a new mission.

Searching for a solution is the most interesting phase in problem solving. This is where thinking activity reaches its peak, with creative imagination taking the lead role (this unique ability will be described in the following chapter). The inventor's ability to find a new solution is a function of the ability to see in the mind's eye images not yet realized in the physical world. This great mystery is not fully understood, yet it seems that here, too, human activity derives its power from a higher creative imagination that serves supreme intelligence in increasing complexity and gives birth to the thousands of new forms we find in the animal and plant kingdoms. It is the power of imagination that allows inventors to construct new structures and examine them; in fact, they are able mentally to simulate the activity of a system that has yet to be constructed. The greater one's powers of visualization, the more precise and reliable the experiments will be. We shall touch on this subject again later by using practical examples.

This active stage may last as long as the solutions to the problem keep growing in complexity. Yet what happens when inventors feel they cannot reach a breakthrough? What should we do when we feel that our actions are sterile and that we cannot advance? The best method is to let the matter rest for a while, since normal thinking finds itself channeled into fixed paths and cannot rise above them. The mind must let go and allow the traces of the inner paths to dissolve so that it may move in new paths.

Moreover, this dissolution is not the only benefit of letting go. Resting and, especially, hours of sleep may seem like a waste of time from the perspective of one racing toward a solution. Is it not surprising, then, that the most innovative ideas arrive after sleep or even in a dream? Our thinking is not put on hold when we sleep; even when the day's consciousness fades into dark oblivion, intelligent activity continues on planes hidden from daily consciousness—hidden, yet not necessarily without intelligence. Modern psychology explains that the power of the "unconscious" is an important factor in forming human behavior, yet psychologists know little about the behavior of the "super-conscious." One of the missions of this book is to point out the movement of this intelligent activity. It is not merely a residue of personal experiences that has sunk into the unconscious world of the private soul, but rather an intelligence that spreads its wings to planes of universal intelligence, where it can find the knowledge it needs. This is the great secret of human intuition, which is capable of expanding beyond the circles of experiences and the boundaries of human knowledge.

Intelligence tests measure personal aptitude, limiting human powers of intelligence to familiar circles of personal experience. This allows some experts to believe that we are born with a certain degree of intelligence and are unable to change and expand it. My own experience of life, however, reveals that our capacity for thinking and creating changes over time, sometimes from one day to the next. Intelligence is not a product of "inner-cranial computations," as brain researchers sometimes claim, but the expression of very complex activities of the soul that, on one hand, are linked to the physical body and, on the other, are rooted in inner, uncharted planes of existence. Furthermore, the soul's creative activity is supported by a physical body and an array of life forces that course through it. These life forces maintain the physical body and take part in thinking and memory activity. We have all had days when our energy just dropped, letting us slide into inaction and lack of creativity, and we experience other days when creative thinking rushes forth as if from an inner spring, and "things just seem to take care of themselves."

The power at the disposal of human intelligence depends on more than the random energetic movements of life forces that support the organism. Because individuals are rooted in a higher plane of intelligence, we have access to tools that allow us to break through the boundaries of personal experience and knowledge and to open ourselves to the transformative influence of a higher intelligence. We admire robust athletes who dramatically improve the performance of their physical bodies. Why should we doubt that we can equally and as dramatically transform our intelligence? Although the physical body has reached the peak of its realization through human evolution, the thinking soul, supported by life forces, is a flexible, still-unformed essence, and this is exactly where the human potential for change lies in our time.

Chapter 6

The Power of Imagination

"Some look at things that are and ask why?
I dream of things that never were and ask why not?"
—George Bernard Shaw

Educators and thinkers tend to see human imagination as an essential component of human creativity, and yet they are united in their admission that they know almost nothing about it. Looking at the buzzing activity of children in kindergartens, where students are constantly busy painting, sculpting, arranging castles made of cubes, and engaged in other creative activities, it becomes clear to us that, with few exceptions, much of the creative impulse of childhood is missing from our adult life. When we travel to places we have not visited before, we try to draw a bit of satisfaction by encountering a new experience. Boredom typifies our Western culture, and we constantly chase cheap substitutes for the feeling of natural richness we lost.

Young children, however, are never bored. Just notice the inquisitive looks with which they study adults, the way they throw a pebble into a puddle and flush with excitement at the splashes it makes. In the thinking aspect at least, it is clear that encountering the world of phenomena constantly invigorates children as they create new concepts for the new phenomena they meet. Children do not know the meaning of the phenomena or how they are connected to the rest of reality; their intensive activity is necessary to connect the bits of information into a satisfying, conceptual whole.

According to Rudolf Steiner, sensory impressions flash briefly in our consciousness. This brief flash leaves as soon as the impression is gone. However, an intermediary world, a sheath of subtle substance—etheric forces, as Steiner calls them—exists between the conscious soul and the world of impressions. The impressions are printed on this sheath as they are received. These impressions do not dissipate immediately but leave behind afterimages. From now on, the observing subject will be able to experience an echo, or memory, of the original impression by watching the imprints on the etheric sheath, and will not require the original, direct experience of the senses.

When the soul is aroused to reexperience a past event, it does so by connecting to the etheric imprint, not to the event itself. Memory is not etched into our brain, as natural scientists believe, but in the etheric substance. This substance is a life force that, in addition to its capacity for memory, fulfills many other roles, which we will consider later.

A skeptical reader may reasonably object to such claims. After all, scientists researching the brain have already proven the connection between reasoning activity and the brain. They have shown clearly that the creases of the brain folds are etched as human subjects use their thinking ability; they have measured the electrical currents that shoot between nerve junctions as we think. Is not all this ample evidence that the brain is solely responsible for thinking activity and the storing of information?

The human brain is indeed vital for our thinking activity, but do scientific findings prove that it generates this activity? According to Steiner, thinking activity needs the physical brain to "reflect" it into human consciousness, just as the ground is needed for walking. The etching on the creases of folds is not the result of the brain's activity but the result of the imprints that etheric activity leaves on the physical brain.

Try closing your eyes after staring intently at an object for a minute or two. You will probably be able to perceive the remaining inner impression. This impression will remain in consciousness for a long time if one's soul is calm; if the soul is turbulent, the impression will quickly dissipate. Though somewhat faded in comparison with the original image, the afterimage is a real figure. As the stability of our attentive capacities grows, our memory also grows more alive and becomes more readily available. We think and remember better when these forces are vividly active, and grow absent-minded and forgetful when these life forces temporarily leave us. Even without suprasensory perception there are many signs that the center of our intelligent activities, our imagining and recollecting capacities, are first and foremost linked to our etheric life forces, which thread back and forth through our physical body.[1]

---

1 *Etheric forces:* In the human being, everything that appears to the external world of our senses, what we can see or touch, and what science can observe, spiritual science calls the "physical body." What enters and weaves the physical body, what prevents a person from turning into a corpse between birth and death, is called the "etheric" body, the body of life forces. The outer human being consists of physical and etheric body together. The third component, which withdraws during sleep into undefined darkness, is called the "astral" body. The astral body carries desires and suffering, joy and pain, impulses, and wishes—the feeling, daytime human soul. The fourth and central part of the human being—the "I"—exists in the astral body

Not everyone sees the power of imagination as a blessing; there are always those who are willing to deprecate it. Those for whom the boundary between the real and the imaginary is blurred are often mocked as "spaced out." The faculty of imagination is held by many to be a creator of illusion, a force we would be better off without. Would we?

Later on, we will discuss the process by which we identify with images in our mind and the damage this identification causes to our overall balance. It will, however, be far more precise to say that a *measured* identification of our attention with the impressions entering our consciousness is absolutely necessary; otherwise, the mental images created there would not register in our memory at all. The problems seem to stem from over-identification, not from the mere existence of the identification phenomenon. A disproportional trust placed in these images of our imagination binds our attention to them to the point where any vestige of our self-awareness vanishes.

Young children make healthy use of their imaginative powers. They are able to create meaningful mental images using the impressions of their senses as a basis and actively combining these with their powers of intuitive thinking. Without the presence of our active power of imagination at the crucial junction of impressions and thinking, our inner world would be void of formal images. Human imagination is a tool capable of organizing sensory input from the outside into meaningful images. More advanced spiritual seers are capable of organizing inwardly received messages from divine reality into inner images. The ability of our imaginative faculty to put information into images is a hugely important gift. We discussed the importance of imagination in the concept-creating process of children, but what about adults? Great artists do not generally replicate nature as captured by the senses; they try to express the imaginary content that exists invisibly in the soul. Raphael's art is a good example; it is not simply a copy of material reality, though he was a master of drawing physical organs precisely. His paintings excite us by conveying the spiritual experience that lived in the artist's own soul.

One may wonder how that experience got into the artist's soul to begin with. Similarly, how did the prophet Ezekiel receive his vision of the dry bones? We see that human imagination is capable of creating images based on information that may come from two different sources: one, the sensory information received from the outer, physical world; the other from within, stemming from the soul's meeting with a suprasensory reality.

The soul's amazing ability to draw images out of suprasensory reality has been witnessed throughout history. In addition to Ezekiel, we have Daniel's prophetic visions and, centuries later, John's Apocalypse, which vividly describes suprasensory events to which human eyes and consciousness are usually blind. The prophecies of Nostradamus were experienced as suprasensory images; their later realization verifies that they were not random hallucinations created by a feverish imagination, but proof of the ability to perceive spiritual truths as images.

Spiritual teachers in modern time all attest to the ability of creative imagination to serve suprasensory reception. In his allegory, *Beelzebub's Tales to His Grandson*, G. I. Gurdjieff defines Teskuano as a "being's vessel of observing" events that occur elsewhere in the universe. In the writings of Sri Aurobindo, including the previously quoted excerpt, we read of the "Empire of Vision" that exists in a divine plane of reality from which we may draw bountiful cosmic knowledge. Rudolf Steiner gives the most fruitful and fascinating modern "imaginations" in his many books and lectures. He does not satisfy himself with describing his experiences, but instructs his students to examine how human capacities for awareness can be developed so that the truths of the spirit world may freely flow into our consciousness as divine images.

Suprasensory perception, however, was never limited to teachers and prophets. Scientists and inventors have created and discovered much using the images derived from suprasensory experiences. Nikola Tesla (see appendix 2), one of the greatest modern inventors, is said by his biographer John O'Neill to have received the idea of the alternating current motor as a suprasensory, imaginary vision. The chemist Friedrich Kekulé, who discovered the inner structure of the benzene ring, reported his discovery in this way:

> I turned my chair to the fire and dozed. Again the atoms were gamboling before my eyes...long rows sometimes more closely fitted together, all twining and twisting in snake-like motion. But look! What was that? One of the snakes had seized hold of its own tail, and the form whirled mockingly before my eyes. As if by a flash of lightning I awoke.[2]

Albert Einstein was another scientist who often lauded his ability to see images suprasensibly; he called it his "greatest source of inspiration." One notable quote from his writings expresses it thus:

> The most beautiful experience we can have is the mysterious. It is the fundamental emotion that stands at the cradle of true art and true

2 Quoted in Alan J. Rocke, *Image and Reality: Kekulé, Kopp, and the Scientific Imagination* (Chicago, University of Chicago Press, 2010), p. 194.

> science. Whoever does not know it and can no longer wonder, no longer marvel, is as good as dead, and his eyes are dimmed.[3]

Indeed, a sense of wonder is a necessary condition for the free flow of divine images into the field of human consciousness. A consciousness charmed by the activity of mental thinking and led astray by it cannot be creative. Just as a computer requires a camera so it can process a picture and edit the information to complete its set missions, so does mental thinking require creative intuitions to construct technology and the exact sciences.

The inventor who borrows ideas from one field and applies them in another has been mentioned; yet we haven't discussed which faculty allows him or her to make these virtual reproductions. The power of imagination certainly has a major role in fulfilling this function. Human language researchers speak of "analogous thinking" or "use of metaphors." Aristotle was the first to recognize the importance of analogous thinking, saying, "The ability to create metaphors is the surest sign of genius."

Earlier we asked: What is it that defines a table or desk? This led us to an object's practical function as its essential character. It is therefore not surprising to find a "desktop" on our computer or to understand that when someone "turns the table" on another person it is a move that gives one superiority over the other in a competitive context.

Analogous thinking, however, is not a uniquely human creation. Inner resemblances are abundant in all levels of nature. Did you know that professional photo analysts have a hard time determining the height from which aerial pictures of shorelines are taken? This is because shorelines show the same regularity, in different scales, from different heights. Lacking other points of reference, it is sometimes impossible to determine the altitude of the photographer based only on image content. The picture (fig. 1) shows virtual shorelines seen from varying distances. This virtual photograph displays this principle in the form of fractal geometry, yet reality is not much different in this sense.

A previous chapter discusses the geometric spiral, which is represented in the structure of huge cosmic nebulas, cyclones, the structure of tiny shells, and Archimedes' screw. The Fibonacci series is expressed in the structure of leaves, sunflower seeds, and pinecones. The Golden Ratio proportions can be seen in the butterfly's wings, in schools of fish, and the ancient architecture of Greece. All these and more reveal a striking similarity that exists both throughout nature and in human thought. These principles are expressed, at

3 Einstein, *The New Quotable Einstein*, p. 199.

times artistically and at other times mathematically, in the fascinating works of Mario Livio in his book *The Golden Ratio*.

An amazing discovery in the field of researching patterns and similarities took place in the 1970s, when the works of Benoit Mandelbrot and his colleagues in fractal geometry (see appendix 2) were first published. This geometry describes how it is possible, using relatively simple manipulation that constantly feeds itself, to create an entire universe of shapes that never once exactly repeat and which all share a property of inner resemblance that merges them all and points to their equal source.

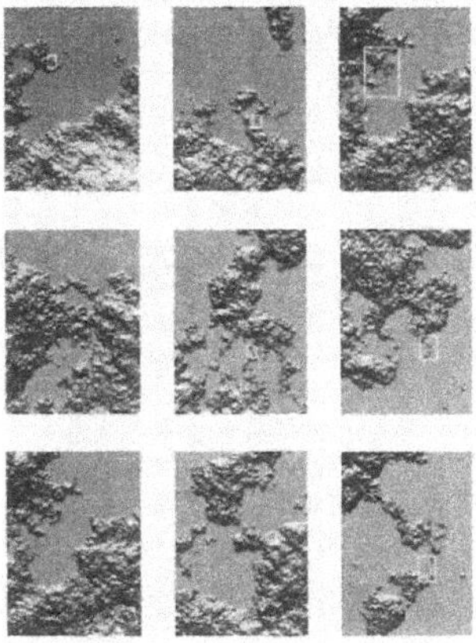

1

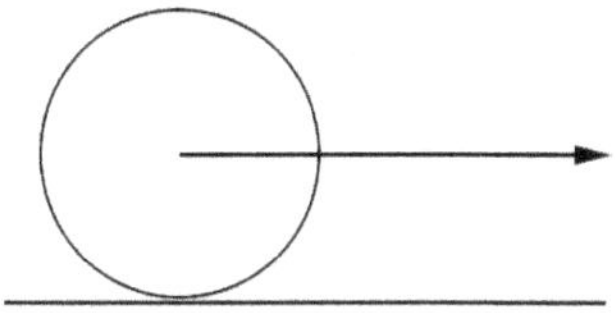

2

The straight line and the circle—an archetypal principle of moving a cylinder on a plane.

One of the conclusions to be drawn from these examples is that the power of imagination is actually involved in the actions of creation. According to all esoteric traditions, the human being is destined to be "an aid in lower worlds"; it is therefore no wonder that we have been given powers analogous to those of our Creator, which allow us to continue the process of creation in our human world. To demonstrate this, let's have a look at the path of the circular shape throughout nature and the history of human creativity.

We will start with the beetle that rolls a ball of food, mentioned at the beginning of this book. What physical or geometric principle is applied here? When a ball or cylinder is placed on a horizontal surface and rolled, its geometric center remains at a constant distance from the horizontal surface. This principle can be expressed by the relation between a circle and a straight line (fig. 2) or between a sphere and a plane. This geometric idea can be used in its physical aspect because the motion of a sphere or cylinder on a horizontal surface is frictionless. This means that if the sphere or cylinder were perfectly shaped and completely hard, rolling them in perfectly equal speed over a perfect horizontal plane would require no effort and would be independent of their weight, since their center of gravity never changes its vertical distance from the plane.

The beetle, of course, does not think in the human sense, yet its creative activity is neither random nor the result of mechanical evolution, as some modern Darwinist thinkers believe, but rather a practical expression of a higher intelligence that directs the beetle's actions from a higher plane of existence.

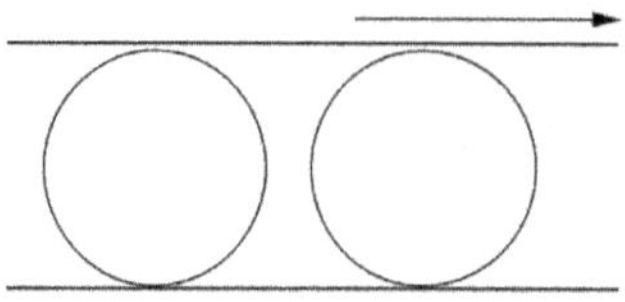
3

4

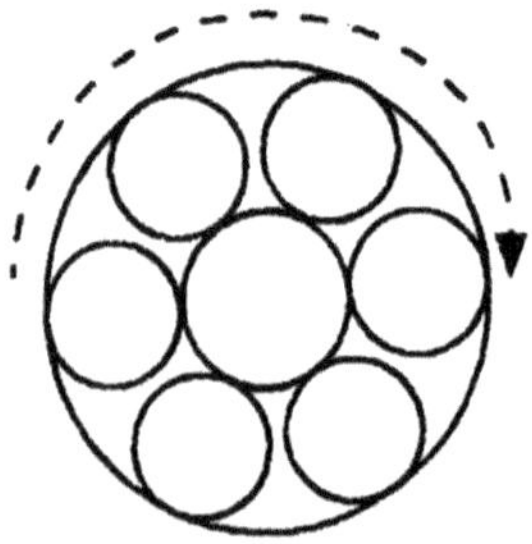
5

In ancient Egypt, large cut stones were transported by rolling them over cylinders placed under their lower horizontal surface. In this way, the Egyptians moved one intelligent step ahead of the beetle, since the idea at the base of this mode of transportation (fig. 3) is that of two horizontal planes moving in relation to each other with a number of spheres or cylinders between them. Here, too, the distance between the planes is constant and therefore no effort is needed to move them aside from the force pressing them against each other.

Now, let's have a look at the ball bearing (fig. 4), 50 million units of which are produced daily around the world, and analyze its fundamental principle. We could say that what was just described in regard to two planes and a number of interceding balls is, in the case of the ball bearing, "bent" into a closed circle. The archetypal principle at the base of the bearing stems from the combination of two geometric facts: when two rings of different diameters are placed around a common axis they maintain a constant distance from one another (fig. 5); in this interval between rings a number of balls or cylinders of equal diameter can be inserted so that the outer ring can revolve in relation to the inner ring. From the physical perspective, the small balls roll on the surface of the rings and they move one around the other without friction and independently of the pressure applied from the outside.

Have human beings created the principle according to which the center of gravity of the upper plane does not rise or drop in relation to the lower plane while they mutually slide? And have human beings alone created the inner law that forces the bearing's rings to revolve around a common axis once equal-sized spheres have been inserted into the gap between them, as the principle of circular sliding dictates? Cosmic Intelligence made the laws of creation and the laws of logic and geometry that eventually gave rise to the human initiative of applying them in the ball bearing. Nature, imbued with cosmic intelligence and much unpredictability, naturally has great creative freedom. Imbued with divine intelligence, nature is the great inventor, realizing its intelligence in its multitude of works. Human beings, imbued with this very same divine intelligence, continue nature's creative activity and find thousands of new ways to express it. In this sense—and only in this sense—can we invent anything truly new. This is the only possible conclusion when we consider the human being's ability to create anything new.

Modern chemistry can synthesize new materials, yet matter's innermost structure is still a great unknown. Biotechnology practices interbreeding and cloning of plants and animals to create new life forms, yet science has no knowledge of the very spirit of life that animates these beings. Continuing nature's creation, humankind supports the general impulse of reality to evolve in thousands of new forms of existence; and indeed it is the intent of cosmic intelligence for thousands of new forms and expressions of its rules also to be expressed through the works of humankind.

Chapter 7

Creating Out of Universal Consciousness

"For this is the difference between intuition and intellect, that intuition is born out of direct awareness, while intellect is an indirect action of knowledge which constructs itself with difficulty out of the unknown from signs and indications and gathered data. But what is not evident to our reason and senses is self evident to the infinite consciousness." —Sri Aurobindo, *The Life Divine*

Musicians and researchers of cognitive faculties cannot explain how an artist can hear a musical composition as a whole before it has been played or even written. This unique phenomenon is so unacceptable to our logic that some doubt its veracity. Others construct "rational" theories to accommodate this amazing ability of, for example, composers such as Mozart. In his book *Brain, Thinking and Creativity*, Howard Gardner, a neuropsychologist who writes much about the development of creativity, raises the following hypothesis: "Where Mozart differs is in his claim to hear a whole piece simultaneously" (p. 365). As I try to understand this claim from my distance in both space and time, I believe that Gardner did not mean this literally. I don't think Mozart could hear a twenty-three-minute piece in just a second or two. Gardner was using a metaphor—a powerful and accurate metaphor. What I believe he meant to say was that the whole organization of the composition, its detailed architecture, was perfectly formed in Mozart's brain. The important decisions—when the different parts would begin and end, when the different instruments would begin to play, when the musical themes would return—all these he could perceive as if they happened simultaneously.

November 26, 2006, the television show *60 Minutes* featured a person born in 1991 to an Israeli mother living in New York. The young man, Jay Greenberg, had composed five full symphonies by the age of twelve. Composer Sam Zyman claimed, "We are talking about a prodigy of the level of the greatest prodigies in history when it comes to composition. I am talking about the likes of Mozart and Mendelssohn and Saint-Saëns."

My interest was sparked by the fact that when he was a child Jay's parents sought professional help to deal with him because his obsessive writing was irritating his schoolteachers. This "problem child" now writes from inspiration that observers cannot comprehend. He is able, to quote the original program, to "finish a piano sonata before our eyes in probably twenty-five minutes." Despite the speed at which he composes, he has no need to rewrite and edit the composition. He never goes back to the notes and changes them, because there is no need to. The boy says that he does not know how the music entered his head, but it comes written in full, that the various parts "seem to come in by themselves if they need to. It's as if the unconscious mind is giving orders at the speed of light. You know, I mean, so I just hear it as if it were a smooth performance of a work that is already written when it isn't." It has also been noted that the boy can play a Beethoven sonata effortlessly from end to beginning, an almost impossible trick that Mozart was also known to perform to amuse his listeners.

Similar cases have been noted in other fields. Exceptional painters and inventors state that they have sometimes seen their creation—whether a painting or invention—perfectly formed in their mind's eye before they rendered it in earthly form. Such reports are compatible with what I have previously stated about archetypes, since human vision can indeed rise to such a level that the whole creation stands before the creator's eyes prior to its taking any material form. Yet we somehow find this phenomenon from the field of imagination and visualization less astounding than that from the musical field. It is not incomprehensible for a painter to translate a suprasensory figure into one we can see with our physical eyes, yet a musical creation can't be described separately from the dimension of time, since the sounds are revealed to us one after the other, and not simultaneously, as in paintings. How, then, can the array of sounds evolving one out of the other throughout the sonata be condensed into just a second or two?

Let us return to phenomena we know from our own lives to investigate this matter. People who have a near-death experience sometimes say that their whole lives passed before their eyes in just a second or two, like an enormous panorama. I myself had a moment like that years ago, while taking a casual walk, though I was in no danger at the moment. It sounds unbelievable, but we should recognize the fact as it is reported and try to understand it deeply, rather than supply feeble "rationalizations," as scientists often do.

Spiritual science provides us with an unusual standpoint from which to examine this matter. We've already mentioned Rudolf Steiner's assertion that memory is registered in our etheric body rather than in our physical brain. When we recall a chain of events, its components are arranged on a time line; that is to say, we cannot remember two events simultaneously. This is so because the nature of associative recollection is a result of the relationship of the physical and etheric bodies; the physical body prevents direct access to the etheric sheath. Otherwise, we would be able to approach its memory content directly rather than through associations. This is the reason that when we have a near-death experience, as Steiner was able to report—since his suprasensory sight allowed him to view this phenomenon directly—the etheric body is partially separated from the physical body. The thinking subject can then contact the etheric body's memory content at once and directly, without mediation by the physical body.

This raises a practical question: can we intentionally nurture this kind of separation in ourselves? Esoteric practice proves this to be possible. In the following chapters about practice, several exercises will be described that allow practitioners to strengthen their etheric forces in a way that makes thinking somewhat independent of the physical body; this allows our awareness to acquire new abilities. When our attentive energy is gathered and focused, we will sometimes be able to see some of the passing day's memories lying one upon the other before our mind's eye rather than one after the other, as they are usually seen through our normal awareness. This is somewhat like reading the paper in front of you when you can directly reference this or the other article, according to your own choice, without having to go through the pieces one after another according to their prearranged order.

We become aware of the fact that higher awareness, somewhat free of its total identification with the physical body, is free of the aspect of time, and things are presented to the viewer arranged together in space rather than one after another through time. This fact, which we can directly experience, may teach us much about the subjectivity of our normal awareness and about the special character of the time dimension. In the current chapter, however, we will limit our discussion of this subject to aspects pertaining only to the creative process. Once we are capable of grasping time's relativity and its dependence on the human vehicle that experiences it through the physical brain or etheric body, it no longer seems unacceptable that a whole musical composition could appear before the composer as "a refined picture," to use Mozart's own words. Our daily awareness, to which we are so thoroughly accustomed, is incapable of grasping this; it takes a contrary experience, brief though it may be, to crack the wall of blind trust that we have developed in the messages of this regular awareness.

Spiritual science's descriptions make us aware of a supreme reality that contains the roots of all of human creation. What to us seems fragmented and arranged on a time line appears as a united and constantly moving whole where all things exist in their archetypal form. It is only through a gradual cosmic involution that this spiritual whole becomes visible to our eyes and audible to our ears. In the supreme worlds exist "spiritual sight" and "spiritual hearing," which the physical senses cannot perceive. Great teachers or initiated individuals report that consciousness that is being developed to higher levels is capable of directly encountering spiritual sights and sounds, without a need for our normal organs of perception. This phenomenon, which Pythagoras experienced as the "music of the spheres," Ezekiel as the "vision of the dry bones," and John as "the Apocalypse," is seen again in the New Age in Sri Aurobindo's and Rudolf Steiner's reports, which describe these levels of reality as the true source for creative life.

Reading the works of humanity's great teachers may bring readers a new perspective about the meaning of human creation and where it comes from, and about the potential for methodically nurturing the tools of perception. Patient, devout nurture, according to the principles of spiritual science, may lead to the discovery of supreme wisdom and creativity, which are expressed through human vessels.

Chapter 8

Human and Cosmic Creation

"We should submerge ourselves in the things and enter their inner thought activity. If this is done, we gradually become aware of the fact that we are growing together with things. We no longer feel that they are outside us, and we are here inside our shell thinking about them. Instead, we come to feel as if our own thinking occurred within the things themselves. Once we have succeeded to a high degree in doing this, many things will become clear to us."

—Rudolf Steiner, *Self-Transformation*

Various traditions describe the human being as a microcosm, analogous to the macrocosm that is the universe. This analogy will naturally find its place in our discussion of human and universal creative power. Unlike materialistic theories that view events in the world as the random results of a mechanical system of blind rules, esoteric knowledge perceives the creative processes at work in our world through processes of evolution and involution, as well as through powers of will and awareness that act through all planes of reality, including those not accessible to normal human awareness. Unlike mechanistic thinking, such as the theory that presents the beginning of cosmic history in terms of a "big bang" and blind processes of integration and disintegration, the spiritual-scientific approach recognizes a supreme, intelligent reality from which creation descends and to which it returns after going through complex processes of development and various degrees of materialization that last infinite periods of time in human terms.

Spiritual research does not focus on the supreme Unmanifested One, transcending human perception, but on the creation of reality, which derives from divine unity and gives birth to differentiation and change, from the highest planes of existence to supposedly dead matter. The complex regularity of the processes of development and materialization is included in the priceless supreme knowledge expressed in ancient traditions, as well as in the teachings of modern teachers. An overview of all these various approaches would require more space than the present work can accommodate. Therefore, we shall limit ourselves to a single aspect in which humanity has a unique role: the powers of creation.

Previously, we mentioned Plato's *world of ideas* and the concept Pythagoras presented as the "Music of the Spheres" as examples of the "super-reality," which exist in the cosmos in connection with the human world of concepts. I claimed that for Plato and for the great teachers of our own time, the notion of the *world of ideas* is not an unreal, abstract concept, but a divine reality with supreme consciousness and supreme will, inseparably merged, that leads divine unity into the world of plurality and back to the One.

Willpower and awareness are usually perceived as two different and separate qualities, yet in the plane of existence discussed here—the supreme world of ideas—these two fundamental forces are aspects of the same being and, in accordance with supreme law, are thus able to give birth to the different worlds that descend, one from another, down to the material world revealed through our senses. This set of rules appears in different forms in all the ancient traditions. Among other places, it is described in the Kabbalah of Rabbi Isaac Luria's writings, which offers a basis for understanding these general laws that also work in the human being. In G. I. Gurdjieff's important epic, *Beelzebub's Tales to His Grandson*, the Law of Three and the Law of Seven appear as the fundamental bases of the processes of evolution and involution that create world reality. This important cosmic knowledge is also expressed in the Vedas and the Upanishads of ancient Indian culture and was revived by Sri Aurobindo, who expressed it in a way more accessible to modern people. Although esoteric knowledge is essentially inconsistent, presenting cosmic processes in many forms and from different points of view, all of its shades and forms are unique in outlining humanity's place in the general panorama of reality and in deriving the meaning of human creation as part of the general process of universal creation.

While human civilization perceives its works—both technological inventions and artistic creations—to be related either to the search for welfare, or to the need for original human creation, esoteric knowledge sees human creativity in a much broader context. This science examines the cosmic interest in infinite creation and strives to understand how humanity fits into this pattern.

Looking at their lives and the phenomena around them, human beings ask, "What is the *cause* of this creation?" The wonder and mystery of creation are unsettling, and we feel that our life is unsatisfactory until we have at least some understanding of the purpose of universal creation and our own lives. The desire to know *cause* is shown by the fact that the creation story appears in many different versions, each wearing the particular attire of its spiritual tradition.

According to the Jewish Kabbalah, the Creator wanted to pleasure his creations. That is to say, he felt that, without someone to lavish his gifts upon, his existence would not be perfect. That is why he created a "will to receive," the inner essence of all creation. In *Beelzebub's Tales to His Grandson*, this matter is explained differently, through a myth about the destructive effect of time, which the writer calls the "Most Great Heropass of Time." According to this myth, the Creator, looking around him at his world, "Sun Absolute," noticed that it was being reduced, owing to the activity of the time factor (Heropass). Therefore, it was necessary to change the existing rules to allow reality to rearrange itself into semi-autonomous activities, from which it would be able to compensate for the lost substance. The new cosmic organism was admittedly supported by the Creator's will, but since a new set of rules was inserted into it that included the possibility of coincidence and chance, the cosmic organism began to maintain *itself* to some extent, and to create forms that had not existed before.

Creative reality, according to Beelzebub, is a movement between two poles, the Divine Absolute on one end and a lower Absolute on the other. Creation flows in both directions, as *involution* and *evolution* composing unified law. This law-abiding, cosmic process is called the Law of Sevenfoldness, and is described in detail later in Gurdjieff's tale.

Reading Sri Aurobindo, one is struck by the similarity between what he expresses and the words of Beelzebub. The same is true for the cosmology detailed in the Kabbalistic tree of life, in the creation stories in Rudolf Steiner's *Outline of Esoteric Science*, and in most spiritual traditions that we know. Although the process of creation includes a mechanical element and the possibility for error and conflicts of interest among various powers of creation, they can all be said to serve a supreme, divine interest, and so creations's movements are not blind and random, which is the kind of evolution and mechanical entropy presented by the conventional natural sciences.

Yet, how is human creation connected with the supreme interest of the general world of creation? Are human beings nothing but external observers in the process of creation, developing their technological and artistic work out of their own world for their own comfort and pleasure? Those with an appropriate feeling for the world around them will refuse to accept the chill emanating from the cold theories labeled "scientific," which disallow any meaningful connection between human creative activity and the forces of cosmic creation that flow, wave after wave, in an endless motion of infinite creation that never repeats itself.

Humanity's mission is connected with the unique structure intended for us. Just as the universal structure includes different hierarchical levels of reality, one inside the other, so does the structure of the human being include a hierarchy of essences, the lowest of which is that of our physical body. Yet the physical body is only the seat of a higher essence, the soul, which wants, feels, and thinks; this essence operates the physical body and uses its organs to come into contact with the "external" world as both an emotional and cognitive experience. However, if the soul had to satisfy itself only with the impressions and nurture of the earthly world, its life would be limited to subjective, animal-level experiences alone. Human beings are unique in that a higher world sheds its light into our soul, filling it with life forces and giving it an exceptional possibility—to create through its own powers.

Thus, the human soul is fed by two worlds simultaneously. One is earthly and presents its impressions through the senses connected with the physical body, while the other is a spiritual world that connects the soul with higher levels of existence. The human entity is therefore a bridge between the supreme, spiritual levels of existence and the earthly levels. We imbue the earthly levels with the blessed influence of the spirit, and at the same time enable the spirit world to experience the material world through our humanity.

Revealed reality, however, is far more complex than that described by this simplistic scheme, because our human role as a reconciling world between the divine and earthly levels is not fully realized. The creative flow of the spiritual world does not find a worthy tool in humanity, at least not as we appear in modern times. The two-directional flow needed for the perfect functioning of universal reality cannot be realized effectively through the human entity, although this was, in fact, the very reason for the creation of humanity.

Because of cosmic influences, as human beings we have developed an element foreign to our original nature: self-centered, egoistic consciousness (the story of that revelation is told differently in various spiritual traditions). There is a missing link in our very own hierarchical constitution. Since the necessary continuum does not exist fully in our being, we cannot fulfill our important role in the universal continuum, and so our place in the cosmic flow is left vacant. This fundamental flaw of the modern human being will be further described in the chapter about attention, where we shall discuss our tendency to identify with the images created by sensory impressions, with endless inner chatter, and with bodily sensations, both pleasant and unpleasant. Strengthening the unique power of attention may encourage the appearance of a new "self," one that gives the human being inner stability and awareness of both earthly and divine forces acting through it. A genuine "self," embedded in the physical body, is the very missing link that I have mentioned, the one necessary to firmly place humanity where divine will meant us to stand.

Why, one may ask, should there be a genuine "self"? What's wrong with our normal, present "self"? We eat, learn, think, and enjoy life. We have created governmental institutions and instituted cultural enterprises. We fight for our liberty as autonomous individuals and maintain a dignified existence.

The coming chapters on meditation and practice will give readers the opportunity to experience the realization that may dawn in someone whose inner field of awareness is beginning to open to the surprising realization about the true nature of what we mistakenly call our "self." One of the missing aspects of the present "self" is that it is unable consciously to grasp its own existence or its unique position within the general panorama of reality. The subjective "self" of the modern human being (we are all modern in this sense) cuts itself off from general reality, is blind to its connections with the external circles of life and is therefore unable to comprehend humanity's essential role as a vital link in the general chain of creation. This "self" cannot, on its own, open to universal powers of creation or to the act of creating. We call it our "self" because we do not know the feeling of the essential, intimate, genuine "self" that we can experience under the right conditions.

Those who listen to their soul's inner demands may find that one demand is to search for our true identity; not the identity with a first and last name, but the living, essential one that gives our life meaning as creating individuals—creating both in the inner and outer sense. We create brilliant technologies and make amazing scientific discoveries, and at the same time are blind to our mission as human creators, meant to carry out, on our earthly planes, the mission given us by divine intent. Our external creation cannot stand on its own merits; it must be combined with the inner creation of a conscious "self," properly fulfilling its calling. External creation can be realized while consciously remembering our presence and listening to the voices calling us from higher planes of existence. Those planes, we should remember, are ceaselessly at work in us; yet we do not listen, locked as we are in the terrible illusion of an independent "self" that does not recognize a higher authority and presumes to speak for our entire being.

There is a deep schism these days between the scientific, technological community and people of spirit and religion. The creators of modern technology occasionally look down upon those they see as being blinded by spiritual ambitions—and not without good cause. The desire to deepen our inner life is undergoing a process of cheap popularization and, in extreme cases, becomes an ambition to live a life cut off from the hard ground of reality. Yet this deep schism has come about only because the profound connection between inner creation and outer work is often misunderstood, and thus it is beyond the ability of many people to combine the two poles. The lives of those who create modern technology would be no less productive if their time were divided between professional creativity and doing what we should do in our roles as human beings. "Render unto Caesar what belongs to Caesar; render unto God what belongs to God." This phrase, first uttered 2,000 years ago, takes on new and penetrating meaning today in relation to humanity's betrayal of our role as creators and as attentive vessels to the powers that seek to find expression through us. Wise old sayings such as, "One who knows how to properly thread a needle knows everything," or "One who knows how to drink a cup of tea has found the Tao," point us to the idea at the heart of this book—integration of the modern person's external and internal creative life. We will return to this subject later.

Heaven and Earth meet in the human being. Though we receive our spiritual impulses from supreme planes of reality, the unique structure of that reality provides us with our own independent living space. The human being is not merely a relay station for spiritual influences traveling into material plane, but rather a sovereign entity able to choose and create independently. In the Hebrew tradition it is said that "man is an aid to his maker." This idea is also expressed in *Beelzebub's Tales* and other esoteric teachings and systems. On the one hand, human beings are capable of autonomous thinking that connects them with the universal source of thinking, and on the other provide us with human concepts derived from the earthly world of senses. We are capable of moving between two planes of thinking—an intuitive plane derived from the intelligence of the divine world of ideals, and a logical plane that stems from the sensory images that arise in our soul in reaction to contact with earthly reality. Imposing our will on this world of dynamic thinking, we are able to direct it toward research, technology, or art, and thus create a new world of phenomena. This world, while new, obeys the inner regularity of supreme intelligence, just as all of creating nature does.

The deviations that can be seen in ugly works of art or destructive technologies do not attest to the lack of supreme, intelligent laws in human creativity, but rather to wrong use of this creativity—they are the result of misused autonomy. Creators who are attentive to supreme planes of reality will find more appropriate use for their powers of creation. Their art will share the harmony that exists in supreme worlds; their technological activity will be used for the betterment of humanity and our surroundings; scientific research will continue to strive to understand reality while expanding its field of activity to other planes of existence that are at the very base of our being. The human creator and universal creation are bound to one another, yet modern humanity has separated them. The call of our time is to find the union once again.

Chapter 9

Fresh Approaches to a Riddle

"The beginning of Science is the examination of the truths of the world-force that underlie its apparent workings such as our senses represent them to be; the beginning of philosophy is the examination of principles of things which the senses mistranslate to us; the beginning of spiritual knowledge is the refusal to accept the limitations of the sense-life or to take the visible or the sensible as anything more than phenomena of the Reality."

—Sri Aurobindo, *The Synthesis of Yoga*

The approach presented in this book is somewhat different from the one more commonly taken with regard to the subject of creating and inventions. This difference, however, does not stem from disregard for or ignorance of the ways in which modern science and technology think and act. In my youth I was fervently enthusiastic about these fields. When I was a child, scientific and technological thinking reached me through the erstwhile *Ma'ayan* encyclopedia, the science magazines of the time in Israel, and especially the "build your own" publications, my loyal companions in childhood and the source of inspiration for everything that I learned later. My technological studies were completed at the Technion, Israel Institute of Technology, where the latest physical and mathematical theories were taught.

My search for knowledge led me to lectures on philosophy at Tel Aviv University and to psychology books by and about Freud, Adler, and Jung. Yet all along, I felt deep in my heart that what I had encountered was not enough to explain the world around me and the meaning of my own existence within it.

My soul, thirsty for understanding, gradually came to perceive three separate fields of knowledge: science, art, and religion. It appeared to me that those worlds were cut off from one another, each separately concentrated within itself, each regarding all of reality from its own point of view. No approach provided a complete understanding of united reality. The philosophies that I had learned did try to connect all three areas, but even there

I could not find the deep, complete understanding that I was looking for, at least not in the theories that I seriously researched.

When I later became acquainted with the world of esoteric knowledge, its treasures began to open to me like a broad panorama that included the understanding of universal reality complete with the understanding of humanity within this whole. I began to see the laws of nature and science, principles of aesthetics and art, and the meaning of life and religious outlook as aspects of the same universal reality. The artificial walls that modern civilization erected between these fields gradually began to seem like the result of partial and limited knowledge by subjective observers rather than characteristics of reality itself.

It is often thought that esoteric knowledge comes from mystical experiences and cannot be scientifically and objectively tested. This thought is a mistake, implanted in modern thinking by biased scientists who fail to consider esoteric ideas seriously. It is an inexplicable tendency of the scientific community. Unlike natural sciences, which are taught as external knowledge, esoteric research cannot be carried out from an attitude alienated from the object of research. Esoteric knowledge is "experienced knowledge"; the researcher, the object of research, and the laboratory are all part of the same living experience. This is why spiritual researchers cannot externally "prove" the veracity of their findings. Does this detract from their credibility?

Western society has experienced a new wave of pseudo-esoteric movements that bring a kind of fogginess and mysticism into the subject. Those unwilling to go the extra mile to and accept the necessary commitment often wander from one mystic workshop to another, chasing the promise of cosmic knowledge and suprasensory capacities provided quickly and at affordable prices. Yet spiritual-scientific research has nothing to do with fogginess and mysticism. Spiritual researchers are not required to abandon the rules of logic and bathe in ecstasy that lacks self-awareness. Spiritual-scientific research begins at the level of daily thinking and gradually rises to higher planes, losing none of its sharpness and clarity.

In the natural sciences, researchers are required to make their every assertion open to examination by others. Spiritual research does not object to this iron rule. Once individuals have developed the appropriate capacity, their investigation will attain the same level of intent. In this sense, esoteric truths are no less objective than those of the natural sciences. Yet since the laboratory in which this research is conducted is none other than the scientist's soul, it is only natural to request that those who check the conclusions should prepare themselves for the demands of research before stating an opinion.

Zvi Yanai, a former director of Israel's ministry of science and technology and editor of the magazine *Thoughts*, publishes articles in a wide range of areas: science and technology, arts and aesthetics, philosophy of science, and many more. No doubt his vast knowledge in so many different areas makes him an exemplary representative of modern Western thinking. A quotation from Mr. Yanai's article, "Living with Uncertainty," makes clear his adherence to old ways of thinking:

> Life on Earth was able to survive for four billion years and develop a certain variety of species against all odds, a success attributable in no small measure to lack of guidance, leadership or purpose.... Though belief in universal law and order allows us to plan for tomorrow as if nothing is more expectable, this answer, important though it may be, is nothing more than a heart's desire.[1]

If we were to ask the question at the heart of this book—where do creative ideas come from—what kind of reply would he give us? A viewpoint that ignores the fact that human thinking does not act on one plane alone, as view that lacks the perspective in which human thinking is seen to be firmly established in universal intelligence, simply cannot provide a satisfactory answer. This kind of viewpoint cannot get to the bottom of scientific progress, though it professes affection for the world of science and technology. How does materialistic thinking explain the astounding correlation between the rules of geometry and the world of phenomena, which acts according to the very same mathematical regularity? The astounding depth of reality, the deep intelligence within it, the sense of mystery that Albert Einstein often praised, is here explained with a mechanistic model of "natural selection," guided by no intentional intelligence save the individual need of a species to survive!

What meaning could human existence have in such a cold, barren model? What meaning could human creation in art and technology have if human evolution happens without "guidance, leadership or purpose?" Modern civilization must find its way back to an overall understanding of reality. Science, art, and religious life have been artificially separated because of modern humanity's failure to recognize the supreme intelligent foundation at the base of all three areas.

1 Zvi Yanai "The Eternal Search," *Talks with Scientists*, Tel Aviv: Am Oved, 2000 (translated from the original Hebrew).

In the previous chapter I attempted to compare human thinking to artificial intelligence, pointing out the vast difference between the two. I briefly demonstrated that human intelligence is not limited to calculating abilities alone, and that the process of recollection and identification involves other faculties of the soul—feeling and willing. Therefore, what makes us human is the fact that no thinking activity, however simple, occurs without the involvement of our faculties of will and emotion. For example, the recognition of written characters, singly or assembled in words, cannot be accomplished without the participation of emotion. If one cannot observe this, a lack of subtlety in one's perception is to blame.

Modern science's approach to this issue can be seen in a conversation between Mr. Yanai and Professor Yadin Dudai, transcribed in Yanai's book, *The Eternal Search: Conversations with Scientists*:

YANAI: "If it's okay with you, I'd like to look at this issue from a different direction: what is memory made of—protein?"

PROFESSOR DUDAI: "No, not protein. In the fifties it was wrongly assumed that memory was coded in proteins. Proteins are necessary for memory, but are not enough." (Ibid., p. 7)

Further down on the same page, responding to a question about the way in which an image received through the eye becomes a chemical, which in turn is translated into an abstract concept, Professor Dudai says:

> The stage we're at now allows us to follow the process: the brain gets information from the eyes, ears, hands, nose, and mouth and translates them into electric activity. This activity moves through neurons and reaches various centers in the brain, where it is processed. We say that that is where computations of representations of electric activity are made. Now, many chemical activities arise in the processes that occur between sensory reception and electrical activity.

YANAI: "I still don't see how information is translated from one medium to another. For example, how does a canary's song become a chemical process, and how does a structure like memory release a song?"

PROFESSOR DUDAI: "Generally speaking, we know that when a bird wants to sing it pulls the song out of its memory. To this end it operates networks in its mind that supply it with electrical information. When it hears a song, the connections between the components of the network should undergo changes. These

> are chemical changes, and the memory of the particular song the bird is about to sing is coded in the neural network, which is now different from the network before the song was coded into memory." (Ibid.)

Any modern designer assigned to develop a computer-operated mechanical bird would probably build it according to exactly the same principles that Professor Dudai describes. Materialistic science does not see that the soul's faculties are inseparably linked, or that stereotypical thinking is not proper thinking for human beings. Take the model of electric currents and chemistry that Professor Dudai offers, affix it to a metal skeleton, and you have a robot, not a human being.

After years of research that brought no significant breakthrough, brain researchers have concluded that the human brain is so complicated that its mystery cannot be tackled from only one approach. Scientists specializing in different aspects of human thinking—psychologists, sociologists, biologists, and brain surgeons—have recently begun to cooperate in attempts to cope with what seems to be the deepest mystery of the human being. The unique findings of a professor who heads an interdisciplinary center for brain research were presented to the public in a recent television interview. In this interview the professor described the miraculous complexity of the central nervous system and the enormous difficulty in understanding how it functions. He then described experiments that measure electrical processes that occur simultaneously in different brain cells. The experiments were done with scientific expertise and their results were displayed as a visual-musical graph describing electrical activity in the brain of a monkey drawing colored circles on a white sheet of paper. At a later stage of the interview the scientist was asked some questions about brain activity that were broader in scope, such as what connection brain functions have with emotion and will, and whether he believed in the existence of a human soul.

At this point we were given what the scientist himself called a "qualified opinion," which is relevant to our subject just insofar as it points to the erroneous way of thinking that has slipped into modern materialistic science. According to the professor, all of our soul's life, including the faculties of emotion and will, is a product of complex electrical activity in our central nervous system; the relations within the system, their amplitude and inner regularity, determine all of our soul's activities. For example, replying to the interviewer's question about feelings of love and hate, the professor replied that these are complex pulses, and it is their organization that creates the feelings. As to the question of personal responsibility between one person and another, he replied that it is the complex organization of these pulses that makes us help others in order to insure our survival, since otherwise the human species would be extinct. How can human intelligence bear the opinion that moral laws, the emotional wealth at the base of a society, a tribe, or the human family, are no more than a product of the complex, systematic activity of neurons that ensures the survival of the human race?

The same basic error in this mode of thinking is repeated time after time in scientific theories that try to explain universal reality while completely ignoring anything that is not matter—anything that can't be measured using mechanistic tools. Such theories fail to recognize the intelligent essence that exists beyond material reality and imbues it with life, consciousness, and intelligence.. Materialistic scientists see emotion as a mechanical activity of our brain cells; they believe that if we just take the computation activity of a number of brain cells and multiply it enough times a "breakthrough," an "act of magic," or call it what you will, can occur and the result will be emotion, willpower, the sensation of life—anything that belongs to our soul's world and wasn't there to begin with! This mode of thinking is no different from that which claimed, until a few centuries ago, that if we were to mix up enough mud, worms would be created. Don't scientists feel that emotional essence cannot result from computational activity? Can't they feel the life forces that course through their own bodies, making them happy or sad, feeling desire or aversion? How could these feelings be the result of computational activity of our nerve cells, no matter how complex this activity is?

This very erroneous way of thinking sneaks into mechanistic theories of the origin of the species. Evolutionists believe that a completely random process in which molecules of matter meet, which they believe has been going on for millions of years, created intelligent beings. That is, take a huge number of encounters between dead molecules of matter, filter the unsuccessful ones, and there you have it—life, feelings, intelligence, and everything else! The theory of worms born of mud survived the cultural development of the twentieth century and is still found among those who lead scientific research in the twenty-first century; incredible but true.

Materialistic thinking sees evolution as a rising scale: primal matter > random formation > first appearance of the element of life > appearance of thinking, feelings, and awareness. Spiritual science, however, sees things the other way around. It is the supreme spirit from which all creation springs; there is nothing but spirit, and even apparently dead matter is in fact condensed spirit. Through a process of involution the spirit has become an essence of soul (astral existence) from which the life forces were born; these later thickened and became the matter of the physical world. Everything we find as lifeless matter (at least according to our superficial perception) is no less than a spiritual force that has become corporeal through many eons of gradual development. At the same time, according to the ascending law of evolution, physical matter evolves toward the Supreme Source through the power of spirit itself, richer and ever growing in complexity. Evolutionary and involutionary processes are elaborately linked, and through ceaseless conflict give birth to the variety of phenomena we see around us.

The Israeli scientists quoted above are not islands unto themselves in the ocean of academic research. An entire multinational community researches human cognitive faculties, yet hasn't the insight to send its questing eyes beyond what can be measured as electrical currents, communication between neurons and chemical secretions, and so on.

The theory about the creation of all of our faculties gets more complicated every time new "computation centers" are discovered. A major discovery was made by Professor Michael Gershon, head of the cellular anatomy and biology department at the Columbia University Medical Center in New York. Professor Gershon found that human beings have another "brain" in addition to the main brain in the cranium.[2] This brain is also capable of memory, learning, and feelings. According to Professor Gershon, intestinal organs and the primal brain begin to develop from the same cell tissue in the early stages of the embryo's development. As the embryo grows, cells go through a process of differentiation and develop different forms and characteristics; some will become the central nervous system, also called the central brain, while some become the enteric nervous system, which we may call our "intestinal brain." These two systems work mutually, communicating through the vagus nerve. According to the professor, the intestine contains more nerve cells than the entire peripheral nervous system. Almost all chemicals involved in the brain's activity have also been found in the intestines.

I do not question the potential of lab research to make fascinating deductions about human physiology; our physiology is indeed a masterpiece, diligently created by supreme intelligence over whole eons of evolution. Yet, in

2 Gershon, *The Second Brain: A Groundbreaking New Understanding of Nervous Disorders of the Stomach and Intestine.*

researchers' conclusions about how this wonderful system functions, we can easily find the usual mistakes that characterize materialistic thinking. For example, in an article published in advance of Professor Gershon's visit to Israel, we find the claim that when the digestive system reports a problem to the central brain, it translates it to emotional phenomena like tension, anxiety, and so on, while when the central brain "communicates" a problem to the digestive system, it translates it to physical phenomena such as stomachaches, constipation, diarrhea, and the like.

Here again, nerves appear to be responsible for thinking and feeling. The mode of thinking that sees brain cells as responsible for creating "emotional reactions" is naively simple, since it completely ignores the only faculty that can sense "emotional reactions"—indeed, the *only* faculty that can feel any emotion. Our emotions are not seated in physical nerve cells, and are certainly not created there. The field of activity for emotions, and that of thinking activity, is the human soul, whose essence is not even related directly to the physical body, but through an intermediary—the etheric sheath's life forces. This, at least, is the claim of spiritual science.

For example, consider what happens when we blush. Whereas blushing manifests as a change of one's skin color, we know that the cause of blushing is the sense of embarrassment one feels. In other words, it is an activity of the soul that belongs exclusively to the soul's field of activity. Would anyone even consider claiming that some nervous computation unit is responsible for the change in color? The same is true for anxiety and feelings of distress that take control of our body and create changes in the serotonin balance. The fact that anxiety attacks can be treated through medication should not confuse the logical thinking process that goes with the scientific findings: our soul's life is merged with our physical organs; they influence the soul's life and are influenced in return. Those who wish to find an explanation of all the soul's phenomena in the nervous system are unscientific, though they would claim otherwise.

In his book *Art, Mind, and Brain: A Cognitive Approach to Creativity*, Howard Gardner, another scientist, reports his research, which was part of a prestigious project at Boston University School of Medicine. In that project, scientists gathered enormous amounts of data and analyzed them one by one, in order to verify or refute dominant current theories about consciousness. Gardner advanced an original theory of "multiple intelligences," according to which human intelligence faculties consist of seven patterns of thought function that cooperate to include all human intelligence. In describing his conclusions, he included phrases such as "music is an autonomous intellectual faculty," and, "like language, music is a separate intellectual faculty." The scientific approach expressed in the book mentions "computation units" and learning functions that represent all of humankind's intelligent activity.

Is music indeed an intellectual faculty? Can we really see musical creation as something produced by a "computation unit?" And how would this theory explain the existence of musical geniuses who start composing incredibly complex pieces at a very young age? How does this theory explain significant breakthroughs in science and technology? Indeed, when thinking that calls itself "scientific" reduces itself to what it finds in the material world, it is no longer capable of understanding originality. When it ignores the invisible forces that work in the human soul and bind it to wider intelligent activity that lies at the very base of all reality, it plods in the world of dead, mechanical "computation units," which have nothing to do with the sensations of wonder, inspiration, original thinking—the very building blocks of human creativity.

In the following chapters we will discuss human creative powers from the viewpoint of a humanistic science, a science that sees thinking, feeling, and willing as universal essences in which human beings have a role as active participants, not as sole creators. Only this approach will allow us to uncover at least part of the deep mystery of reality and link our creations as human beings to the whole array of creative forces at work in the entire universe.

Chapter 10

Genius and Madness

"Its madness is a wise madness of Ananda, the incalculable ecstasy of a supreme consciousness and power, vibrating with an infinite sense of freedom and intensity in its divine life movements. Its action is supra-rational and therefore to the rational mind which has not the key, it seems a colossal madness. And yet, this that seems madness is wisdom in action that only baffles the mind by the liberty and richness of its contents and the infinite complexity in fundamental simplicity of its motions; it is the very method of the Lord of the Yoga, a thing no intellectual interpretation can fathom."

—Sri Aurobindo, *The Synthesis of Yoga*

Western culture has long been aware of the supposedly odd coincidence between genius and madness, overflowing creativity and psychic insanity. Artists, scientists, mathematicians, and unusual inventors occasionally appear on the stage of human civilization, leaving their unique mark, not only because of their creation, but also because of the unbearable suffering and psychological difficulties connected with their creative life. Scientific research was directed to the problem without definite results. Nevertheless, details of a recent research project carried out in Hungary by Szabolcs Keri were published recently.[1] The main focus was Neureguin 1, a special gene that is responsible for a variety of inner processes of the brain.

It was already known that this particular gene is actively present in people suffering from schizophrenia and bipolar disorder, but the recent research investigated its existence especially in creative, healthy students within the local academic community. Genetic blood testing of approximately two hundred creative individuals showed beyond doubt that this special gene was present to a high degree in these subjects, beyond the general norm. Although the scientific finding is clear, the essential cause for this

1 "Genes for Psychosis and Creativity: A Promoter Polymorphism of the Neuregulin 1 Gene Is Related to Creativity in People with High Intellectual Achievement," *Psychological Science* 20,9 (2009).

correlation between creativity and madness is still a great mystery. It would be interesting, then, to observe additional aspects of the question based on the ideas of spiritual science.

One of the best-known stories of genius and madness is that of John Nash (see see appendix 2), who was portrayed in the 2001 movie *A Beautiful Mind*. Nash's achievements in mathematics won him the Nobel Prize for Economics in 1994. The work that earned him the award was a theory about the equilibrium of a singular point within a system of dynamic forces, which had occupied him in his youth as part of his interest in game theory.[2] His theory was later found to have value in the field of economics. In this branch of social science, which deals with the production, distribution, and consumption of goods and services, participants with conflicting interests are motivated by human considerations, not necessarily by rational considerations. John Nash started having unusual mathematical intuitions in his childhood; at the same time he started displaying symptoms of what his doctors would later diagnose as paranoid schizophrenia.

The part of this story that is most relevant to our topic is Nash's testimonies about the drugs he was prescribed and how they affected him. Nash said that, whereas the drugs did relieve his suffering and released him from the delusions that haunted him, they also reduced his vitality and his ability to connect to the sharper intelligence that he possessed before he was hospitalized. Watching a filmed interview of Nash, my impression was that he was not at all happy about the drugs, even though they helped normalize his life. He seemed to have been in love with the rich streams of insight that flowed into him without medication, and their loss, caused by the drugs, took away something vital that gave reason for his existence. The Nobel Prize he received was for work he did in his youth, before he was hospitalized. Although once "cured" he was given an academic chair and returned to teaching, his productivity at this stage in life wasn't nearly of the same capacity and quality as in his youth.

Nash's story, of course, is not the only example of this phenomenon. Other geniuses have displayed various degrees and symptoms of dyslexia, autism, manic depression, and suicidal tendencies, among whom we find musicians such as Beethoven, Schumann, and the modern pianist David Helfgott; the writers Ernest Hemingway, Charles Dickens, and Tennessee Williams; and the greatest inventor of modern times, Nikola Tesla. Until the age of seventeen, Tesla saw blinding, painful flashes of light and strange visions, which

2 "Equilibrium Points in N-person Games," *Proceedings of the National Academy of Sciences* 36 (1950), 48–49.

caused anxiety and ruined his psychological stability. The intensity of the attacks lessened only when he turned his interest toward creative inventions.

My friend Georg Kühlewind was interested for some years in what he called, "special children." He described their unique qualities in his book *Star Children*. Kühlewind believed that our era is marked by the appearance of unusual children who show special qualities such as rare intelligence, unusual sensitivity, and sense of individuality—characteristics not normally found in children their age. On the other hand, these children often suffer from hyperactivity, lack of ability to focus their attention, stubborn rebelliousness, and introversion. According to Kühlewind, we should understand this phenomenon within its spiritual context rather than rush to administer medication that only causes these special children irrevocable damage.

Though I am not very knowledgeable in the fields of psychology or education, the unusual experiences I have had in my life and conversations I have had with friends in those fields have led me to ideas that are somewhat different from those common in the professional world of psychological health. These are ideas about the strange connection between works of genius and the maladies of the soul that on unusual occasions may afflict a creator. I would like to share these ideas with you.

We tend to go through life half asleep, and so in a certain way we are calm and rested; we are not at all aware of the intense nature of the reality beyond our awareness. This is not because this reality does not exist; it is because our present structure of consciousness cannot withstand its dazzling light. Its activity is so intense that if one is not prepared in one's soul to withstand it, it might harm one's faculty of consciousness. Many who practice meditation experience the peace and quiet that it brings; yet this is not all there is to it. In more advanced stages of esoteric development, students may face spiritual powers that try to penetrate their soul and body. Spiritual reality naturally strives to transform earthly planes and raise them to its level; it is a supreme cosmic goal, and human beings have an important and vital role in its fulfillment. The process of transformation occurs through gradual descent into the human vessel, with the spirit purging the murky places—in both soul and body—on its way down, thus creating a new and higher substance, the fruit of its intense activity.

Though we generally remain unaware of the fact, this transformative activity is constantly at work among humanity and, to a lesser extent, with nature in general; this transformation of humanity occurs over long spans of time, hundreds and thousands of years. The essence of esoteric practice, which is the inner obligation of individuals, is to accelerate this process so that individuals who take up the commitment of self-initiation will see the fruits of transformation appearing in their lives. The essential process of transformation requires more than strengthening our attentive power (as I will describe in a later chapter). Whereas this part of the process is vital, it is only a stage of preparing for the advent of a higher power that reaches the body's layers through its own initiative, dissolves constrictions in body and soul, and imbues the earthly levels and human body with the spirit's vitality.

The structure of our soul, and especially that of our vessel of consciousness, is built in such a way that we do not perceive what we are not yet ready to assimilate. We are asleep, daydreaming if you will, with our attention focused mostly on the impressions of the external world of phenomena. Yet even when the soul turns inward, it perceives only associative thoughts, images, and inner chatter; it cannot see beyond those. Our vision is twice limited, both inwardly and outwardly, by an impenetrable screen; the suprasensory existence beyond the screen is stopped before it reaches the bounds of our awareness. Those who have not had the appropriate training and try to look inward find that they cannot do it at all. We fear the silence, fear the unknown, and so we fall asleep or turn back to the world of external impressions; this is the way of a dormant soul.

The wall that we have constructed around us to fend off the fierce intensity of higher planes of reality is the very thing that cuts us off from these planes of activity, from the infinite source of creation to which our soul is linked in its inner sanctum. The essence of esoteric initiation is that it prepares the soul for penetration by the powers of supreme consciousness; it cleanses the human vessel—both body and soul—and strengthens it so that it is able to encounter supreme reality and not be harmed. The kabbalistic story about four individuals going into an orchard (*pardes* in Hebrew), with only one, Rabbi Akiva, emerging whole in body and mind, reminds those who delve into esoteric wisdom of the dangers lying therein for those not suitably prepared.[3]

And cases do occur where blinding reality penetrates an unprepared soul with too much power, causing irrevocable damage. A friend who is a clinical psychologist and a companion on the path of inner development once said, "In the hospital where I work there are some patients who have had turbulent spiritual experiences that caused them irrevocable damage; I can point to no clear genetic or physical factor that could be a direct cause for

3 The Hebrew word for "orchard," *PaRDeS*, also serves as a four-letter acronym: P = *Pshat*, "simple;" R = *Remez*, "hint;" D = *Drash*, "search"; and S = *Sod*, "secret." Together these represent the four levels of understanding in esoteric initiation, from the coarsest to the most subtle.

their deterioration." It is possible, then, to claim that while the delusions and disruptions that these patients manifest after their harsh experiences might attest to a disruption in the soul or body, this disruption is not the source of malady but rather a result of an inner experience.

Dealing with the process of acquiring new concepts, we mentioned the necessity of having a fully developed conceptual world. The process of using concepts becomes so efficient that we no longer suspect their reality. Becoming sure of their authenticity, we begin to have confidence in our inner, logical world and lose the ability to stay for a while in a moment of silent questioning, a dimension that is void of words. Indeed, this organized world of ideas is essential for practical behavior; nevertheless, it closes off our daily consciousness from being nourished by a higher realm of thoughts where genuine reasoning sounds.

Great artists and scientists very often prove impractical in their personal lives. Their trust in logical consideration is not as firm as that of ordinary, practical people. They suspect any given "truth" and fail to fulfill their duties in social life. Paradoxically, this very weakness of their conceptual world makes possible a refined attentiveness to sounds and visions that ordinary people cannot perceive.

The most striking aspect of creative genius is not illness, however; rather, it is a powerful connection to higher reality. We cannot understand the ability of creative genius to compose musical pieces, including complex instrumental partitas or to create entire inventions, complete in all their details, without the concept of a universal intelligence at the foundation of human existence as described in previous chapters. Despite the sorrow and pain we feel when we encounter these unusual stories of the madness connected to genius, they can teach us things that are relevant to us all:

- To bring the creative element back into our lives, we need a way to reconnect to the intimate reality at the base of our being. The soul's true healing process begins when we start searching for the lost connection with this creative world that seeks paths of expression in our soul, yet encounters only a stubborn insistence to maintain our present state.
- To make this essential transformation, we need measured, patient, and devoted practice that will allow us to benefit from the fertilizing activity of the power of supreme consciousness and will, at the same time, avoid premature exposure by keeping our feet firmly planted on practical ground.

Chapter 11

Suffering and Creation

> *"If you take in hand the development of your will like this, so that you in part make of yourself what the world would otherwise make of you as a person, then the vital thoughts into which you have found your way by meditation and concentration take on a quite special aspect for your experience. That is, increasingly, they become painful experiences, inward experiences through suffering, of the things of the spirit. And in the last analysis, no one can attain higher knowledge who has not passed through these experiences of suffering and pain."*
>
> —Rudolf Steiner, *Self-Transformation*

In the previous chapter, which reviewed the creative lives of tormented geniuses, we referred to the aspect of pain and suffering in their lives. For some geniuses, such as Mozart and Picasso, their creativity overflowed with abundance and ease. In most cases, however, we encounter artists like Dostoyevsky, Thomas Mann, and Richard Wagner, for whom creating was extreme anguish. Friedrich Nietzsche's phrase "What does not destroy me serves only to make me stronger" has long been a favorite motto of people whose lives have led them down a road of struggle and misery, who have endured the torrents of harsh fate, yet who walked this path willingly, seeking to transform the quality of their being and their art.

Although the close connection between suffering and creativity has been mentioned frequently in relation to the lives of outstanding artists and inventors in human history, it seems that the essence of this connection is still barely understood. Some have proposed that the anguish and pain in the lives of artists such as van Gogh or Franz Kafka arose from their failure to gain recognition during their lifetimes. Others believe that the impracticality in their daily lives led them to failure on the material plane, even leaving them at times on the edge of starvation. The connection between suffering and the creative process should be considered on a deeper level, beyond the eye of ordinary consciousness, accustomed to searching the outer surfaces of life.

Several years ago, I attended a lecture about the creative process in which the Israeli author and playwright Yehoshua Sobol described his own creative process. "The creative process starts when something stirs and bothers me inside," he said. "Sometimes it goes away by itself, and sometimes it comes back. When that happens, I know something has started to grow. The process of fertilization continues, as different details of my outside life begin to connect to the original issue and enrich it. This is the 'pregnancy' stage. At some point, I know that I have to give birth to the work, otherwise it will die before birth."

This description points us in the right direction; the birth of a work of art is not the result of a random idea passing through the inventor's brain, but something deeper that, in a way, forces itself on the creator from the inside; it does not stem from analytic reasoning, but from the unknowable depths of one's soul. We can see that what comes from the depths, sometimes emerging through conflict and pain, is rich with significance. One who has a discerning eye may know when a piece of art has been created out of the easy flow of pleasurable creation; when it was created out of intellectual thinking; and when the process of "pregnancy" began in the essential recesses of the soul.

How can we tell? Do we have a tool that allows us to reliably determine the background from which a work arises? We do. For example, when we regard the works of a painter, if we are attentive to the inner content of our soul as we look at the paintings we may very accurately feel where the work reverberates within us. This is especially easy to verify when we listen to musical pieces, yet it is equally true in other areas of creativity, such as painting and sculpture, choreography, theater, and even architecture. The principle of resonance, mentioned in previous chapters, is at work here as well, and it serves as a reliable tool in our estimation of the nature of the art, perhaps even its value.

Art conceived in the essential depths of the soul has a unique feel. We sense a certain superficiality, that something is lacking, when we encounter the work of a writer specializing in comedy who writes to entertain readers or viewers; we sense that this reality has nothing to do with our inner essence. It leaves no valuable trace behind, and the next day it is forgotten. On the other hand, comedy that contains a subtle shade of sadness, since it reflects an essential aspect, a certain truth about the heroes—and by necessity, about us—is of greater value. We cannot escape the fact that the life of all humanity, and of each and every one of us, is tinted with want and pain. Yet, what do want and pain contribute to our lives? Do they play a valuable role not revealed to casual observation? The ancient traditions and modern teachers of humanity illuminate these questions from several angles.

According to G. I. Gurdjieff's Fourth Way, human development is based on two main principles: *conscious work* and *intentional suffering*. A student of the Fourth Way is guided to choose conditions that will not allow a comfortable life, but to choose instead a life imbued with struggles and conflicts. The disciple chooses voluntarily to fulfill this task. In doing so, it is not others that one confronts, of course, but one's own whims and desires.

These principles from Gurdjieff are expressed in the inner work that students undertake to fight their own selfish forces. Students learn to observe the hidden content of their soul without bias. They discover how their selfish tendencies block the deeper layers of the soul, how their thoughts run around in closed circles, and how their emotional stance navigates between fixed, unchanging patterns and positions. The Fourth Way discipline is intended to stir students, to push them into seeing what they hide unconsciously under a protective cover of "I'm right," "I know," or "I can." Disciples are presented with the ideal of "wake up, die, be born," or, in its ancient Hebrew version, "die before you die." This does not aim at physical death, of course, but the death of ego powers linked intimately to the disciple's soul.

Fighting the powers of the ego causes students tremendous suffering, since these selfish powers respond, refusing to relinquish their hold from every corner of one's soul. The unprejudiced vision developed in the course of esoteric initiation puts everything students don't want to know about themselves right before their eyes; the deeper and more essential this sight, the greater the suffering that comes with letting go. Disciples of the *Fourth Way* are familiar with Gurdjieff's saying, "One who has a soul [in the sense of a fully developed individuality] is happy; one who has no soul is happy as well. Pain and suffering come to those who have only the primal seed of the soul." It is letting go, and the pain and suffering involved in it, that creates new powers never possessed before in the disciple's soul. Through subtle alchemy, new, conscious powers develop in the disciple's soul, revealing new aspects of one's being that previously struggled under the burden of selfish forces. In this sense, suffering is conducive not only to the growth of the disciple's being, but also to one's ability to create something of value out of one's inner, newly-revealed essence.

The reader may quite justly claim that artists whose lives have been marked by pain and suffering were not disciples on the path of esoteric initiation—that they suffered individual hardships at the hand of fate, were bereft or suffered illness through no choice of their own. How can we say that the imposition of suffering contributed to the quality and depth of that suffering?

Anthroposophic spiritual science illuminates the subject of suffering and expands the area of observation to wider circles than "voluntary" suffering and human suffering in general; it also considers *universal* suffering. To study the need for suffering in the development of the species, we need some prior description based on several spiritual concepts. Although explaining the entire anthroposophic conceptual world is beyond the scope of this book, it would be impossible to penetrate this deep mystery—the role of suffering in universal creation—without providing some basic description.

A previous chapter discussed the array of etheric, life forces that interweave living reality and sustain it. Yet, in addition to this array of forces that supports corporeal reality and protects it from disintegration, there is a subtler entity called the "astral body," which supports the etheric sheath, or layer, and maintains its proper functioning. The plant kingdom is sustained by etheric life forces, while animals, including human beings, are penetrated by both etheric and astral forces. Sensory impressions that living human entities experience go through the etheric layer and become inner experiences in the astral entity, the abode of the living soul.

In this stage, when impressions enter the living body, spiritual science reveals a deep mystery that evades sensory investigation: external impressions such as light, heat, or sound cause a partial, invisible destruction of the outer layer in the physical body. This is almost imperceptible damage, and only the spiritual eye of the spiritual researcher can observe it and the way it affects the assaulted physical entity. Spiritual researchers report that a miniature confrontation develops at the place of assault—a confrontation between external forces of destruction and the etheric forces that arise to defend the physical body and heal the damage. The living soul senses this struggle as pain, as suffering that results from the struggle between external forces of destruction and the life forces countering them. Yet the surprising thing about the resulting process is the unique fruits that develop as the result of this struggle—a new consciousness, a new spiritual life that the living entity did not previously possess. This, then, is the source of a more conscious inner life, which evolves and grows in complexity through a subtle alchemy. The key to understanding the evolution of life is therefore in this struggle of the living entity with external natural forces, a struggle whose fruits are both pain and a more conscious, complex life.

We can therefore see that pain is a vital constructive force, and its blessed activity finds its actual expression not only in esoteric initiation but also everywhere that spiritual life exists. Khalil Gibran expresses this idea in his short story "The Pearl" in his book *The Wanderer:*

> Said one oyster to a neighboring oyster, "I have a very great pain within me. It is heavy and round and I am in distress."
>
> And the other oyster replied with haughty complacence, "Praise be to the heavens and to the sea, I have no pain within me. I am well and whole both within and without."
>
> At that moment a crab was passing by and heard the two oysters, and he said to the one who was well and whole both within and without, "Yes, you are well and whole; but the pain that your neighbor bears is a pearl of exceeding beauty."

Even without supreme powers of perception, experience allows us to confirm the special effects that disease, suffering, and pain may have upon us. One who has been sick and then recovered recognizes that during the healing process and after it, one is accompanied by a sense of clarity, a sort of inner cleanliness or alertness. People who have recovered from a life-threatening illness often declare that their malady changed their life; they say that their illness was their inner teacher. Suffering seems to have a double effect on us; it cracks the walls of security that selfish identity provides us and allows the soul's essential contents to find their way up to the surface of external life. At the same time, suffering creates stronger, more intense powers in our soul, and therefore enriches our creative abilities with the essential expressions of the soul.

The biographical descriptions of the lives of artists who have endured great suffering are accompanied by a sense of their gratitude for the anguish they were forced to suffer. Though perhaps not always aware of this, deep within their souls they sensed the vital inner process that preceded their work. Whether their suffering was the result of a unique personal fate, or whether it had to do with disease and injury to their bodies or those of their loved ones makes no difference; what's relevant in the context of this discussion is that the best and deepest of human creations were preceded by pain and suffering.

We cannot hold this observation within the limits of a purely theoretical discussion; each of us, in our own particular ways and measures, creates—in the arts, in technology and science, and within the family and in the nurture of children. There are elements of pain and conflict in each of these areas. And so we can choose, as we often do, to remove the problem or ignore it when it arises. Yet there is another, more intelligent attitude we can take—approaching the problem as a lesson, meant to teach us something we don't yet know. If we approach the problem with animosity, we will find that our attitude has only added to the original difficulty and created a new burden; however, if we approach the conflict with a brave, accepting attitude, we will find the inner difficulty colored with a new shade. A struggle that has become a means for self-transformation is no longer the suffering we knew. It becomes a source for new life forces, for richer and more intense creation.

Chapter 12

Creation, Destruction, and Evolution

"Nature goes to its limits and when it realizes that it cannot advance, it destroys everything and starts afresh."
—Mirra Alfassa (the Mother), *Words of the Mother*

In the previous chapter, we discussed the close relationship between suffering and creativity. Now we will consider the other aspect of this issue—the forces of destruction that cause pain and suffering. Observing the infinite process of creation that forges reality, we cannot but wonder at the destructive processes within this complex whole. We usually regard them as hostile factors to be resisted. Considering them to be the root cause of suffering, we often wish to negate their existence, or at least to narrow it as much as we can.

However, observing the natural processes around us, we sense that things might not be as simple as our initial, naïve thoughts would have us believe. For example, seasonal flowers die every year and others bloom in their stead; animals, though not dying and regenerating with the seasons, do follow a regular cycle of death and rebirth; and what of human beings? If we believe in reincarnation, then do human beings not materialize time and again in new bodies? Do we not strive to advance stage by stage through the experiences of each lifetime? That, at least, is how esoteric wisdom describes human development. Furthermore, if we observe perennial plants, we can see this principle occurring in a single plant's life: its growth stops, a branch dies and is replaced by another. The plant's development is not linear but follows a complex regularity that intrigues us and makes us thirst for understanding. Why does the plant's development depend on a branch dying and the growth of a new one? The engineers among us might say "What a waste! If I had created the world, processes would be consistent. Such a waste to begin anew every single time."

By looking at this process more closely we realize that the end of one phase—the destruction of what already exists—is a necessary precondition for the creation of something new. Inventors and artists recognize a stage in their process when they feel that something can go no further, that the process does not advance. This is not necessarily fatigue or an end to their resources, but rather the feeling that something has reached maturity at a certain level and every attempt to advance it even more will involve some kind of coercion of the creative process. An intelligent artist knows when to leave a work alone: at times erasing it, as Picasso used to do, at times forgetting it and starting again—each according to one's own intuition. Sri Aurobindo wrote his immortal epic poem *Savitry* twelve times, starting anew every time. Why would one whose infinite inspiration stemmed from the highest worlds act in such a way? We cannot find the answer to this secret of reality without looking at all its levels, including those not revealed to our day-to-day awareness. The process we must examine is only partially revealed to our senses, while another part of it, no less important, exists on a different plane of reality. The cycles of existence are living, breathing processes shared by both worlds, one standing before our eyes while the other, subliminal, supports it from "behind," motivating and fertilizing it, imbuing it with life, yet remaining hidden from our sight.

Lying in bed at night, tired and at times stressed and unhappy, we fall into deep sleep. Morning finds us charged with new energy. More than feeling refreshed, our outlook toward a problem has also changed. Intelligent decision makers know they should avoid snap decisions; their motto is "I'll sleep on it." And they're right. Spiritual science maintains that when we sink into our night's sleep, essential components of the soul let go of their hold on the physical body to connect more freely to a higher plane of reality. That we do not consciously experience this does not negate the findings of spiritual science, which indicate a flowing of spiritual powers into the tired soul, imbuing it with renewed life forces and preparing it for a new day.

Daily life cycles resemble the greater life cycles between death and rebirth. Spiritual science illuminates the various processes that the soul undergoes through this latter cycle. Human evolution does not proceed in a straight, continuous line; rather, it passes through complete life cycles. Spiritual science perceives these patterns in the stages of our planet's evolution as well as in human evolution. Processes of evolution, on all levels of reality, occur in consecutive stages of development, building upon one another separated by pauses—a sort of spiritual breath.

As human creators—inventors, painters, composers, or writers—we can learn from the mysterious process through which universal creation is realized and apply it to our own work. We should learn to experience the creative process as a breathing process. Usually, when an idea rises in us, we do not stop and wonder, "How did it get here?" Instead we often take it for granted and immediately try to apply it, in painting, writing, or another form of expression. This is our first mistake—the desire to pick immediately the fruits of our spiritual process interrupts this creative process and cuts it short. If only we could learn to listen to the mysterious plane from which this idea springs, if we could fight our tendency to transform the archetypal idea into the hard currency of form or written words, we would sense that the hidden thread between our two levels of awareness does not have to be cut. Patient practice of this principle, along with concentration and meditation exercises, to be described later, may create an open inner channel between the "spiritual womb" and its fruit on the material plane.

One way or another, the creative process has been started and we begin the hard work of fulfilling it. We shape and polish it, forge it in the flame of logic's critique, or put it into form and render it complete. In following this path, often we do not feel satisfied. An inner voice whispers that our work is still not perfect, that we can make it better. We hover around it, looking from this angle and that, hoping to find some other aspect we have neglected—another possibility for development. This process of creative action, or its development, is essentially stopped. This is the point at which we sometimes make our second mistake: we do not know how to stop. Here, the word *stop* should be understood in the widest possible sense; we may erase a painting, tear up a rough draft, or destroy a sculpture or prototype, but perhaps such violence is unnecessary. Sometimes we can simply set the matter aside, try to forget it, and return to it at a later date.

Frustrated with the apparent failure, we often ask ourselves, "Has all my work been in vain?" This could be our third mistake: we ignore the fruits of our labor at this stage of the creation, failing to realize that the results are not in the ruined canvas or text, but on a subtler plane residing unseen in our soul. Now that our mind is no longer occupied with the subject, the fruits of our labor are transformed to a higher plane, a sort of superior consciousness that maintains our existence, though it is not recognized by our limited awareness. A higher intelligence will take care of the fruits of our labor from now on, and return them to us processed and enriched so that we may begin the creative process anew. It is important to be aware of this unique behavior of our inner essence, to pay attention to its existence, and, most importantly, to develop trust in its powers. Since the power of such consciousness is incomparably greater than the limited powers of our subjective soul, this is the best way to develop our creations and our own selves. A universal power of evolution imbues creative processes on all levels of reality, and *knowing* this secret is a necessary condition for a fruitful life of creation, not only professionally but in our personal life as well.

In addition, we are asked to change our attitude toward the destructive processes we encounter in life. We are asked to recognize their necessity, their contribution to the evolution of the species, to the development of human and universal creation. Destructive processes on the plane of the physical world are a precondition for growth on the complementary, hidden one. In fact, what seems to be growth in the physical world is only the withdrawal of higher forces, while what seems like deterioration and destruction may later be revealed as the liberation of those forces for a new, more complete creation. This is how Anthroposophy views the process of flowering and decay.

Reality moves from the perfection of creation to another, higher, perfection; each stage is in itself whole and complete. We must not look for "final perfection" in any preparatory stage: final perfection will arrive only when there is no longer anything to be destroyed—and as life shows us, that stage is very far ahead of us, indeed.

Chapter 13
Creation and Will Forces

"In every world there should be the power of knowledge and of will, which out of endless possibilities determines and dictates relationships, develops the effect from the cause, manifests the great rhythms of the cosmic law, and rules the worlds as supreme seer and governor."
—Sri Aurobindo, *The Life Divine*

In the field of human creation there are those who shine brightly: artists, whose work is infused with inner daring, with a hidden force that finds its way out through their writing, painting, and architectural work. Even their thinking, an area often considered to belong to the field of philosophy, has the timbre of an inner power that we cannot find in other thinkers. Arthur Rubinstein, Pablo Picasso, Antonio Gaudi, and Friedrich Nietzsche are all examples of such characters. Anyone who ever watched or listened as the elderly Rubinstein struck the keys of a grand piano, filling the hall with expressive sound, felt that the music contained an overflowing human power out of any scale with his advanced age. Picasso's work, expressed in various genres, also overflowed on the canvases and pots upon which he painted with a thrust and originality that seemed to demonstrate he was never satisfied to rest upon the reputation he had obtained through his earlier works. The same is true of Gaudi, Nietzsche, and other great creators who left us not only their works, but above all left a deep impression of human power, flowing out of the existential depths of the soul and expressing itself as form, sound, an architectural structure, or a thorough examination of reality.

Human creation is normally considered to be the result of our faculties of thought, imagination, and feeling; yet these artists' works point us toward another aspect, one that often eludes superficial observation and hides behind other forces that motivate human creativity—will forces.

Alongside the previously mentioned creators who were blessed with inner power are others who are gifted with intelligence and bountiful imagination, yet lack the inner power that characterizes the above-named artists. Artists who do not have this inner power have a hard time realizing their creations, and when they do succeed in creating something, there is an intangible sense of something missing in their works. The inner weakness of artists can be seen clearly in their art. As noted in previous chapters, artistic life is often interrupted with suffering and grief. In addition to biographies in which suffering brought about blessed fruits, in many others the creative processes ended with self-destruction, sometimes leading to the artist's tragic end through suicide.

Having indicated the existence of will forces that participate in the formation of human creation, try to appreciate their uniqueness and variations. In some works, whether musical or visual, we can see an inner power that expresses mainly lust and instinct, waves of emotion, or sensuality. We find such qualities in the creations of many people, from Africa and South America to the works of quite a few Western artists. For example, the paintings of Gauguin and the unique performances of Jim Morrison of The Doors have taken the sensual experience to ecstatic heights, while the listener or observer can easily sense the unusual nature of the impulse that impels the work and provides its vitality. On the other hand, when we look at Raphael's paintings or listen to the music of Pergolesi, Mozart, or Fauré, we find not only a subtler shades of emotion, but also a very different motivation for the most part. It will therefore be well worth our while if we strive to understand these differences, since understanding them will enable us to better understand the very forces that motivate us and the possibility of transforming them into higher forces.

What, then, is this evasive impulse of the human structure? What is the role of will forces in the artistic, philosophical, or mechanistic formation of human creation? We cannot rely on our superficial observation or even on science to help us with these questions. Rudolf Steiner best expressed this difficulty when he spoke of our being awake with regard to thinking; being dreamy with regard to feelings; and being completely asleep in regard to will forces. In simpler language, the will forces that work within our essence are completely hidden; their activity does not reach our daily consciousness. We usually think of our will forces only in relation to the soul's desires—we want to eat, to succeed, to fulfill ourselves, and so on. But have we ever asked ourselves what it is that makes our feet move when we dance? Have we ever asked ourselves what makes our lungs move when we breathe? Or what makes our metabolism run or our heart beat? Is the notion of mechanical muscle impulses directed by the brain a satisfying answer?

Will forces are indeed the most secret element of the human being, the one that is most difficult to observe. It is so because these forces never reach our consciousness, although every single process in our being—body, soul, and spirit—contains an element of will force. Will force is not only an attitude of the creative person, a motivating force of one's soul, but a fundamental element imbuing the physical body, down to its very cells.

What does *wanting* or the force of one's will have to do with the building blocks of the human body? Esoteric knowledge regards the element of will in a much wider perspective than do the modern behavioral sciences. Physiologists observe the hand's action and see a muscle contracting after receiving an order from the "control center," the brain; they see a purely mechanical response system. Spiritual science, however, understands will forces as the universal element that, while indeed causing the physical body to operate, at also imbues the very structure of the cells. The system of Lurianic Kabbalah maintains that all created reality is made of different levels of a universal Will. The same essential element of created reality underlies both the material infrastructure of our physical bodies and the forces that move our bodily motor system—the essence of will force.

Rabbi Isaac Luria's Kabbalah directs us to transform our will to receive for ourselves a tool for receiving in order to influence, or giving pleasure to the Blessed Creator. According to this principle, we should place the cultivation of the attitude of service at the heart of our practice.

When I studied architecture, I often looked at the extraordinary works of Antonio Gaudi in Barcelona. My eyes were drawn to close-up images of some of the towers constructed by this unique genius. Though the towers are quite distant and cannot be observed with the naked eye, their outer walls are decorated with great attention to detail, as though they were intended to be scrutinized from only a few feet away. Why, I wondered, would he bother to decorate these elements, which are so far from human eyes? Though I did not realize it then, it was my first meeting with the principle of the "will to receive" described in Luria's Kabbalah. Many years would pass before I could come into direct contact with the content of this experience.

Delving more deeply into this idea requires a wider frame of reference than is possible here. However, the sense of such transformation can be alluded to as follows. The unique shades we find in various artworks indicate the diversity of the creative impulse. When we compare the facet of sensual creation with the finer hues of works that strive to express a higher principle of reality, we see a secret duality hidden within the human being. This ancient truth, expressed in the great spiritual traditions, as well as in the teachings of modern masters, indicates that the human soul opens its doors to essentially different sources of influence. One influence is connected to the physical body, and therefore to the planet Earth, while the other is connected to a higher, inner world, a universal reality that unites all of the human species and originates in divine planes of reality. The earthly influence has its own unique shades, connected with sensory perception and bodily desires. Divine influence aims at a subtler longing, a desire for the uplifting, for the moral, and for the beautiful. The soul therefore is motivated by various impulses that penetrate its field of activity from both directions.

The circumstances of a human being would be comparatively simple if one's motivations came only from those two sources of influence. In effect, however, the human soul itself contributes to the play of forces within its field of activity. New impulses derived neither from the body's direct needs nor from the direct influence of the spiritual world have arisen from the tendency to recycle pleasures and satisfactions, the longing for an autonomous definition of the soul's uniqueness, and its tendency to protect what it perceives as its exclusive assets. Human will forces are therefore saturated with impulses, desires, and longings that eventually dictate the nature of our creations, expressed through color, sound, thought, and poetry.

A short comparison of animal motivations with those of human beings provide an example of the simplicity and immediacy of the animal kingdom in contrast to the complex and somewhat disturbed human world. Predator animals are not necessarily motivated by impulses of hate or vengefulness, and certainly not by the desire to shine above others of their species. Animals do not eat when they are satiated, nor do they exhaust themselves with bodily exercises when such exertion is not required. In a sense, human beings seem inferior to the forces that motivate animals. This comparison of animals and human beings is incomplete, however, and ignores humankind's unique advantage: our ability to learn and improve. Moreover, it ignores the human ability to consciously transform inner motives!

Our ability to learn can almost be taken for granted, but what about our ability to change the direction of our will? This seems inexplicable, and perhaps even appears to contradict what was said previously about the tendency of will forces to elude our daily consciousness. However, the esoteric path of initiation, a practical path aimed at transforming the human being, allows its followers to gradually change their current motivations and to replace them with new will forces, different from those they had previously known.

The Darwinist principle of species improvement contains a deep truth whose broader scope and meaning are learned through initiation in the esoteric schools. All planes of reality, including nature, are under constant pressure from a higher consciousness that creates within nature a rising evolutionary direction, a transformation going upward from the physical level through a vital level (the life forces), and later on the mind level, up to the divine-spiritual level. As microcosms, human beings are thus presented with a unique opportunity to hasten radical inner change according to the same law; to allow a transformation of the present essence of our being, including the physical, vital, and mental aspects; and to evolve to higher levels, which, as noted, has already begun to blossom in those who have given their time and effort toward making such a transformation happen.

Conscious divine will, which originates in the higher worlds, appears as a new factor in the modern path of initiation. From the spiritual heights it finds its way downward to the human sheaths of body and soul in order to transform them, to give birth within the human being to a new essence with a quality of being that is different from anything it has known before. Disciples of esoteric schools of initiation can meet this force and open themselves to its impact, allowing it to replace their own will, which is driven by selfish desires and wants. Such a force seems to melt both physical and soul resistance. Instead of a frozen, contracted essence that hides within the boundaries of its own forgetfulness, this transformative activity gives birth to a finer being who is open to the planes of higher reality. Disciples are filled with awe toward the new will forces that come to dominate one's soul. They sense its superiority and cherish its blessing. Gradually, the souls will develop a new attitude toward what they sense as a higher reality and try to serve it, just as Gaudi and many others have done. In this sense, we can understand the Kabbalistic concept of changing the subjective, egoistic will into a new impulse to serve a Universal Cause.

The transformative experience is not limited to disciples' motives or to their inner attitude because divine willpower is not limited to changes in the soul and in the array of life forces. These aspects of the human being are relatively transparent and put up less resistance to penetration by the will. At the height of such a transformation, the effects of divine willpower reach into the very physical body, right down to its living cells. Like a sharp scalpel, divine will finds its way into the body's matter as though a porous, silken fabric. It melts murky, ignorant areas within us and breaks up contracted tissues, filling and enriching the body's cells through its presence.

But it is not only the cells that are enriched; something is released from the loosened contractions and a new subtle matter is formed. What before had been impenetrable matter now returns to its superior state—a subtle, formless, self-conscious essence that can assume any shape. In this sense we may regard the new creation as a universal process in which the human race can take a creative part.

What is it that allows for the dramatic penetration of divine willpower into the dense essence of our physical body? Why does this physical matter resist its penetration? The deep mystery of matter is tested when the forces that brought about its formation now fight over what they have attained, over everything that was achieved over a long and patient process—form, stability, and self-definition. The victory of divine will, the possibility for its penetration into the thickness of matter, can be understood through the esoteric view found in all ancient spiritual traditions; divine will forces and the physical body's matter arise from the very same essence. The essence of Universal Will, an emanation of the Universal Creating Being, a service to a divine cause whose full scope they do not yet comprehend, but that they long to serve with all the fruits of this inner transformation, are all seen in the student's gradually changing attitude. Esoteric students' trust in the forces found in the soul will henceforth guide their attitude, their deeds, and the nature of their creation. Creators imbued with the rays of creative will forces will sense that something more is expected of them—an inner attitude, a yet-to-be-understood service to the divine, and a longing to serve with all one's heart and vigor. From their previous attitude as selfish creators who considered themselves the source of their creations, such students now strive to be channels for a flow directed at the wider circles of society, which need a subtler quality of nourishment, while serving the Divine Impulse seeking to transform earthly planes of existence into a richer, subtler, and more perfected world.

Chapter 14

Vibrations and Discontinuous Processes

"All of these changes can be viewed as the result of vibrations, or waves, that start in the center, the absolute, and then spread in all directions, crossing each other, clashing and merging, until they completely stop at the end of creation. According to this view the world is therefore made up of vibrations and matter, or matter in a vibrating state, vibrating matter. The frequency of vibration is at opposite relation to the density of matter. In the absolute, the vibrations are faster and matter is least dense. In the next world, vibrations are slower and matter denser, and so on—matter becomes more realized and vibrations become slower accordingly."

—G. I. Gurdjieff[1]

The relationship between our world of ideas and universal law was first mentioned in the chapter discussing the human world of concepts. In creating our concepts, with all their complexity and variations, we dissect and analyze the continuous flow of world phenomena, needing to enclose it within defined conceptual boundaries. This, we have said, is a necessity, a precondition for the creation of communication and of an evolving human civilization. Yet the unity of existence is not really a formless continuity. If that were the case, there would be no distinction between the various phenomena; indeed, our world could not exist. It is a fact that the world of perceptible phenomena contains a huge variety of distinct forms and essences that seem to be defined.

The diverse variety that we see in the world of phenomena does not lack an inner order, and nature's creative processes are not random, but follow an unseen, inner regularity. Some illustrations from the worlds of minerals, plants, and animals may help to clarify this.

The Mendeleev periodic table describes the elements as they exist in the natural world. Following a slight reorganization of the table, these elements are currently arranged according to the atomic number that represents the

1 Quoted in *In Search of the Miraculous,* p. 170.

number of protons in the atom's nucleus. The table shows a developmental line that rises in whole and separate numerical units, so that there is not a gradual rise but a rise in numbers that jump. The rise in the atomic number is not continuous, but develops from one place on the table to the next. After all, we do not find hybrids between two adjacent elements, but whole, separate elements. A more thorough observation of this table reveals another regularity, which has to do with the elements' inner qualities, such as electronegativity and the ratio of ionic energy.

From the scientific point of view, the worlds of color and sound also include a periodic cycle whose basic units are separate; each is distinct and defined. The notes of the musical scale signify the frequency of the sounds. These ratios of frequency are not random; rather, they interrelate with regularity (as we shall describe later on). We cannot sing tunes, even if we compose them ourselves, unless we set our voice exclusively to the tones included in the musical scale. Anyone who tries to sing a false note intentionally finds that it is almost impossible to do; if only one note of the musical chord is off, the listener will easily spot it. There is analogous regularity in the colors of the rainbow, revealed in all their glory on rainy days; though in the process of revealing themselves the colors develop gradually, it is still possible to clearly see the center of gravity of each color. As we can spot a cyclical "sound octave" that ranges from lower A to higher A, we can also spot a "color octave" that ranges from one red to the next red that appears in the cycle.

In the plant world as well, the creative process has typical stepping-stones or stages—sprouting, growing, blossoming, flowering and dying. The process is continuous, yet its centers of gravity are clearly distinguishable, both morphologically and with regard to their role in the growing process.

The Darwinist evolutionary ladder is based on two main supports: the principle of mutation and the principle of natural selection. The central idea of Darwin's theory—that this complex world process develops blindly, with no guidance—is losing its dominance in modern culture as the only acceptable theory for the development of the species. However, the processes of mutation, even when we observe relatively short intervals, reveal that the forming of the species occurs through crossing the boundaries between different species, even though there are few cases in which researchers identify one-half or even one-quarter of a transformation between one species and another. Research points to an astounding similarity between the whale's fin, the bat's wing, and the human hand. We do not know whether one evolved from the other, yet it is glaringly obvious that there are no examples of animals with limbs that are a combination of a fin and a hand or of a wing and a hand. If it is indeed one evolutionary process, then there are distinct, separate stages. Research based on fossil evidence distinguishes about 250,000 separate species; what inner regularity directs the processes to jump from one stage to another, to move ahead in whole ratios and not in a gradual, continuous way?

Though the human growth process is much more complex than that of the plant, with human beings it is also possible to see separate developmental stages, like the notes of a rising octave. The anthroposophic theory of education states that the first seven years of a person's life are devoted mostly to the development of motor functions; the child's organs and ability to move are at the center of development. Some would say that these years are devoted to the development of language, but during this period the development of language also has a motor character; the child learns to speak mostly through imitation rather than through intellectual thinking. The next stage of seven years is devoted to the development of the child's emotional world. Conflicts in encounters with the environment, and later, the development of romantic relationships with the opposite sex, all gravitate around one center—the emotional life. Only as we begin to approach our twenties do we become capable of truly thinking. At this early stage of adult life, the spirit of curiosity fills us with the desire to discover the secrets of the universe and to understand the meaning of our own life.

It is often thought that the creative process that produces a mature human being ends with adulthood. Esoteric wisdom, however, tells us otherwise; additional stages of development take place that have to do with human awareness and spiritual life. Developing into these stages, however, depends on one's initiative. Describing these stages and the inner regularity at their base is beyond the scope of this chapter; for now, we shall satisfy ourselves with pointing out that such stages do exist, and that they are a natural continuation of the first stages we have already mentioned.

How does this development manifest in the area of human creation? All creative people are familiar with the discontinuous nature of the human creative process in the arts, technology, and science. When the main idea begins to crystallize, it does not appear immediately. Many creators speak of an incubation period, in which the primordial idea coalesces in the soul's intuitive depths before it matures. Once it has matured, the second stage begins, in which the creator tries to realize the idea in different ways. One carefully looks for the path, setting a cautious foot down in one direction, then pulling it back and trying another; or sometimes one simply stops and waits. Every creator has a unique path; each creation has a unique birth.

The human creator is familiar with moments when the creative process reaches a dead end. Impatient creators tend to give up when this happens, dropping the idea and trying something else. Yet anyone who has had enough experience with these things knows that it is best to let the matter rest, and to wait. Amazingly, the original idea may rise anew with fresh energy once it has had sufficient rest. The creative process may now move to a more mature level, gathered and focused around a central axis, and the creator will sometimes feel that it was during the resting period, when she let the process sink into the unknown part of her being, that something matured. My own experience shows that the creative process is a living one, and does not stop even when the product, the fruit of development, has reached the stage of industrial or marketplace fulfillment. Even when it seems that the product or invention is ripe for marketing, new blossoms may appear in the depths of intuitive thinking, suggesting new possibilities for development. The creative process never stops. It's not for nothing that marketing people often tell development teams that "the enemy of good is better!"

As we have seen, hidden forces that determine the nature of a process, and the relationship of those hidden forces with complementary processes, lie at the base of human creativity. The questioning reader may ask, "Do the laws of discontinuous processes hold also in the invisible world, or with the basic particles of reality?"

As recently as the late nineteenth century, the science of physical matter had always considered energy flow to be a continuous process. Then an investigation was begun to research "blackbody radiation" (the radiation of a body that does not return light when gradually heated). When physicist Max Planck attempted to measure this phenomenon, he found no way to calculate the data until he had artificially divided the flow of radiation into separate quantities. He called those artificially created portions "quanta" (singular, "quantum"). According to his assumption, the measure of such a portion depended on the radiation's energy and its wavelength. Later, following disagreements between the results of calculation and experimental findings, physicists began to understand that the quantity described by Max Planck was not random, nor in accord only with the researcher's mathematical equations, but was a meaningful constant that is part of the mysteries of reality itself. It was Albert Einstein who first implemented "Planck's constant" when attempting to investigate the photoelectric effect—the current of electricity emitted by metal bombarded with a light beam. Einstein and other physicists who took part in the research found that the light was received by metals or omitted in separate units, not in one continuous current. Those light units were defined as light quanta.

In 1911, Ernest Rutherford conducted his well-known experiment. He bombarded a piece of thin, gold foil with radioactive particles and found that some particles went through the foil as if it wasn't there. This experiment later served as the basis for the first model he presented in which the atom is composed of a nucleus with a positive charge surrounded by a negatively charged electron cloud, so that most of the space held by the atom is actually completely empty. Later it became known that the atom receives and emits energy in units, and that these units are arranged according to a set inner order, a basic pattern that typifies the matter to which the atom belongs.

In 1913, physicist Niels Bohr suggested a new model of the atom in which the electrons move in orbits whose distance from the nucleus does not constantly change, but is set in distinct values. Electron movement around the nucleus occurs only in these orbits, and never between them. The quantum idea began to infiltrate researchers' consciousness, and they were amazed by the precision of quantum calculations and verifying observations based on quantum theory. Even if Bohr's model, and later models by Schrödinger and Heisenberg, are not a completely accurate depiction of reality, and even if researchers still do not understand quantum phenomena in depth, the facts seem clear; the basic infrastructure of the universe is a vibrating essence, and the processes within it are discontinuous.

Scientific research, in its quest to understand reality, has for the last centuries assumed that there is a fundamental building block at the base of the phenomenal world. The scientific view is that this building block allows us to understand reality's entire complex array. This way of thinking, according to which the whole array of world phenomena could be composed by joining elementary building blocks, led to the idea that it was possible to find a basic material building block that could not be further divided, so that if we tried to divide it again it would not maintain the material's typical characteristics. This is the most deeply held belief of the materialistic worldview.

These models gradually gained a respectable position in the field of science; first through Niels Bohr's model of the atom and then through more complex models with further subdivisions. However, laboratory experiments later showed that basic particles do not always obey the laws of Newtonian physics. Phenomena that are typical of the world of vibrations, like interference and diffraction, began to appear in experiments, and have fundamentally undermined scientific belief in the particle composition of the universe. The emergence of quantum mechanics has gradually taken over modern scientific thinking, and there are fewer and fewer adherents of particle theory left.

Esoteric wisdom was never infected with the materialistic way of thinking described here. It is a known principle, in all esoteric paths, that the infrastructure of reality does not consist of material building blocks, basic units with no consciousness that are randomly joined to compose the infinite diversity of reality. Esoteric thinking is holistic by nature; it develops from the top to the bottom; the conscious unity of the spirit world moves toward an infinite diversity of details.

In addition, suprasensory experience growing in the researcher's soul reveals the vibrating nature of reality. This reality is a world of vibrating processes that thread through one another, mutually strengthening, weakening, or transforming. It is a miraculous, multifaceted world whose nature, depth, causes, and meaning are hidden from thought that relies on the normal sense organs. Any individuals who have ever experienced the vision that develops in the inner field of consciousness will never again believe the illusion of the world's materialism, since they have personally witnessed, through direct, immediate consciousness, a genuine picture of the world, one that sheds a different light on the hidden nature of reality.

For those who would seek to understand the nature of creative processes, the question arises: Is there a building block suggested by esoteric wisdom? Although esoteric knowledge includes the deep truths of reality, it is not always presented as an ordered theory. Disciples who seek to understand the hidden side of reality cannot stop with theoretical study of the knowledge contained in various writings; rather, they must live the truth as expressed in the writings of the great teachers and within one's own soul. What follows is the result of such an effort.

We have already said that the basic building block of reality is not a material particle, but has more to do with the vibrating nature of realities, as we shall later see. Modern scientific thinking cannot be satisfied with descriptions of experience, and requires a more logical and precise characterization. In order to present a scientific critique, we need to define the building block of a process whose inner nature is not material, but is based on inner vibration. Vibrating processes are naturally dynamic, and so are difficult to define using concepts with clear boundaries. When we go back to the basic assumption about the discontinuous nature of creative and developmental processes, we need to define the basic unit as clearly as possible and not be satisfied with a description that is merely mystical in nature.

The following is an attempt to characterize some basic outlines of the vibrating, elementary unit, describing its qualities through illustrations of sensory phenomena. These illustrations do not give us the inner taste of the experience itself, but only point in the right direction:

- The basic unit has a vibrating essence.
- This unit has an inner center of gravity and a particular level of consciousness.
- The unit has a defined, autonomous nature and identity.
- The basic vibrating unit is a stage (somewhat like a note of the musical scale) of a discontinuous process that takes place on a particular plane and includes within it an additional plane of more intense vibrations.
- The relationship between the including and the included units is zero to infinite, similar to the relationship between two different dimensions of the sensory world.

Because the essential nature of the basic unit is a vibration, it would be natural to look for its expression in the world of sounds. In Pythagoras's esoteric school, circa 500 B.C.E., the harmonious relations of human and universal reality were studied. One illustration of these universal relations was the monochord—a solitary string stretched over a wooden sound box. The experiment showed that when the string was shortened to half its previous length, each of the remaining sections of the string sounded a tone similar to that of the original string, but higher. If the string was tuned originally to a C, then both halves also sounded a C. We now know that when the number of vibrations of a string is doubled, a similar note would come from both segments; this range between two notes is called an octave (next page, fig. 1).

Pythagoras experimented further, and showed that when the string was shortened to two-thirds of its original length, a new note would be produced that vibrates harmoniously with the original note. Thus, if the first note was C, the new note would be F; similarly, if the original length was shortened to three-quarters, the resulting note would be G. These intervals are called, respectively, *octave, fifth,* and *fourth,* noting a distance of eight, five, and four spaces from the basic note C. The fact that harmonious relations can be expressed using whole numbers points to a harmony hidden not only in the musical scale but also in the very infrastructure of reality. We shall return to this point later.

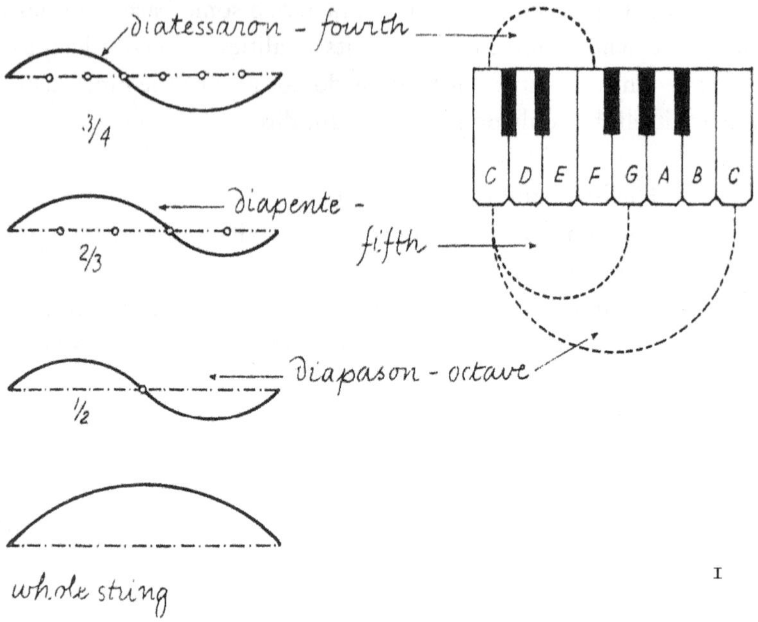

I

The mysterious division of the monochord later reappeared in relation to the quality of the sound produced by different instruments. How is the note C produced by a violin different from the C produced by a flute, since both vibrate at the same frequency? Modern means of photography show that a string vibrating at a given basic note such as C simultaneously also sounds additional notes, mostly F and G, representing intervals of a fourth and a fifth. It appears that besides the basic note C, the string also vibrates at a higher pitch, as if it had been artificially shortened according to Pythagorean ratios while vibrating. These hidden sounds, called overtones, bolster and enrich an instrument's basic notes, and determine their quality and unique shades.

Ernst Chladni, who was deeply interested in reality's inner vibrations, experimented by spreading fine sand over glass and metal plates, holding the plates between his thumb and fingers, and making them vibrate using a violin bow. The vibration created in the plates also made the particles of sand vibrate, and soon the vibrating mass of sand showed complex geometric patterns with a definite inner order. Chladni changed the frequency of vibrations, the type of sand or sawdust he used, and the structure of the plates, and produced a dazzling variety of new patterns.

In 1967, Hans Jenny, a Swiss researcher, refined Chladni's experiments using his tonoscope, a complex instrument he constructed to control the parameters of vibrations—frequency and amplitude— allowing him to achieve amazing results. He found that the higher the frequency of vibrations on the plate, the greater the complexity of the patterns (fig. 2). When he increased the amplitude, the waves rose higher, and at some moments wild beams of sawdust were tossed in the air like water from a spout, or the twirling patterns would destroy the symmetric patterns until total chaos ensued. The vibrating mass continued to move, creating a moving array of waves, and the form of the waves changed while in motion. Jenny next tried to examine the behavior of liquids under the influence of vocal vibrations. A mass of water or turpentine poured onto a vibrating plate began to form itself in separate puddles, divided and arranged in perfect order. Changing the frequency made these separate puddles form elongated bodies, quite like centipedes, which would move on the surface of the plate like living creatures. Amazingly, this continuous mass of liquid arranged itself in discrete units, looking more like solid material particles than like an amorphous liquid—all thanks to the vibrations of the metal plate underneath.

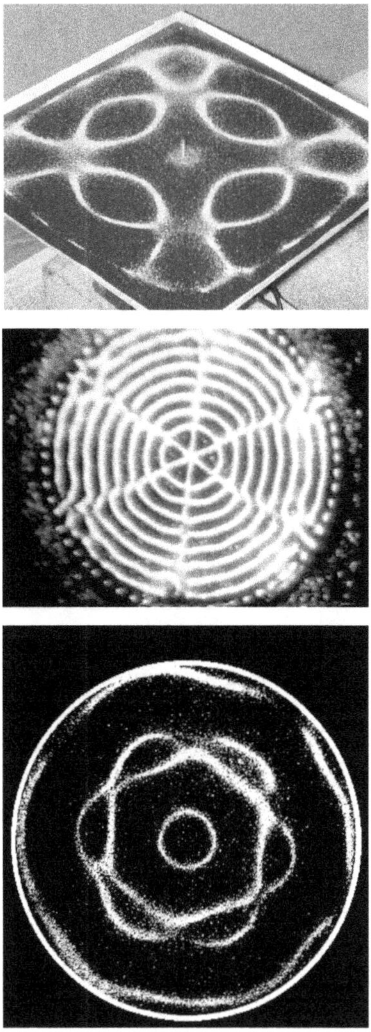

2

As mentioned, Jenny's interest went beyond the world of audible sounds. He also researched the influence of the human voice upon the patterns that emerged from the vibrating mass. He stated in his reports that Hebrew or Sanskrit spoken vowels created shapes that symbolically represented the spirit of the forms of these letters. He claimed that this effect did not occur when using modern Western languages. According to spiritual science, Hebrew and Sanskrit were formed out of a deep spiritual

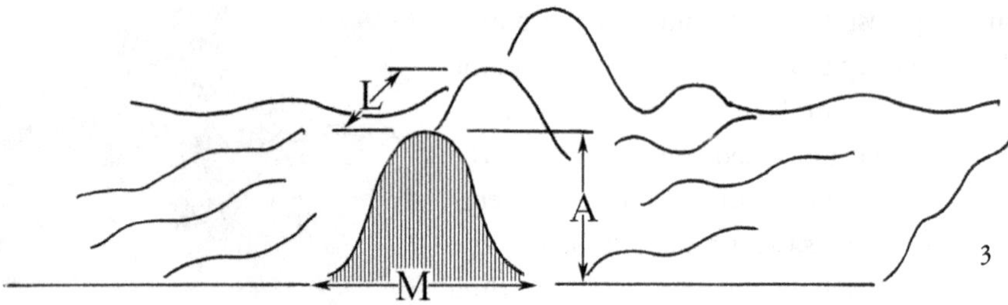

3

knowledge, following the inner principles that define reality.[2] Jenny created an entire scientific niche around his experiments, calling this science Cymatics, after the Greek word *kyma*, meaning "wave."[3]

These examples of experiments in sound demonstrate to a degree the possible nature of the basic unit of developmental processes according to the basic outlines previously mentioned. The images (fig. 2) show sawdust particles rising above Jenny's metal plate, with concentric circles visible around a central axis. As the original *Cymatics* videotape shows, these waves are not static, but rather chase each other endlessly around the central axis. The drawing (fig. 3) shows a virtual slice perpendicular to the axis of movement. The basic unit can now be typified according to the criteria mentioned:

> The basic wave whose amplitude is signified by the letter A develops and disappears at the frequency F. Its width is M and its velocity shall be V = L * F, with L denoting the distance between the peaks of two adjacent waves developing one out of the other. This wave has a semi-autonomous identity and a center of gravity. Other waves may have a curve that is serrated, split, high or low, etc. The basic wave is part of an overall movement that flows over the whole plate, yet is itself formed due to the more intense vibrations of thousands of smaller particles of sawdust; these particles have a frequency, a power and a nature of their own.[4]

This complex picture, visible to our eyes, also exists within another medium of reality, one that is not revealed to the physical sense of sight, yet

2 Detailed descriptions of the relation between language and the vibrations hidden within it can be found in Rudolf Steiner's lecture series on the Book of Genesis, and in other lectures he gave about language and sound.

3 Videos of the tonoscope experiments are currently marketed by Macromedia, including beautiful photographs of the processes described here, and information about truly interesting medical experiments.

4 Hans Jenny, *Cymatics: The Healing Nature of Sound,* Seattle: Macromedia, 1986 (video).

may appear in the inner field of awareness, if one is properly trained. Under the conditions that develop in an expanded field of vision, the physical body is experienced as separate from a subtler essence that lives a somewhat independent life. As it is possible to distinguish oxygen and hydrogen when they are separated from water, so, too, can we see the difference between the physical body and the essence that lives within it—they are two complementary yet separate beings. The subtle essence that imbues the physical body is a fine yet active substance that manifests the life of the soul.

At a higher stage of development, when this field of activity, comprised of different shades and movements, becomes more observable, it is possible to experience an even higher plane of existence glowing in the background, penetrating at chosen moments into the half-obscure substance and accelerating, or rather intensifying, its vibrating quality. This inner state of reciprocal penetration is experienced mostly as an awakening of the soul.

It is interesting to find that the subtle essence is not a coherent substance, but rather contains clearer and murkier areas that live side by side, waging a sort of inner struggle over the territory of the soul. We can see how a meditant's unworthy attitude would support the soul's murkiness, while an opposite attitude disperses the fog so that a higher light may shine forth. This "war of light and darkness" becomes a living reality within the meditator's soul, accessible to direct vision by one's observing awareness. For those who research the basis of their essence, direct observation sheds light on some aspects that have to do with the theme of this chapter:

- The human being contains at least four separate parts, belonging to different planes of existence:
    - the physical body;
    - a sheath of life forces that imbues the physical body and surrounds it with defined boundaries;
    - a soul, which imbues this sheath of life forces;
    - a superior divine being that radiates its influence into the soul and further down, all the way into the physical body.
- The relation between these four planes of existence is zero to infinity, or as mentioned before, like the relation between a line and a plane or between a plane and a three-dimensional body. It is a relationship between different planes of existence that contain each other, vibrating into one another.
- Each plane has its own center of gravity, its own distinct character, and its own distinct level of awareness.

- These separate planes of existence maintain their independence, but they influence one another; in special cases, boundaries are crossed through some mysterious initiative, and a transformation occurs.

These aspects may require some clarification. Whereas the vibrating nature of the subtler sheaths may be observed with relative ease, this is not the case with the physical body. Esoteric traditions hold that even that which we see as inert, lifeless matter is basically a spiritual essence that agglomerated or crystallized to create a new form of existence—one that is aware to a certain extent. When meditating, we encounter the fact that our physical body has its own independent awareness. When this awareness comes to life, it is seen as subtle radiation that imbues the physical body and radiates from it. This radiation has a role within the human being's transformative process, because it allows the crossing of the boundaries previously mentioned. In rare moments the spiritual essence may launch a vibrating force toward the sense of the awakening physical awareness. This meeting is a transformative act, as the spiritual essences penetrate the cells of the physical body, vitalizing, expanding, and refining it, similar to the first rainfall of autumn that saturates the earth after a dry summer. On its way to the physical body the spiritual force also influences the other sheaths of being. The transformation of the human being is the result of this penetration of a conscious spiritual power into the ignorant essences of the body and soul, refining them and making them into worthier vessels for the soul. The reception of the spirit's reviving power would be impossible were it not for the vibrating nature of the spiritual essence on one hand, and the particle-like material nature of the physical body on the other. The crossing of boundaries between different planes of existence is made possible thanks only to the vibrating nature of the essences contained in the human being.

The phenomenal world of daily life also reveals the wonderful nature of vibrations. Two stones thrown into water will raise concentric waves, and as they expand, the waves will meet each other. When they meet, the waves' lines will cross, yet each will preserve its own nature. Radio waves fill space, crossing each other, contradicting or bolstering each other, yet each maintains its original character; if this were not so, all of our communications would be reduced to one radio station. The world of inner essences is even more complex. It is sometimes felt as a vibration; yet if I had to draw the multi-dimensional picture of these waves as it appears in the inner field of awareness, I would not be able to do so. Mental awareness uses defined forms in its activity and is organized up to handle something that is so intense and essentially formless, yet is able to assume all possible forms. Supposedly strange phenomena of telepathy, thought transference, mass panic, or hysteria are possible only because of the wave-like nature of the soul's substance. Thoughts, for example, are not limited to the physical sheath, and can spread like radio waves, each preserving its own unique nature.

This consideration sheds new light on the previous comparison between natural scientific and esoteric research. We have already mentioned the tendency of scientific thinking to describe reality using the concept of a basic building block, whereas the esoteric approach is holistic, starting from the multidimensional whole and deducing the details. This is not the only difference that typifies the approach influenced by esoteric knowledge. Another difference has to do with the relationships that develop between the fundamental units of the processes. We've already seen that the nature of the basic unit, as defined here, is mostly characterized by the inner vibration within it; but we have not discussed the reciprocal influence that every elementary unit has on its surrounding units.

For example, the notes of a musical chord determine the exact location of each note. Once two of the chord's notes have sounded, the third note's frequency is defined very precisely; otherwise we get a noise. The nature of waves in Jenny's tonoscope is also determined not only as a function of the vibrations of the tiny sawdust particles, but also as a result of the reciprocal influence that the waves have on each other. Nothing is self-determined. Each unit, at no matter what level, is partially shaped, influenced, and even determined by its surroundings.

More than anything else in the world of sensory phenomena, the musical scale points to the special relationship between the different notes in the octave. Among the otherwise uniform spaces between notes, we find two exceptions: the spaces between E and F and B and C (fig. 4). You may ask, "Why aren't these intervals between the various parts of the full octave uniform? Would composers not have easier lives if the black keys could fill the spaces uniformly in contrast to the occurrence of the relationships between E and F or between B and C?

We can find deeper engagement with these questions in the esoteric traditions, where the musical octave is seen as an external, sensory expression of a profound principle that underlies all developmental processes. The Fourth Way, taught by Gurdjieff to his disciples, is filled with knowledge regarding this principle. According to this ancient tradition, cosmic processes on all

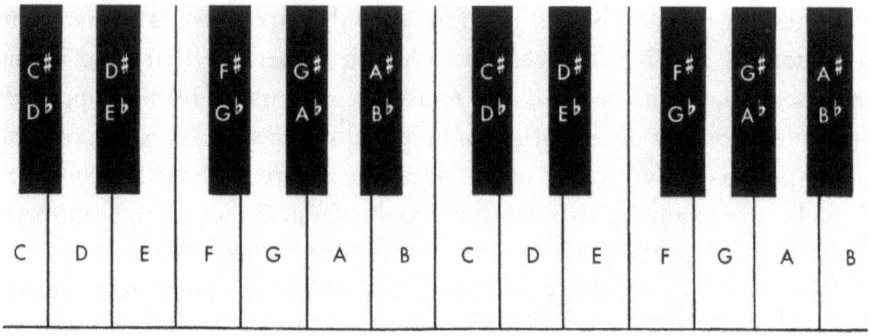

4

levels—from the minute to the universal—follow two basic rules: the Rule of Three and the Rule of Seven. According to this tradition, the full process, the full octave that runs from one C to the one above it, is not continuous. There are two problem zones between the poles of higher C and lower C that do not allow the process to develop in the original direction given it by the primal thrust of the basic creating note. According to the Law of Seven, if the process is not aided by an external factor it will wander off its original path or simply cease. The location of the spaces is intentionally set in a way that provides the entire process with special characteristics that hold essential roles in the process of creation and its maintenance. We do not fully know the manifold suprasensory aspects of this cosmic law; nevertheless, the musical octave, the full scale of colors, and the table of elements are known manifestations of the same intrinsic law.

However, this process does not behave like the laws described by the natural sciences, such as the process of entropy or the evolution of biological species. While these processes are linear in their nature, the cosmic octave develops not only upward (evolves), nor does it materialize only downward (involve); instead, it runs simultaneously between these two poles, including predetermined stations along the way. This law operates vertically between the hierarchical planes of existence; because of its complexity, it is not possible here to detail its inner dynamics and the way in which the Law of Three works to create passages between the common stations. For now, it will suffice to point at the universal nature of this law that can be seen at any scale and level of the vibrating universe, as Gurdjieff first presented it to the West.[5]

The Kabbalistic worldview is based on similar principles. The Lurianic system describes the division of the world into ten spheres (fig. 5), ten worlds that emanate from the infinite and draw from one another according to

5 See Gurdjieff, *Beelzebub's Tales to His Grandson,* and Ouspensky, *In Search of the Miraculous.*

lawful cosmic processes in a downward trajectory, right into the world of action. This trajectory is perceived in part by our senses. In the Kabbalistic worldview, there is a rising evolutionary direction that exists within the involutionary process of creation, and therefore within both *light* and *vessel*, terms used by Lurianic Kabbalah to denote the two aspects of a perfect dualism that analogously appears at all levels and in all details.[6] As in the Law of Three, which establishes, as we have noted, the notes of the octave, every new phenomenon, according to Kabbalah, goes through a four-stage process, after which creative act is complete. Since the structure fashioned according to the ten spheres can be found in all details and all levels of existence, we should not be surprised to find it in the human being, who is but a miniaturized replica of the universe. This concept is extremely important for understanding human creative processes and their significance, as we shall see later on.

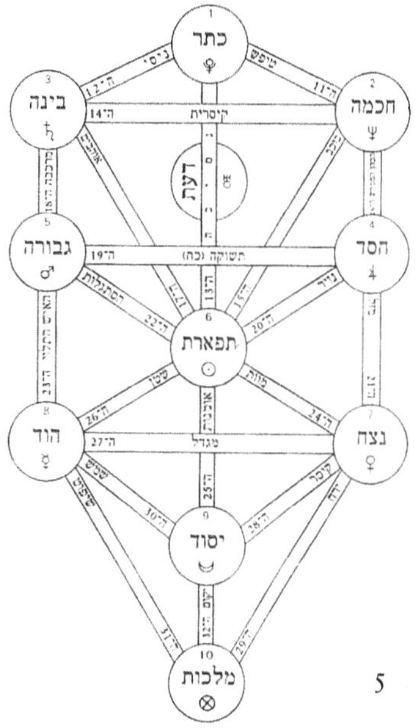

5

We can easily spot the characteristics of the basic unit—a vibrating note, a world, or a sphere, according to the principles outlined in the beginning of this chapter—in the two worldviews mentioned above. The basic unite has a center of gravity, self-identity, and a defined consciousness. Every note or sphere is part of a whole process, and includes a more dynamic, analogous inner process that provides it with its inner vitality. The core idea of this strange bidirectional process appears not only in Kabbalah or in the Fourth Way; its typical characteristics can be found in all ancient traditions, each expressing it in their own way. According to this principle the world of creation is realized between two poles, the higher of which is the Absolute or Infinite World; what Hinduism calls Brahman or pure reality, and esoteric Christianity refers to as the Father. According to this principle, a primordial cosmic vibration develops out of the divine bosom and creates all the worlds that descend one out of the other; it creates the diversity of forms and details in every world, yet itself remains beyond the rule of time and space. This is a process of realization that begins in the worlds permeated with the light of consciousness and ends in ignorant, unaware matter,

6 For more detailed information interested readers may look into Yitzhak Luria, *Talmud of Ten Spheres* (mentioned in the appendix).

whose connection to its fountain, the creating divine essence, is gradually forgotten; this is the involutionary direction.

At the very same time, the stream of cosmic consciousness permeates the descending process of realization, imbuing all levels and forms of the essence coming into realization. The basic unit that we have sought to describe is not, therefore, a physical format of lifeless vibrations, but rather a note with cosmic quality, a relative perfection in which cosmic consciousness vibrates on all the levels where it can be found. According to this view, the universe is not a compilation of elements that have come together randomly, but rather is a living organism that follows divine reasons and develops toward defined goals. Humankind has been set to fulfill a vital role in this living organism.

We can therefore see two worldviews: one presents an evolutionary process of randomly growing complexity, proceeding with no directional hand, through mutations and the principle of survival. This system has no explanation for the cause or purpose of creation, for the appearance of life on the planet, or for humanity's appearance. In this system, the appearance of consciousness is explained as the random creation of nerve cells, and the essence of thinking as the interaction among those nerves.

By contrast, the esoteric approach describes not only a unidirectional process of evolution, but also a bidirectional path of evolution and involution that permeate each other in one multidimensional process. In this complex process there is a key role for cosmic consciousness—an intense divine, omnipotent, and omniscient essence. This essence is at the base of the active life of each component that is part of the universal whole, and itself develops through the infinite interactions of all its components.

This understanding of the function of creativity may point to a possible answer to the question bothering creators of our time in all fields—the arts, philosophy, education, technology, and science. Though they may not express this publicly, or even admit it, today's creators may be bothered by a necessary question: what is the purpose of my work? What is its aim? Surely, the value of work is determined only according to the purpose it serves. And as we can see, new fields of creation have spread over an enormous range—a multifaceted diversity with infinite expressions. Processes of creation have become independent and self-centered, and their connection with an overall basic cause, which ought to underlie their very essence, has gradually been lost.

We have to admit that the intrinsic sense that personal works of art can be created to serve a greater, hidden cause to be realized in manifold manifestations is, in fact, lacking today. Participation in a greater movement supervised by higher forces is an unacceptable idea, although it is, essentially, very true. Nevertheless, human beings serve this greater cause whether we want to or not; we simply do so unconsciously. The quality of our work will therefore change radically when we become conscious of the living impulses that drive our personal work; we become aware of the unity of living forces behind the apparently unconnected aspects of phenomenal reality.

A broader perspective on reality, a deeper picture of the world that encompasses the reasons behind cosmic creation and the inner regularity of the creative process—even if these are studied initially only in theory—may provide creative people with an initial infrastructure out of which they could understand their own work. This understanding is therefore a vital need in our time.

What is the connection between the creator's personal, intimate work and the greater laws of the cosmos? Indeed, unlike the view that human beings merely lowly grains of sand in the infinite reality of a limitless universe—negligible particles that universal reality could easily do without—perennial wisdom and the cosmological philosophies of ancient civilizations point to the fact that humanity is inseparable from universal reality. Humanity is an essential foundation necessary to fulfilling the goals of divine wisdom. In all esoteric traditions, the multidimensional model of the universe is described as "divine creation," which is the vibrating essence of all that exists, realized through a descending process of involution and moving an omniscient, omnipotent reality toward the multiplicity in which human creative life is embedded. At the same time, divine consciousness seems to send its arms downward into the essences sunk in oblivion with little or no consciousness, and uses them to materialize itself in the world of separate details. Reality develops, spreading like a fan to realize goals set for it by divine wisdom: from divine unity to infinite diversity, in which divinity expresses its endless aspects from unity to diversity that is also divine! According to the principles of esoteric wisdom, humanity's role is to help in the process of realization of the divine plan. Human beings, set as we are in the material world, yet bonded to the spiritual world, have a special role—helping the Creator materialize creation.

Esoteric knowledge, to which this chapter is only a brief introduction, can help us find the meaning of our existence and with it the meaning of our personal creation. The study and integration of esoteric knowledge through direct experience may summon a magical contact between the human being and the cosmic infrastructure at the bottom of one's very soul. A transformation of the soul, its awakening, its awareness of its noble origin, makes it into a tuned instrument, a monochord of the soul that vibrates at the same frequency as the divine music.

In such conditions, creators are imbued with inner fire, and their work expresses depth, a universal dimension, that provides it with meaning; the work is no longer a random expression of the individual, but rather a cosmic creation expressed through a human vessel.

PART TWO

CULTIVATING THE CREATIVE FORCES

Chapter 15

Nurturing Creative Thinking

> *"It was my great debt to Lele that he showed me this. 'Sit in meditation,' he said, 'but do not think; look only at your mind; you will see thoughts coming into it; before they can enter, throw these away from your mind till your mind is capable of entire silence.' I had never heard before of thoughts coming visibly into the mind from outside, but I did not think either of questioning the truth of this possibility, I simply sat down and did it. In a moment my mind became silent as a windless air on a high mountain summit and then I saw one thought and then another coming in a concrete way from outside; I flung them away before they could enter and take hold of my brain and in three days I was free. From that moment, in principle, the mental being in me became a free intelligence, a universal Mind, not limited to the narrow circle of personal thoughts as a laborer in a thought factory, but a receiver of knowledge from all the hundred realms of being and free to choose what it willed in this vast sight-empire and thought empire."*
>
> —Sri Aurobindo, *Sri Aurobindo on Himself*

When Wolfgang Amadeus Mozart was already a known composer, a talented and ambitious boy, whom many saw as Mozart's inheritor, was brought to study with him. "I want you to teach me to write symphonies!" said the boy defiantly. "That is not quite so simple," said Mozart shaking his head, "Perhaps we should begin with sonatas." The boy stamped his foot impatiently and said "Didn't you yourself write your first symphony at age six?" "Yes, of course," said the genius, "but I never asked anyone to teach me how to do it."

Creative talent is indeed a necessary starting point for any artist or artisan. There is little debate over the need to cultivate talent, but how is this done? Professional and academic specializations can be acquired; the student needs to know a sum of knowledge and have some practical experience. The creative professions, however, do not rely on any knowledge bank—though knowledge may be useful—nor on mere exercise and experience. Creative activity is not based on the known; by its nature it emerges from the unknown, permeating the field of known activity.

In our intensely technological age, creative powers are strongly encouraged in some fields. It begins with enrichment courses for children and youth, and later continues with government help for start-up companies in technological greenhouses, assistance from the Office of Science and Technology, scholarships, and more. Yet good intentions regarding aid and advancement are challenged where creative individuals are concerned. Society senses that its knowledge is not deep and encompassing enough to directly aid the creative forces within individuals.

We live in an age that worships analytical thought. Our culture tries to apply it in every field, even those that are essentially antithetical to analysis. For example, consider how art critics demonstrate their vast knowledge at every opportunity; instead of employing their subtle feeling perception to observe the art itself, their critiques tend to be full of names and dates and bits of information, relevant or not.

Professional literature and workshops for empowering creative thinking and especially inventive thinking bloom like daisies on the green pastures of the education system, filling the pockets of writers and leaving the paying public wondering, "How much has my creativity really improved? Did the way I think change fundamentally or did I just learn a few tricks?"

Dr. Alexander Chernobelsky's book, *Systematic Inventive Thinking for Technological Problem Solving*, is based, according to the writer, on the vast activity of Prof. Heinrich Altshuler in advancing inventive thinking, and especially on his book *Creation as Exact Science*. In a chapter about rules for the development of mechanical systems, Chernobelsky claims that the main requirement for developing systematic inventive thinking for problem solving is a systematic approach based on the rules of technical systems development, which allow for considering and solving contradictions. The writer defines "technical contradiction" as a state in which improving one operation of the system will cause a deterioration of another operation.[1]

Dr. Chernobelsky's book is interspersed with many examples of beautiful creative solutions, but I failed to see in it any method for developing creative thinking. And why? Because such a method cannot be devised. Would you, dear reader, even consider leashing your essentially intuitive creative

1 *Systematic Inventive Thinking and Technical Problem Solving*, p. 50.

thinking with the chains of an ordered method of the mind? Are not method and intuition diametrically opposed by nature? Certainly, systems for data processing may be used; this is the blessed contribution of discursive thinking to technological and scientific creation. Yet can one be replaced with the other without leading to a muddy mixture—a mixture that is neither creative nor methodical?

Dr. Chernobelsky's book is mentioned here only to demonstrate the basic misunderstanding of the essence of creative thinking today. It involves an inability to recognize the various essences that merge in intelligent human activity—their diversity and the planes on which they take place, at times supporting one another, at other times getting in the way of one another, as we shall see.

A more structured Western approach, which is nonetheless guilty of the same basic error, is Dr. Roni Horowitz's ASIT technique. It is intended to improve the creative capacities of those who buy the author's books and tapes or participate in his workshops. Here, too, problem-solving strategies are offered, interspersed with interesting cases in which surprisingly creative initiative has been used to solve a problem that at first glance appeared unsolvable. It is true that anyone watching the charming video the company produced can learn something. Using problem-solving strategies can teach us something about the approaches that may be more or less appropriate in a given case. Yet I cannot think very highly of a method that sums up all the particulars in every case presented and then presumes to outline a plan that is supposed to work for all these cases. When we think up an original solution in a given circumstances, we are really using our intelligence, but if we try to apply a solution we learned in a creative-thinking workshop because someone else used it before, it may be efficient but we will not be using the fruits of our own thinking and will therefore not advance our creative abilities.

The attempt to impose systematic programming on the creative impulse derives from, among other things, the misunderstanding and therefore distrust of the intuitive element of inventive thinking. For example, Peretz Manor is a well-known supporter of systematic inventive thinking, claiming that in most cases people describe the inventive process using foggy concepts such as "sudden inspiration," "enlightenment," or "creative outburst." Whereas we can admit that such descriptions may be accurate in describing the inventor's inner atmosphere at the time of invention, they have no practical application because they do not help in reconstructing the creative process to solve future problems. In the practical exercises to be introduced in coming chapters we will see that inspiration and enlightenment are "foggy concepts" only for those who never learned to observe their essential content. For those with the appropriate capacity, inspiration and enlightenment involve a clarity far beyond what is possible on the planes of discursive thinking.

The examples thus far should be enough to convince readers that the focus in developing creative thinking must be on the creative being and one's ability to allow the inner creative forces to be expressed. Neither data organization nor thinking strategies, as their inventors call them, will do. Methodical systems deal with the products of thinking, its findings or conclusions, not with the thinking human being.

Understanding of the need to go beyond systems in creative thinking is now beginning to emerge through the prolific work of Dr. Edward de Bono, who has written books, produced television series, and advised corporations such as I.B.M. and DuPont. In his book, *Teach Your Child to Think*, he observes that our thinking is not one unified stream, but something much more complex. De Bono writes, "Instead of excluding emotion, as is normally the case with the teaching of thinking, we must find ways of allowing emotion and feeling to play their proper part in our thinking." Of the various types of thinking he says, "It is surprising that we persist in believing that logic is the basis of thinking. This arises from our reactive thinking habits. You put material with ready-made perceptions and information in front of students and then ask them to react. Clearly, logic is important since the perceptions are provided. In real life, we have to form our own perceptions."[2]

His book does indeed try to deal with the thinking entity, not the thinking system. De Bono offers his famous hat-changing exercises, which allow practitioners to break out of their narrow-mindedness and examine the problem from various angles simultaneously—something they wouldn't have achieved taking routine paths. Despite de Bono's relatively independent inquiry, the way he treats the subject of creative thinking is naturally influenced by common Western academic thinking, which is tainted with error and misunderstanding regarding the inner nature of thinking. We should be aware of some of these errors.

In Edward de Bono's chapter "Principles for Thinking," twelve guiding principles of thought are listed. Among them is the following suggestion to the reader, "Detach your ego off from your thinking, and be able to stand

---

2 *Teach Your Child to Think*. pp. 18–19.

back to look at your thinking."[3] This principle's importance can hardly be overstressed. Our thinking is, indeed, deeply tainted by our subjectivity. Disconnection from our subjective being is the goal and desire of Zen Buddhists and disciples of Gurdjieff's Fourth Way schools. These seekers work for years in order to gain, at least partially, an inner position that can impartially face life's reality. Western people, however, cannot adapt this approach just because they stumble across it in a book. Our habits and patterns of thinking are stronger than a moment's wish. As soon as readers put the book down their habits return, and force them to act once again in a one-track manner. In fact, most readers don't even know what an ego-free approach is—they have never experienced it or received the necessary tools to understand what it means. The subject has great importance when we attempt to explain the nature of creative thinking, yet if one does not offer a practical way to adopt such a position so that it can become a habitual part of the reader's daily practice, the aforementioned lines remain no more than an impractical recommendation.

Similar things can be said of other guidelines de Bono offers his readers: "Always be constructive"; "Think slowly and try to make things as simple as possible"; "Be able to 'switch gears' in your thinking. Know when to use logic, when to use creativity, when to seek information."[4] All true, but how are these recommendations to be applied? Are these suggestions enough to make readers let go of their hold on thousands of behavior patterns, rooted in their souls for years? It is hard for someone who has not gone through a path of practical experience in a serious esoteric school even to understand the difficulty in changing habits and thinking patterns that have accumulated within them and have brought them to the present state in which their creative powers are imprisoned—barred from flowing into their inner world with all their richness.

It is not so easy to cultivate our hidden creative powers. We will have to pay a higher price than that charged for short weekend workshops. The creative forces will not be unleashed until the entire human being goes through gradual transformation. Those who want instant change will never find the magic key to the world of creation in lectures and random workshops, educational though they may be. Such workshops can only provide new outlooks or original lines of thinking. The desired changes can come only as the result of devout, thorough self-improvement over a

3 Ibid., p. 220.

4 Ibid., pp. 220–221.

long period of time—possibly an entire lifetime. We have examined the fundamental building block of universal being and considered the essence of creativity. Now we will look at how we can develop and encourage creative thinking.

Chapter 16

Exercising the Imagination

In Light-and-Air of Spirit-Land
There grow the roses of the soul.
And their raying red, downpouring
Into the weight of Earth
Fashions the human heart.
It rays again in the force of blood —
The rose-red of the Earth —
Forth into the Spirit-fields.

—Rudolf Steiner, *Verses and Meditations*

Observing the world, we need to understand that impressions, by themselves, provide us with one aspect of the world. The complementary aspect is provided by thinking, which organizes the impressions of the senses in an intelligent array of mental images and meaningful concepts. As stated previously, this thinking faculty is basically intuitive, at least as it appears in the child, while the ability to observe the world of concepts and consider its principles is more active, and is acquired at a later age.

Observing the world of concepts, perceiving each concept's essence, understanding its principles and its connections with parallel principles—generally understood as analogous thinking—requires the active participation of our imagination. Imagination should not serve the stream of mental images that rush through our awareness as we daydream, but should be an active force, putting its ability at the service of guiding intelligence.

One of my favorite pastimes may also serve as an effective means of practice: observing archetypal principles—both their nature and how they navigate within human consciousness. Examining the appearance of external reality is not enough, and one instead learns to observe the inner, ideal aspect of the phenomenal world. A cynical reader may consider this a speculative game with illusionary creatures of imagination that have nothing to do with outside reality; yet the unprejudiced reader, interested in investigating this possibility, will gradually find that practicing thinking in this way creates a kind of inner flexibility and an ability to perceive thinking essences as objective beings, not a random creation by the thinking subject.

For example, consider the statement above by looking at a geometric image. We can accept as fact that the validity of the concept of a triangle cannot be shaken by the judgment of a thinking subject. A triangle is a triangle for any thinking person, regardless of one's upbringing or cultural background. It becomes more difficult, though not impossible, when we consider concepts that are the basis of fabricated objects. The key to understanding here is that the human inventor's thought existed as the basis of those objects even before they took material shape. Seeing ideas behind the general world of phenomena—trees, animals, processes of becoming, and anything that is not made by human hands—can be achieved by only a few, since it is not human thinking, but rather divine thinking, that lies at the foundation of all creation.

Although in its present state our thinking is not capable of directly observing the world of ideas, we can develop some measure of sensitivity to the independent existence of the world of archetypal concepts, and see how they are expressed in different contexts. Once we stop and look at a basic concept, like "resonance," we are already committing an unusual act of initiative. In our daily routine there are hardly any pauses; our attention moves from one activity to the next, fluttering over the surface of phenomena and concepts, hardly paying them a moment's attention. However, when we intentionally stop the flow of activity and refuse to let it rush on randomly, we are raising an amount of thinking willpower that, we shall see, is necessary for the activity of creative thinking.

For example, in order to "feel" the essence of the concept "resonance" within our thinking, we begin to look for its manifestations in the phenomenal world. When we strike a tuning fork tuned to the tone of C, the C string of a nearby piano will begin to vibrate, while all the other strings remain silent. Likewise, most of us know the phenomenon in which wooden doors in our house begin to tremble when a large airplane passes above. The explanation of these phenomena will be left to the reader's active thinking, since the effort used to understand phenomena is more important than the explanation itself. We can look at some archetypal phenomena in a way similar to the approach we used in the chapter titled "Concepts in the Creative Process." We considered the concept of the self-resonance of swinging objects, and showed how rhythmic winds can topple enormous bridges, and how a swing's motion grows by pushing gently at proper times. We have even discussed the suprasensory aspect of resonance and how it functions to cause transformation between different levels of suprasensory reality.

Having considered the different expressions of the resonance principle, we can begin to apply it virtually to objects constructed by our imagination. Let us juxtapose two imaginary objects, cause one of them to vibrate, and try to imagine (with closed eyes) how movements of the first object contribute to motion of the other. We must note that while the objects were created in our imagination, the way that the first object moves the second is not random, but must obey the rules of resonance. In this way we become aware of the limits of human creative freedom as inventors or creators in any field. We do not have absolute creative freedom, even in our imagination, and are bound to the inner regularity of physical reality. While we may be the makers of the objects, the regularity according to which they act on one another is determined by superior intelligence beyond our understanding, and we are obliged obey it.

Let us create additional virtual situations based on the resonance principle. For example, let's imagine an innovative instrument that transfers its vibrations to a distant object. What would this instrument look like? Try to imagine its active principle, and then try to imagine that the force of transmitted vibrations grows to infinity. What will eventually happen to the receiving object's mass? We can expect it to disintegrate, since the forces connecting its various parts won't be able to withstand the sharp motions we have transferred into them. In effect, we have virtually created a powerful weapon. While the destructive instrument we have just described has not yet been invented, modern medicine is already making use of this principle to smash kidney stones without the need for surgery. A special tube with a transformer transmits ultrasound vibrations of the same resonance as that of the hard objects accumulated in the kidney, and thus disintegrates them without causing any harm to the soft organic tissue. The disintegrated matter is washed out with the liquids passing through the kidney, and the kidney returns to normal functioning without the need for surgery. Recently, we heard that an Israeli company called Insightec developed technology that uses this principle to remove myomas (fibroid tumors that are usually benign) from the uterus. The patient lies inside a scanner that provides 3-D images of the tumors and guides the vibrations to the right spot. Ultrasound waves heat the tissue and destroy it without harming neighboring tissues.

Observing archetypal concepts is more than just an exercise for our thinking and imagination. It teaches us something about the reality we live in. In other words, it is a research tool that can expose new aspects of life.

Now, I will take a break from writing and sink again into contemplation of the concept "resonance" and will share the content of my mind during these moments with the reader....

Now I'm back with you, dear reader. I have just raised the image of the concept "resonance" in my head again and have allowed it to hover there for a moment. I noticed that it does not rest quietly as it is and wishes to change shape. How interesting, I thought, there is no pause in the world of supra-sensory concepts; everything is in constant motion, one thing affects another. One thing becomes another. The concept "transformation" appeared first. I allowed this new concept to stay in my consciousness for a while without pressuring it, letting it reveal its essence by itself—a typical position when in a meditative mood, which is something we will discuss later. The concept "energy" appeared: the energy of water crashing down a waterfall and transformed into the kinetic energy of a turbine, which transforms it into electric energy, which is later transformed into thermal energy, or back into kinetic energy, and so on and on. Then I started seeing a beautiful fractal produced on a computer, and that turned into a unique animated movie, and then from there, into Antonio Gaudi's buildings (see appendix 2) in Barcelona, metamorphosing into one another.

Now, I will let the two concepts, "resonance" and "transformation," dwell side by side and see how they respond to each other. Vibrations grew harmoniously and reminded me of another animated movie I had seen, *Cymatics: The Healing Nature of Sound.* Following Ernst Chladni's experiments with sound and form (see appendix 2), later experiments were made by the Swiss physicist Dr. Hans Jenny, using metal dust spread over a taut membrane and causing it to vibrate it at different resonances. As noted in a previous chapter, the vibrations were created by playing different instruments, or by using an electronic generator. The dust began to move and assumed the shape of waves of one kind that transformed into waves of another kind. Truly a sight to behold.

I allowed the memory images of vibrating dust particles to transform before my mind's eye for another moment, and new thoughts began to appear. Though words are a crude means to describe them, I will do my best to give hints of them. I thought, *How do the sounds of a flute become the visible, harmonious movement of particles? Is not all of reality a constant transformation of vibrating substances from one level to another?* I was reminded of the experience regarding the PlanTower vibrating pump (discussed on page 199), and with that a new insight arose: the principle of transformation imbues the entire universe—the plant world undergoes constant transformation, from sprouting to growing, maturing, blooming, and finally dying. The Darwinian evolution of the species and the geological development of our planet, all express this universal principle. Then I thought about how these are all horizontal examples, taking place on one level, and then remembered the pictures of "imagination" that Rudolf Steiner described.[1] Here reality is also created through vertical metamorphosis: one level becomes another—once in the involutionary direction, once in the evolutionary direction—and the two are merged. The concept of metamorphosis began to acquire a deep meaning, full of inner grandeur, which filled my thoughts with intimate warmth and a feeling of awe. Later, the concept ceased to exist as literally, but instead assumed a transparent, airy shape, lit by a pale inner light, flowing out like an endless streaming fountain.

I have described, in the first person, the chain of inner events that passed through me as I practiced meditating on the concept of resonance in order to demonstrate more vividly for the reader what may develop out of this sort of practice; yet to be fair to those unused to this manner of thinking I must say that they should not expect similar results at the first stages of practice. What I have described became possible for me only after long years of practice. I would ask interested readers to find the right pacing and style for their needs and to wait patiently for the results. We must remember that patience is a necessary condition without which no rewards can be expected.

Any readers who would like to experience some of what I have suggested in this chapter might try doing so with the concept of symmetry. The concept of symmetry naturally connects with such phenomena as order, aesthetics, natural structures, and spiritual science.

Dear reader, try to follow the subject in its mathematical contexts; what forms of symmetry are there? "Rotation symmetry" (rotating a shape by a certain degree allows us to create a triangle, a square, a pentagon, a hexagon, and so on); "reflection symmetry" (changing a shape on both the left and right); "glide reflection" (creating symmetry by gliding a shape).

Now, in the world of nature, consider how the deep laws of reality are expressed not only in mathematics, but also in the plant and animal kingdoms: the sea star with its pentagonal symmetry, the beehive with its hexagonal symmetry, snowflakes with even more complex hexagonal symmetries, and so on. What is the meaning of reflective symmetry in the human body? Why are there intentional flaws and what seem to be errors in this symmetry?

Consider symmetry in the world of art. Think of architectural structures such as the Taj Mahal in India or the Alhambra in Spain; both combine

1 Cf. Steiner, *The Stages of Higher Knowledge.*

rotation symmetry and reflection symmetry in the same building. Cornelius's paintings and Bach's compositions also express the same wonderful regularity, which, as we can see, can be found in more places than just shapes.

Likewise, esoteric cosmology also expresses the principle of symmetry, in the famous saying "as above, so it is below," meaning that the inner world and the outer world of phenomena are built analogously so that the same laws govern different planes of reality. This can be seen in the relation between humankind (microcosm) and all reality (macrocosm) in the Kabbalistic tree, and in many other examples.

Devote to this exercise the time it deserves; undertake it with enjoyment and passion. Later, try to connect this archetypal concept with the concept of transformation, as I have described above, and see what results. Several useful new directions of thinking may be found through exercises of this nature. Once the different aspects of the concept have begun to live in your soul, you should introduce this concept to the concept of metamorphosis, and wait for the results of the encounter.

All inventive planners have their own methods of contemplation; inventors seeking creative solutions or scientists seeking an explanation for the reality they find may reach a breakthrough while practicing contemplation. Inventors may, in the course of their work, create a virtual reality and allow its various elements to interact according to inner law and thus find new possibilities. This is an effective method that relieves the inventor of the necessity to draw up or build an entire system just to see if it is feasible. Thinking, supported by the forces of imagination, may be the most practical field of experimentation; virtual experiments can be made and conclusions reached even before the first prototype is built. I invented the Selectogal, described in chapter 24, by virtually flooding beams of light through different prisms and examining the results within my own imagination. If I had not had this ability, I would have had to invest thousands of hours in cutting and experimenting, and even then I might never have reached the solution.

There is an even stranger phenomenon that I have encountered several times while developing inventions. Once I have found a reasonable solution to a given problem and am ready to apply it as a practical prototype, I often feel that a better result can be achieved and I ask for some extra time to rebuild the ideal concept. Clients tend to say in these cases that "better is good's worst enemy." This refers to the inventor's difficulty in saying goodbye to the inventive process and letting the product go on to mass production. Customers who want to see the invention realized are no doubt right; if they do not end the inventing process, perhaps quite bluntly, the process of development could last almost forever. On the other hand, this experience points to the fact that the object of an invention has a life of its own. I have experienced this situation more than once. The concept, in its idea form, already exists in your thoughts; after a good night's sleep, you find it there in a somewhat improved version. Several days later, perhaps not having even thought about it, the concept rises again in your soul, this time in a different version. For example, you may find that an item can be made smaller, or that its parts can be assembled in a different order, and so on. It is a similar feeling to that of growing a plant in your garden; the plant grows and develops by itself, displaying new and sometimes surprising forms, without your constant supervision. No doubt, part of the processing of the concept happens while we sleep, whereas it seems as though our intelligence is inactive. This mysterious fact implies that inventors (or, indeed, those in any creative field) carry out their creative activity using a higher plane of thinking, which unlike daily thinking never shuts down, not even in sleep. In fact, there are indications that it is even more active while we sleep.

Having spent some time going over the different expressions of any principle—in both the physically manifested realms and those not revealed to subjective thinking—we begin to sense that this archetypal principle has a life of its own. Esoteric wisdom claims that this life stems from a higher intelligence that is at the very base of the laws and regularity of corporeal phenomena; it is therefore just as real as its outward expressions. We can train our thinking to function as a new "sense," beyond the physical senses—a sense that consciously perceives an intelligent reality, established within a world of its own.

In order to train our thinking, imagination can be exercised in additional ways. For the first and most simple exercise, it is best that the practitioner go out into the open countryside, though this can also be done indoors. You should look around you and scan the scenery in a given area, keeping it small and contained at first. You should not look at objects, and certainly not try to mentally memorize them, but rather allow your soul to make a natural, effortless impression of what is there. After a minute or two, close your eyes and try to envision the scenery as well as you can, also without effort. You will probably find that there are pieces missing in the puzzle, while some areas are quite clear and sharp. Then, open your eyes and compare the original with what you remembered, paying special attention to the pieces that were missing the first time. Again, close your eyes and try to envision the scenery more accurately.

This practice can be repeated in different directions and at different times, according to your needs and energy. You will soon find that your ability to remember complex landscapes is getting better. Quickly reviewing a part of the landscape will be enough to hold on to a relatively vivid image from which you will be able to draw miniscule details that hadn't reached your thinking when your eyes were open. This is another way of discovering what I have already described as our etheric forces. Landscape images leave a kind of imprint on this etheric sheath without involving the mind—what I have called an "afterimage." The greater the inner calm and stability of attention that the practitioner acquires, the more this afterimage grows solid and vivid, until, as I have said, it is possible to draw even the smallest details from it.

We can continue the practice with another exercise practiced in esoteric schools. Rudolf Steiner offered the following version to his students several times. In the evening, we review the day's events, one by one, not in the normal order but from the most recent back to the beginning. We envision the latest situation and then try to recall the one preceding it, then the one preceding that, and so on. Practitioners find that the reverse order causes them unusual difficulty. After all, our mind is used to linking events in chronological order. When the order is reversed, thinking is revealed in its laziness, lacking the strength to "go against the flow."

This exercise is enormously important, and it is impossible for me to discuss its inner consequences in depth in this book.[2] Still, even one who does not devoutly follow this practice in an esoteric path of initiation may draw practical benefit from it. The afterimages stored in the memory reveal hidden aspects of the practitioner's conscious life. We may recall a certain situation in a rich, vivid way, while finding that other periods have been completely "erased" from memory. "How can that be," we wonder; "after all, I was equally present in both situations!" The key to understanding the difference is in discovering a wonderful capacity of the soul that will be discussed in a later chapter on the power of attention. Our level of alertness is much influenced by the intensity of the action of this subtle energy, as is our memory. When the power of attention is drained by its almost complete identification with its surroundings, impressions pass through us, leaving barely a trace. Or, to put it in a different way, when the subtle life energy into which impressions should be imprinted is unstable, our memory capacity weakens, and even tends to disappear. Strengthening our memory can be done using attention-enhancing exercises, which will be mentioned in the appropriate chapter.

Provided with conclusions reached during practice, practitioners may go through the following day with an inner decision to be more present in what

2 Cf., Steiner, "The Backward Review, or 'Retrospect'" in *Start Now!* pp. 119ff.

they do. They will not get lost in the sweep of outside events, and will reserve a measure of attention to themselves to become observers who remain in the present moment and maintain awareness of their own existence to the best of their ability. They will be surprised to find that their life has become richer and their ability to think colorfully firmer and more stable. Trying to remember events in reverse order strengthens inner powers of the will of which few are even aware. The practitioner gains the ability to hold a mental picture and channel it as one wishes, instead of letting outside events dictate a chaotic, spineless chain of thoughts.

Imagination is therefore a vital component in the array of intelligent forces; human creation could not develop without it. What I have written about imagination doesn't even scratch the surface of this wonderful creation of the Maker; trying to disperse just a little of the fog that surrounds it, we discover that the mystery only grows.

Chapter 17

Habits and Patterns of Thinking

"The next object of self-observation must be habits in general. Every grown-up man consists wholly of habits, although he is often unaware of it and even denies having any habits at all. This can never be the case. All three centers are filled with habits and a man can never know himself until he has studied all his habits. The observation and the study of habits are particularly difficult because, in order to see and 'record' them, one must escape from them, free oneself from them if only for a moment. So long as a man is governed by a particular habit he does not observe it, but at the very first attempt, however feeble, to struggle against it he feels it and notices it. Therefore in order to observe and study habits one must try and struggle against them."

—P. D. Ouspensky, *In Search of the Miraculous*

To what extent do habits dictate our lives? How often do we find that our thinking runs around in set patterns and that we are forced to repeat these patterns again and again in vicious cycles? I can assure those who have not examined these questions impartially that they have no idea how deep the problem is. This is not because they lack a certain kind of intelligence or do not care to know, but because our modern mental world is such that we cannot know, even when we want to. Our habits of walking and eating, just like our habits of thinking and feeling, are preset in well-defined patterns that block the enormous range we could enjoy without them. The inability to create new ideas is no doubt the result of the thinking patterns that prevent us from seeing the world vividly and offering our own creative forces in return.

People will not be convinced by such claims until they experience their truth personally. To that end, we need an indirect way to confront the practitioner with the facts. Why indirectly? Because our field of awareness arranges things in such a way that we do not see what we do not wish to see. As soon as we notice in ourselves a shortcoming or flaw, some inner imp leaps to the front of our consciousness and arranges our viewpoint so that we look "okay," so we can stay perfect in our own eyes. We must therefore trick ourselves and reach the truth in a roundabout way.

The following exercise, which provides a new outlook on our system of habits, can be of use in this roundabout way. Set aside five to ten minutes during the day for a walk along the street or through a field. After walking for a while, intentionally change your pace to half the previous speed and keep going. Pay careful attention to what happens shortly after the change, as this is the moment when you can gain interesting insights into your motor habits. Let us leave what you may discover to your own direct experience.

Why is this exercise a roundabout way to discover the power of habits? Because it offers the possibility to gain a new insight that results from a disruption inserted into the routine of motor habits. At the moment of changing from a routine pace to a forced half-pace, an amount of attention may be released, providing us with a rare impartial observation of ourselves. The term *impartial* here refers not to an observation uninfluenced by prejudice, but to the gradual adoption of a position in which the practitioner feels the gaze of a hidden, supreme witness. On the esoteric path of initiation, this new power of observation is used to better know the student's body and soul—a task that cannot be accomplished in any other way. Just as we used this conscious power to examine our walking habits better, we can also turn it to any other pattern of behavior and find what was hidden from us.

Changing our pace is something that can be done several times and in different ways. We can either speed up or slow down, checking the scope of influence that motor habits exert on our behavior without our knowledge. Walking is not the only area where we can use exercises to examine our habits. For example, we can change the location of our wristwatch, wearing it on the opposite arm from the one normally used. Discovering some of our automatic reactions by this means is a longer exercise, and you can choose the time and circumstances under which you may wish to try this.

Our patterns are not limited to motor habits alone. For example, as an exercise, why not try to avoid using the word *I* for a while, whether within your own mind or while talking to others. One quickly discovers the extent to which our thinking is conditioned by the language we use. Omitting the use of this precious word has a more profound effect than merely breaking a habit. It becomes such an intimate experience that it is best to leave it to one's personal inner dialogue.

Other possible exercises in the same vein can be as simple as stopping for just a second every time we are about to cross a threshold, and then completing the crossing; or we can decide in advance that we will have our next meal silently, not saying a single word until we have finished. Creative readers can pick other options, according to the principles described, once they have experienced the potential of these exercises.

The essential value of disrupting the bond of habits relates primarily to knowledge of the self; nevertheless, an additional interesting fruit of these exercises is that being partially released from these inner limitations provides you with a more sensitive attention to the inner fountain of creative activity. This will surely be felt by the serious, persevering practitioner who uses methods borrowed from esoteric ways of initiation.

There is another aspect to the relationship between mental and bodily thinking. Like Japanese Zen painting, calligraphy calls for the student's spontaneous expression. A person who spends many years learning a technique of writing or painting may find that they have become enslaved to acquired patterns and habits. In such cases, they may be advised to leave calligraphy for a while and do something else. When they return to the practice of calligraphy or painting after a period of absence, they will find that their basic ability has naturally taken root in their behavior and they no longer need to exert their mind to control the technique. Freed from the bonds of habit, the process of creation can arise spontaneously. It is fascinating to see how skills we have worked hard to acquire throughout life cease to be managed by our intellectual thinking and are instead led by our body's intelligence. Bodily intelligence is much faster than the mind's intelligence; it is efficient in its performance of bodily functions and frees the mind for other tasks.

Dancers are well acquainted with this relationship between the body and the mind, which they experience when they learn a new dance. The different moves are learned through the mind's intelligence, yet a dancer's motion will assume spontaneity and grace only when the intelligence of the body takes over. Fourth Way movement classes are an excellent example of how this happens. In the Fourth Way schools, very complex exercises are practiced in accordance with the principle of "breaking habits." Exercise students, arranged in lines, are asked to perform, along with music, complex movements that somewhat resemble Eastern dances. The movements include unusual positions that the practitioner's body has never experienced. Later on, a count is added to the movements, regular, backward, and in canonical order (1–2–3–4; 2–3–4–1; 3–4–1–2; 4–1–2–3; 1–2–3–4...) so that the existing patterns of thinking and movement are completely disrupted and practitioners are able to experience themselves impartially, as they really are—body and mind. In the school of the Great White Brotherhood, founded by Omraam Mikhaël Aïvanhov (1900–1986), the movements are performed together with prayers that give the exercises additional depth.

Practicing with the group, the student is required to perform complex movements, and new moves are added all the time. At a certain moment the mind's ability to control reaches its limit. The student then faces two options: one is to make a mistake or quit performing the exercise; the other choice is to learn to rely on "something else." That something else proves that the body's conscious ability to perform complex exercises is greater than that of the mind. Students find themselves in a new environment, outside the thinking and moving patterns they are used to, and find that they can perform the complex movements very efficiently, and with a sense of freedom and spontaneity.

Those not connected with an esoteric school can also gain from even partially breaking habits, since habits not only limit the wealth of human expression—they constrain our whole life.

Observing unusual phenomena of the kind we have described may teach us something about our professional lives. Most people tend to concentrate their occupations in one field. Others add one or more complementary artistic abilities. The conscious decision to change our habits occasionally may help us break our patterns. If this is impractical for personal or professional reasons, then we should at least make a change in the complementary areas. For example, a painter may choose to leave painting behind for a while and learn to play a musical instrument. Later, after returning to the paint and canvas, one finds a refreshing new quality in the art. Playing a musical instrument can also improve a scientist's performance or an inventor's creativity, instilling one with an inner flexibility that counters the tendency toward the physical and rigid thinking that can grow from routine activity.

Chapter 18

Broadening Our Scope

About Love

"I wish to observe and find my ignorant self;
Trying to act, I realize my incapacity to perform;
Wishing to love I find myself, just as I am—
a self-centered being.
Anticipating a miracle,
the reversal of consciousness provides me with a key—
I give up observing and find the supreme witness,
failing to act I suffer the Force
overcoming my resisting nature,
Bathed in its very substance,
why should I care to love?"

—I. B.

Being able to broaden our scope is vitally connected to our previous subject of changing our thinking patterns and habits; it is our fixed and self-centered thinking patterns that prevent us from seeing thinking clearly and in proper perspective. We tend to approach things from one angle, and then another, so that we always see only part of the picture. While this limitation may not disrupt our simple, routine activities, when we approach more complicated questions, such as choosing a profession, a place of residence, or a life mate, we must do so with a handicap that stems, at least partially, from a lack of the ability to have an overall, comprehensive view of the problem.

For example, those who favor a certain sports team see the sport only in a partial light, while matters of policy are seen partially through a lens of political identification. This is true in all areas; most conflicts in the world and in private life could be avoided if we were wise and compassionate enough to see the world with less partiality.

Some who are aware of the seriousness of this problem have offered exercises that can help free us from the bonds of biased observation. For example, students in Tibetan monasteries often learn religious precepts by arguing for a certain view of the text, trying their best to convince one another that they are right. At a certain point, they change sides, now making their best case for the opposite view. This sort of debate is easily tested, and the reader is encouraged to try it with someone. Couples who constantly quarrel over a supposedly insoluble issue can gain great benefit by trying, even just once, to "switch hats," as Dr. Edward de Bono calls it in *Six Thinking Hats*. Each takes the other's side with conviction, giving it their best argument. The result may be quite surprising.

Modern planning teams use a similar technique, known as "brainstorming." According to this system, several planners get together to mutually enrich each other's ideas. When a problem is presented, each raises the wildest ideas in turn. The atmosphere is uncritical, and the question of feasibility is left for a later stage. In this way, one person's ideas may break another's fixed set of patterns, resulting in a very rich pool of solutions. When I participated in such groups myself, I occasionally asked everyone to take a break in the process and go off on their own for a while to digest the material. The process is most fertile when it swings between two poles—on one extreme, the greatest effort is put into finding new solutions; on the other, individuals do their best to listen openly to all ideas. This exercise is intended to improve originality in a planning process, but it can also be used for deep research into oneself. To do this, we must not only turn our attention to the subject of research, but also notice how we listen and respond to everything in the field of observation. Such a technique can be used in any creative field and can be used as a fascinating tool for self-knowledge.

Another exercise is related to what some call "Goethean observation." Johann Wolfgang von Goethe, famous for his sharp perception, had a way of actively observing nature around him. He used to look at the clouds, study their changing shapes, and predict which shapes might bring rain, which would maintain their shape, and which would dissipate and when. The story goes that he could glance at a cloud and say, "In two hours it's going to rain in the northern part of town." Observers reported that his predictions would materialize with astounding accuracy.[1]

Using the principles of this exercise, a group of students can take a particular object, such as a branch from a thorny bush, and report in turn which

1 Arthur Zajonc, "The Wearer of Shapes: Goethe's Study of Clouds and Weather," *Orion Nature Quarterly* 3,1 (1984) pp. 35–43.

characteristics they notice. The first may report on the shape of the leaves, the second about the capillaries that go through them, the third on how the leaf connects to the stem, and so on. Even when some are convinced that all aspects and parts of the object have been covered, someone always comes up with another characteristic that hasn't been noticed. Some students prefer to practice gradually by going through the different levels of observation. First they look at the physical aspects of the plant, as described above, then go on to aspects of the plant's etheric life—aspects of the motion in its branches, the direction of its growth, the pace at which branches extend out from each other as they grow, and so on. Finally, they consider aspects of the soul: what the plant expresses, what mood it inspires in the observer, and so on. When observation takes place within an atmosphere of quiet attention, the images gradually rise with new, deeper, and broader perspectives. Our potential for deep insight is miraculous, yet it is rarely realized, since the observer often does not have the patience to wait and see more than what appears at first glance. We shall study deeper aspects of this phenomenon in the chapter about esoteric texts.

In a meeting with his students, Gurdjieff once pointed out the importance of organized thinking from many viewpoints. He suggested they pick a particular object and examine it according to the following principles:

1. Its origin;
2. The reason it came into being;
3. Its history;
4. Its main attributes and characteristics;
5. Objects that are in contact with it or have some relation to it;
6. How it is used and its various applications;
7. Its effects and their consequences;
8. What it explains and what it proves;
9. Its future and its end;
10. Your opinion of it, and the cause of this opinion.[2]

Rudolf Steiner claimed time and again that, to discover the essence of objects or phenomena, they should be examined from as many different viewpoints as possible. Truth, he said, never resides with any one viewpoint, but rather where all viewpoints meet.

Broadening our perspective, however, is not just a result of testing the issue from several angles. The unique structure of our consciousness tends

2 *Gurdjieff parle à ses élèves*, p. 142.

to cause us to be intellectual at one moment and emotional the next, critical and then forgiving; in other words, we are one-sided in our approach to just about anything. If we naturally practiced a balanced mode of examination—in which thinking and the body both participated—it could reveal additional sides of the object we are observing or of the problem we are considering. Because this state of balance does not exist, we must work consciously to be present in emotion, mind, and will, uniting them as one force. The cultivation of attention, which we shall discuss in the next chapter, aids our ability to work in this direction; yet we also need to be aware of the importance of balanced seeing. This is always true in regard to all things, even when we are discussing a technological development. A beautiful idea or a new principle arouses a special sentiment in us; we are excited by it, and not just because it may have come from us—we care about it even when someone else originated the idea. Our feelings are for the ideas themselves. Anyone who identifies with this concept can see it as verification of what I have previously said about the universality of thinking and its connection to the greater Mystery.

Observing the world around us with loving eyes is more than just a casual recommendation—it is a matter for practice. This practice begins with animals or plants, and in the next stage we can try it with people—especially those we do not tend to love. I suggest that the reader occasionally go and sit in an open area, full of plant life, pick one plant, and regard it for a long time. You may examine how the leaves grow from the branches, how the capillaries spread out within the leaves, and so on to the finest details. Stay with the observation of the plant until you feel that you know it as thoroughly as you can. Then, relax your penetrating observation a little and allow your emotions to be filled by what comes to you from the plant. After several attempts at this, you may notice that you're receiving something essential transmitted by the plant—not through your eyes but through your emotions. The plant reveals something that is not part of its external form but of its inner essence; something that is not revealed yet to the outer senses. We find that our sentiments become a subtle tool of perception, and when they are coupled with our thinking we get a far deeper and more comprehensive impression of our surroundings.

"Love unites the devout with great Love," says Rabindranath Tagore. This expression, and the poem that appears at the opening of this chapter, point to the fact that a reversal of our consciousness is practically possible. Our self-centered attitude can be gradually replaced with a new one, opening to a wider and deeper reality waiting to be revealed. We may be physically separated from external reality, without hope of union, but this is not true for the higher elements of our consciousness. When we are somewhat released from the limiting power of intellectual, self-centered perception, we perceive the world differently, as full of life and passion. We are no longer separated from it, but feel ourselves to be vividly planted in it.

Chapter 19

Attention

"*Whatever you may want to do in life, one thing is absolutely indispensable and at the basis of everything, the capacity of concentrating the attention. If you are able to gather together the rays of attention and consciousness on one point and can maintain this concentration with a persistent will, nothing can resist it—whatever it may be, from the most material physical development to the highest spiritual one....*

"*And everyone has in himself a tiny little beginning of it—it is given to everybody. But people do not cultivate it.*"

—The Mother, *The Sunlit Path*

The coming chapters relate to the esoteric path of initiation. I shall therefore caution the reader that this material is not intended to encourage personal practice; it is not sufficient as a systematic method of initiation that can be practiced without proper guidance. Descriptions here are meant only to provide the reader a glimpse into areas that have traditionally been hidden from public eyes and practices that have been introduced only in esoteric schools. This information helps to illuminate key points in the cultivation of creative forces as discussed in previous chapters.

Releasing the creative forces within the soul begins with observation: observation of the current structure of our thinking, the flow of thoughts, the origin of ideas. Even a superficial examination reveals that our thinking is not organized and directed, but is conditioned by random impulses that push it back and forth. We try to think about our first goal for tomorrow and find ourselves reminiscing about yesterday's party. We hurry to work and then remember we forgot to take the kettle off the stove or forgot to lock the door. Our thoughts are an endless inner chitchat, a stream of mental pictures spawning others. The first gives rise to the second, the second to the third, and the flow is accompanied by emotion and empathy, hopes and expectations, fears and anxiety, and everything is random, undirected—a ship with no captain.

The elementary capacities of the soul—thinking, will, and emotion—are mixed within us, merged with and disturbing one another so that only rarely are we able to consider things in a properly balanced fashion. For example, when we are tested in school, we need mental clarity; it is just then, in those critical moments, that anxiety takes over and distorts our thinking. We've all experienced this kind of thing. Or, when we need to act out of love for the work at hand, we find ourselves obsessed with considerations of gain. When an act of will, such as making a decision, is needed, our thinking spins round and round, causing us to be unable to come to the needed decision and carry it through. Our personality's center of gravity changes from moment to moment. At times we are rational, at others we become emotional; sometimes we are decisive and confident, and at other times hesitant and incapable of decisions. The pendulum swings from one unbalanced position to another; rarely are our actions truly balanced.

It may seem that this description is exaggerated and unbalanced in itself; that it is not based on scientific research or objective criteria. This claim is understandable. It is the special character of the life of our soul that it does not allow us to deeply look into it, to stand face to face with an unflattering reality. How, then, can we learn the truth? How can we more objectively understand the true nature of our soul's life?

Accepting the assumption that there is a veil over the life of our soul that keeps us from seeing things as they truly are, following the same logic we should look for another factor that counters the veil and allows us to impartially recognize the true reality of our soul's life. This factor is indeed available to us, yet very few notice it without some guidance.

Looking back on our life, we can probably see that it is interspersed with special moments, the kind that we later remember as meaningful. We express these moments by saying, "At that moment I felt present in a different way"—with the emphasis on the word *present*. Or we say, "It was a moment of deep reflection; I saw myself as I truly am." These are different descriptions of the same experience. How can we explain this wonder? What is it that changed in such situations that makes us more self-aware and able to appreciate life from a higher perspective?

The key to this interesting question lies in an essential capacity of our soul's life that is important yet hidden—the power of attention. Attention, which some refer to as "listening energy," is not a voluntary, abstract motion toward one object of our observation or another; rather, it is a reality, or more accurately, a "soul substance" that from one moment to another is turned to different objects of our consciousness in the process of knowing them. For example, when we turn our eyes to a red rose, our soul's essence turns to whatever flows into us through the window of the eyes and is imprinted by it; that is to say, the rose's red impression and complex shape leave their mark on our essence's etheric substance. The soul cannot directly experience the impressions of the senses and requires this mediating substance of our life forces—the etheric substance. We experience the input from this subtle element of the etheric forces within our inner consciousness, adding to it the complementary elements of thinking and feeling that were mentioned in the chapter about the human conceptual world. This inner alchemy has been perceived for some time, and was already noted by St. Augustine. It is considered one of the most important mysteries of initiation into esoteric spirituality.

However, let us return to our practical training of this enigmatic essence. When students detect a chaotic rush of thoughts, an improper emotional attitude, and an ongoing seepage of their attention (caused by unnecessary contraction of one's inner thinking and feeling movements), they learn that there is a possibility of using the will to prevent such a waste of soul forces. In quiet moments, when we are relaxed, yet sitting up straight, we can try to refuse the automatic inclination to identify with the flow of these passing associations and treat them as if their content is unimportant—as it often is. If we practice this with sufficient devotion and determination, we will notice that the associative stream of thoughts is no longer quite as attractive. And when associations and mental images lose some of their importance and interest, we will find that they gradually melt away and disappear. What happens now to the attention formerly aimed at these thoughts? It is still listening. Now it is ready to receive any impression and shape, yet the attention itself has no shape—it is free attention!

This freedom of attention is the hidden key we were looking for. It allows us to observe our soul's life deeply and impartially. Our inner field of vision expands and starts to contain new facts, as well as new impressions of ourselves such as we have never experienced. Freed attention is, indeed, a sensitive tool of awareness, capable of reflecting aspects of the body and soul to which our regular awareness is completely blind.

First we observe the body's position. As I have mentioned, without being aware of it we usually hold unnecessary tension in thousands of subtle muscles. Even during meditation, we cannot let the body truly relax. The body holds an enormous amount of energy, most of which is not put to any constructive use. It could be set free.

When our expanded field of consciousness reveals our excessive contraction, the body is indeed getting freer; thousands of tiny knots seem to open one by one, and the practitioner realizes how the held energy is released and intensified, hovering like a subtle cloud as "observing essence." The disciple's general field of vision expands even more; it seems to intensify, even changing its inner quality. The disciple now begins to be aware of a silent witness, a quiet observer of the inner panorama of one's soul. We feel that this witness is silently present, conscious of the processes taking place within our inner field of consciousness, neither judging nor criticizing, nor trying to improve or remove the flaws that it sees. The worthy and the flawed are accepted with the same equanimity.

The field of consciousness continues to develop naturally when attention is allowed to gather as a steady, viable presence. The different shades of the emotional life are revealed one by one. The silent witness—our very self—begins to see how an attitude of egotistic desiring automatically arises, and how the mood of letting go reverberates in response when one agrees to accept whatever one sees and does not strive to change it.

In fact, the chaos of our thinking doesn't stop with the world of thinking and feeling. Our world of willing is no less chaotic; we can't stop wanting, not even for a moment! We feel that our life depends on constant desire, a sort of "I want, therefore I am." We perceive the tendency to relinquish a desire as a move toward our demise, toward nonexistence, suicide. All this is revealed in a conscious field of observation that has been developed through the consolidation of freed attention.

The reader may now recollect what I said previously about the speculative nature of material, mechanical research compared with spiritual-scientific knowledge. What I describe here is the fruit of immediate experience whose reliability requires no outside support—I cannot scientifically prove it to an outsider.

The field of awareness thus expanded does answer at least part of a question asked in the beginning of our discussion: how can we know the hidden truths of our soul's life? Yet other questions remain unanswered: how can the inner balance between our faculties be restored to our soul's life? Or, how can the creative forces within us gain from such a balance?

Attentive energy is not only a unique instrument of awareness, but also the great healer of the ills of a chaotic soul. Try to clench your fist with excessive force, and at the same time think about something else, such as having a refreshing drink—anything to take your mind off of it. Once you've forgotten about the clenched fist as much as you can, point your attention to it at once, simply examining it and not giving your hand any other orders. You will probably realize two significant facts: first, when you again notice your unnecessarily clenched hand, it tends to relax by itself; that is, the very act of noticing a flawed or pointless state creates a natural impulse to correct the flaw. The second fact is that the relaxed hand still maintains some tendency to keep its present constricted state—it does not completely relax at once. The first fact is typical of the beneficiary influence of awareness, which orders anything unnecessary, anything with a harmful or useless role, to "cease and be gone!" The disintegration and disappearance of anomalies in our body and soul, when they are exposed to the light of awareness, is a fundamental principle of our life; the processes of identification cannot continue to exist under the clear light of awareness. The second fact indicates the contrary tendency: the body/soul system tends to unconsciously preserve its current state whether it is desirable, harmful, or useless.

Thus, our soul's life takes place between unconscious, intrinsically ignorant forces that strive to preserve the status quo and the conscious forces that strive to change it and balance it by harmonizing its various functions. Struggle between these two tendencies takes place constantly, though we may not be aware of it; the knowledge and the exercises discussed in this book aim at taking an active, intentional, devoted part in this ongoing struggle, empowering the conscious forces. We gradually realize that free attention has, indeed, a miraculous influence on our soul's life. The extreme tendencies of our emotions, our thinking, and our desiring grow more moderate; none seeks its own prominence any more. They recognize a higher ruler, a silently observing witness, and subject themselves to the service of the conscious "self" that has begun to make its appearance in the midst of the activity of our soul. The different functions of emotion, thinking, and will tend to cooperate, each making a contribution to the common goal. Our thinking is no longer cold and abstract as it used to be, but rather becomes saturated with emotion, more attentive to the subtler shades of life's flow. It is imbued with will, which stabilizes it and allows it to function effectively and fulfill whatever seems worthy and useful. Our life in general and our creative life in particular benefit from the gradual improvement that comes from practice, since no creative activity can be properly realized without firmness of intention or the inner attunement to create, which requires balancing our forces of attentive energy.

Indeed, the balanced and invigorated activity of our body and soul improves our creative forces. It rids our emotional life of inhibiting forces—fears, hesitations, and blocks—that stop our soul from freely expressing itself. All of these inhibitions gradually dissolve, leaving behind a fertile field in which new intuitions can grow and where creative forces can seek

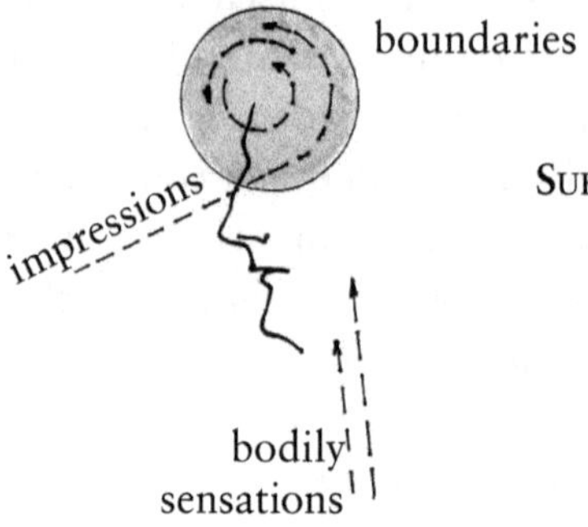

Subjective consciousness

Impressions: mainly sensory
Boundaries: separation from the outside world
Existence: a subjective, self-centered "I" closed to itself

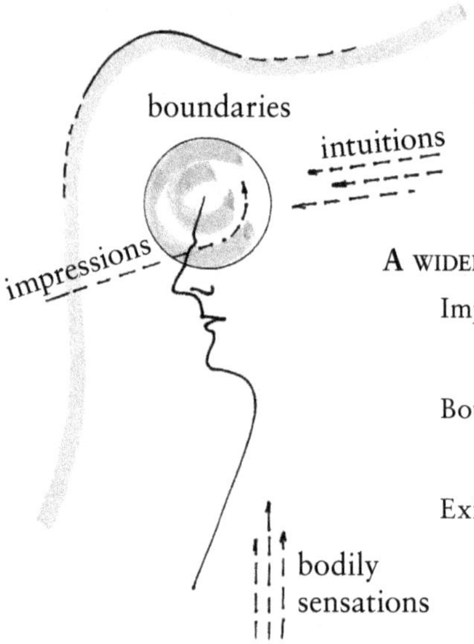

A wider field of consciousness

Impressions: in addition to sensory impressions, direct impressions of being
Boundaries: being immersed in universal existence; intuitions coming from boundless space
Existence: a feeling of self-sufficient "I am"

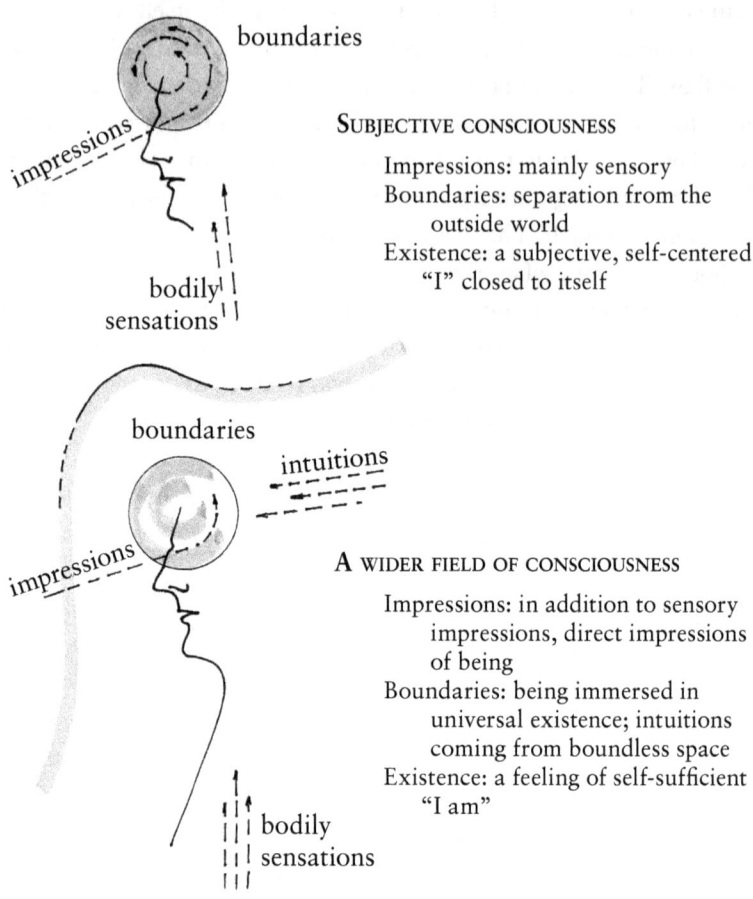

ways into the outside world. Our creative life becomes permeated with subtle shades of emotion, a necessary motivation for every creative act. We learn to love the very act and process of creating, not just the end product. To a great degree, we reclaim the childlike joy we lost while growing up, and realize that the need to create is just as fundamental to the human structure as the need to eat, sleep, or have sexual relations.

"The human being was born to labor!" Many understand this biblical passage as a punishment meted out to humankind that forever set our destiny toward pointless suffering. Some see human labor as an evil, to be rid of as soon as we can. And yet the soul, released somewhat from its chaotic state and inner blocks, finds that human labor is an indescribable source of satisfaction. Human beings create not only to improve our condition, but also because we have a fundamental impulse to fulfill a creative role in the universe. Consciously creating, we begin to consider our creative life as a meaningful mission. Though we may not fully understand this mission, we feel that by taking part in the universal creative flow we serve something higher than our own selfish needs. When we begin to understand our role in this divine context, not only with our mental thinking, but also with the whole of our being, our work exceeds the limits of earthly reality and takes part in a broader, deeper, cosmic movement. Though our creative life takes place on the earthly plane, the force of awareness injected into it lifts it to higher planes of existence to serve the all-encompassing interest linked with the universal process of creation.

Chapter 20

Concentration and Willpower

"What is concentration? It is to bring back all the scattered threads of consciousness to a single point, a single idea. Those who can attain a perfect attention succeed in everything they undertake. They will always make a rapid progress. And this kind of concentration can be developed exactly like the muscles....

"The will, the concentration must be cultivated; it is a question of method, of regular exercise. If you will, you can."

—The Mother, *The Sunlit Path*

What is the force of consciousness? How can we allow its blessed influence to penetrate us? How can we enable the spiritual light to penetrate the world of our being, a part of which knows nothing of this light and does not wish to know?

The esoteric path of initiation uses special methods—those that have been passed down from one generation to the next in esoteric schools and through the ancient mysteries, and those provided in modern attire, suited to the spirit of the new age. Concentration exercises, meditation, and contemplation are still first-rate tools on the path of esoteric education, and all serious practitioners use them, at least to some extent. In this chapter, we will examine the inner value of concentration exercises and meditation techniques, describing the main approaches, the particular nature of each method, and the way they affect the creative forces of the practicing soul.

In the previous chapter, we saw the importance of attentive energy as a cognitive component of our soul life and as a healing and balancing factor. We saw that, when attention does not wander but focuses on external objects, it tends to acquire some solidity and fulfills an active role in the service of our awareness. Yet this self-gathering does not happen without our own effort. Normally, we are charmed by the impressions of the senses and the flow of mental images that pass before our mind's eye—we fall in love with them and give in to them. This neglect of the habits of our so-called active thinking results in the weakening of our thinking power, which then becomes a spineless servant of any momentary whim. We could return the lost component of will to our thinking and stabilize it internally so that it would become able to withstand temptations and refuse them, and to offer its services to a higher presence and the more important needs of our soul.

Engaging our will forces with our thinking power may seem questionable. How are they related? Our thinking has become so dull that we no longer notice the important component of our will that is mixed in with it. For example, observe the way public debates develop and the manner in which social and artistic problems are discussed; we see the extent to which these discussions sometimes lack spine. Speakers do not proceed from one subject to another according to the unfolding inner logic of the discussion, but react emotionally to one another's statements. How many times have you heard the sentence, "I *have to* tell you that..."? It seems to betray the absolute surrender of thinking to the speaker's emotional impulse rather than to the logical need of the subject itself.

Nonetheless, our intelligent life is not completely devoid of will. Driving at a late hour, on a broad and empty road, there is often a tendency to nod off. Once a car appears ahead, or the road curves sharply, we call forth inner powers of will and are able to bring ourselves to a heightened state of alertness. This limited ability is evidence that thinking vitally requires its inner element of will. People who have been through an emergency, such as an accident, can relate the unique quality of their thinking in that brief moment to an utter, inner quiet that had been summoned for the precise and effective action needed at the moment. Why can we not have this quality of thinking in our daily routine and over a long period of time? It must be that our thinking has the possibility to be imbued with will and supported by it, but that this cannot be practically realized.

Coming back, now, to the practical aspect of enhancing our creativity, here is an exercise to be found both in Rudolf Steiner's *How to Know Higher Worlds* and in Georg Kühlewind's *From Normal to Healthy*. We choose an object, preferably manufactured. We examine the object in our thinking, trying to understand its characteristics, its connections with similar objects—in short, we try to limit our thoughts to matters relevant to the chosen object. If the object we choose is a pencil, for example, we should imagine different pencils, think about how they are used, how they are made, and so on. Our thoughts should not roam too far from the main object; it is best to avoid a string of thoughts like, "The color green suits pencils very well.... I got a green pencil from Aunt Esther yesterday.... What a nice woman she is....

She has such a great sense for choosing presents." Such associations are not suitable for this exercise.

This exercise is practiced every day for a week. On the second or third day, we find ourselves returning to the same thoughts, and we now become bored and lacking further challenge or interest. This is the very moment when we need our will to restrict our thinking and avoid wandering outside the predefined bounds. Without exerting effort, we have no chance of completing the exercise. According to Kühlewind, during the following week we should at least be able to hold the concept "pencil" with the same attitude discussed in the chapter on the conceptual world. We try to sense the essence realized in the pencil. In other words, we try to perceive the idea behind it, and we follow that idea as closely as possible. Later, we remove the outer verbal form of the idea and remain only with the idea, devoid of form. What is left of the pencil once the words are gone? Only direct experience can provide one with the answer, since the spiritual essence that stays behind cannot be conveyed with words. Try to remember, dear reader, that when we reviewed the inventor's creative tools in chapter 4, we used the term *archetypal concepts* to describe suprasensory essences that inventors feel, or see in the mind's eye, and that they can use to reach a new solution. This exercise is meant to empower thinking and give it the ability to "see" what the senses cannot grasp although these things are real.

In this exercise, we have again met the power of attention, subject of the previous chapter. Once the observed object no longer interests us, a certain amount of attention is left with no object to disappear into; lacking outside direction it gathers into a formless existence, ready for whatever mission may come. The gathered power of attention answers the call and begins to act through an independent will that is part of its nature. Later, when practitioners have enough power, they will be able to focus the gathered attention in a selected direction in order to perform a specific task.

Esoteric literature contains stories about unusual achievements in this field. Eyewitness accounts of Sri Aurobindo's life often mention his ability to imbue his listeners with powerful silence and deep listening, which they would not have been able to reach by themselves. His disciples say that when he was writing, his room was so full of concentrated energy that even the pouring rain stopped at the open windows and, despite the blowing wind, didn't wet the room. Gurdjieff, in his *Life Is Real Only Then, When "I Am,"* claims that after intensely concentrating his energies he could kill a yak or make an elephant fall asleep from a distance. Although we cannot know how factual such stories are, we can realize the power of concentrated attention in ourselves and turn it to humbler goals, such as those related to our creative life—inventive thinking, musical composition, philosophy, and so on.

Concentration exercises are not limited to manufactured objects. Meditative sentences may raise practice to new levels that are truly suprasensory. This is a meditative sentence by Rudolf Steiner: "Wisdom lives in the light."[1] Sitting comfortably with eyes closed, we relax the body and call the sentence before the mind's eye. The sentence may be meaningless to the normal mind, since we have never perceived a similar phenomenon with our senses. We remain close to the structure of the sentence and fight off the diversions that appear one by one. Once the focus on the sentence is intense enough, we narrow it. We drop the word *lives* and keep "wisdom in the light." Now we feel that the word *lives* is included in the shorter sentence that remains. At a more advanced stage, we also drop the word *wisdom*, and the word *light,* all alone, now contains the whole sentence. The word *light* is now saturated with inner meaning, regardless of the sensory light seen with our eyes, and it begins to appear as a moving image, lit by its own inner light. With one more step we could completely drop any verbal aspect of the original sentence and keep the direct experience of what has come into our being through the growth of attention.

This exercise may seem too advanced to someone who has not tried it, yet it is another means for strengthening our thinking power. From now on, with this practice we will be able to turn this power toward our choice of a wide range of objects and understand them deeply. Students can place key words like *hierarchy, symmetry,* or *transformation* before the mind's eye and wait for the idea behind the words to start moving before their inner gaze, revealing the words' inner meaning, as related in the earlier chapter about the conceptual world. As noted in this chapter, inventors do not satisfy themselves simply with philosophic inquiry about the meaning of each idea by itself; they can bring two or three ideas together, as described previously, and wait for them to interact and create a result that can be used in their creative work.

Concentration exercises and meditation, practiced for a long period of time and with additional aids, can bring about a dramatic change in the structure of consciousness. Inner planes of being are revealed to the expanded consciousness. This is a reality that our awareness was unable to detect when it was limited to mental thinking and its related conceptual world. Whereas before the practitioner's thinking moved in closed circles,

---

1 Steiner, *Start Now!*, pp. 11–12, 176.

in a flat and pale conceptual world, one now sees living reality, with depth and richness that the words connected with mental languages cannot even describe. One begins to understand the limitations of the mental world and its dependence on a plane of being that is part of all of conscious life.

One can now observe the conceptual world that one has acquired with a new perspective, since expanded awareness encounters its inner world in a different, more experiential way, and turns the practitioner's conceptual world inside out. Concepts like "truth," "freedom," "relation," and many others appear in totally new attire. The concept "truth" appears in the mental world as something representing validity, compared to its opposing concept—since without the concept of a lie, the word *truth* would not exist at all. The concept "truth" finds its way to daily use in language, and from that position moves into logic, which it helps to establish. Yet when awareness expands, it begins to include a more intense reality, containing essential layers of reality of which mental awareness is not conscious. Practitioners feel that what is revealed to their awareness in the process of expanding their consciousness has become more real and direct. We begin to see that the conceptual world to which our consciousness was accustomed gave us only a limited part of the whole of reality. *Truth* now becomes the term for a higher existence revealed with blinding inner light, signifying a new feeling that there is something more real at the basis of the phenomenal world—something that contains the phenomenal world as a projected limb of the living reality. *Truth* becomes a goal for our longing, since we feel that it is not merely a mental concept, but a real, divine world, unlimited in its scope, to which we, ourselves, belong.

The concept "freedom" likewise acquires a new meaning, different from what we have previously known. Countless articles and philosophical essays have been written about human freedom. It has been discussed from social, legal, religious, and many other viewpoints. In most cases the discussion was based on comparison and analysis—the difference between "free" and "not free." Later, other concepts were derived from it—free choice, social morality, equal rights, and more are all based on conceptual thinking—always based on the comparison between a thing and its opposite. Just as the concept "truth" cannot exist on the mental plane without opposition to the concept of falsehood, so too, the concept of freedom must be understood as the permission or ability to choose between several alternatives. The concept of human freedom has no separate existence in the mental, conceptual world, and always appears in comparison to something external to it. Here, too, expanded awareness reveals a new dimension of human freedom—not a mental but an experiential aspect. Practitioners whose awareness has to some degree been disconnected from the mental conceptual world feel an existential sensation of being free. We experience this as someone would who breathes fresh air after years in a dank cell. For such a one, "human freedom" becomes a name for being in a field of action, free from fixed patterns of thinking, free from the emotional load and physical burden that previously hung upon one's thinking as weights. One can now move thoughts with ease and alertness, ready to experience the inner warmth of thinking. We experience "freedom" as an actual reality, existing by itself with no need for comparison to anything else. Instead of a mental philosophical concept, freedom becomes an experience in which thinking, will forces, and emotion are combined as one.

Those who wish to enrich their soul life with creative forces must look for this in a higher world, a plane of existence where concepts exist vividly and dynamically, with humankind participating as the inseparable part of the whole that we are. Mental thinking creates a flat, conceptual world that is experienced from the outside; when the field of observation expands, we experience the multidimensional nature of existence and become an inseparable part of the occurrence.

In mental thinking, separation and comparison are the rule; spiritual awareness returns the conceptual world to its original unity. Mental thinking is cold and disconnected; authentic, active thinking is saturated with intimate warmth and inner abundance. Mental thinking exists on a single track, cut off from the unity of being; true thinking is alert activity of all of our soul's faculties—thinking, will, and emotion.

Chapter 21

Beyond Mental Thinking

"Through the power of the Sun, the original light shines into the world. It shines within the human soul as thinking. But we fail to grasp the soul's living element. We perceive the light of thinking—but we do not experience it as alive....

"The bodily organ of thought is a screen that reflects the light of thought, while holding back the life of the light."

Massimo Scaligero, *The Light (La Luce)*

In previous chapters we noted that our creative life could be far richer and more productive if our consciousness worked the way it was meant to work—that is, to create as a service to the wider universal impulse. I also noted the joy that children have in creating, and directed the reader to question, "Where is the child I used to be? Where are the joy, the spontaneity of creative expression, and the warm feelings that came with childhood?" We have seen that an inner field of observation, developing in the course of meditative practice, may lead to the discovery of a limited "self," or "personality," which protects us from the assaults of the outside world, yet also blocks our spontaneous expression and prevents us from living a rich, expressive life. We have examined this self's tendency to classify every new experience and insert it into a well-defined archive of "the known." Caution was also urged, pointing to the deep fear that can accompany meditative practice every time the unknown is faced—fear that eventually blocks our access to the creating, intuitive whole. Yet as important as all these points are, there is a further aspect to understand—the unity of our body-mind system is flawed in more areas than this; the most important block to the spontaneous act of creativity is the structure of consciousness itself.

The human cognitive process is fundamentally based on two essential, complementary elements: the first is the "knowing subject," for whom the instruments of perception were created, and the latter is the "means of reflection," which reflects perceptions to the knowing subject. We could illustrate this with a well-known example from life. When we go to the cinema to see a movie, we don't see the light projected at the screen. We detect its existence only after it has been reflected to our eyes by the thousands of dust particles in the air or by the screen itself. Without the existence of those reflective elements, we would never know of the beam of light thrown by the projector. Certain dance venues employ a new visual instrument that includes a fine net stretched above the crowd, with a complementary laser projector that throws a red beam of light onto the net. The projector goes over the net with incredible speed so that it displays complex shapes. The net becomes a reflective tool, allowing the observing human eye to see the beam of light. In similar though obviously more complicated way, the human "self" requires an appropriate inner means of reflection before information from the outside world can reach its awareness.

In his lectures about human thinking, Rudolf Steiner claimed that the brain is the human tool of reflection. Thinking itself, he said, takes place in the etheric sheath—the array of life forces that thoroughly penetrates the human body—yet the vibrations in the etheric body are reflected in the physical brain. This finding of anthroposophic spiritual science may provoke resistance from scientists who investigate the brain's activity. Neural researchers have learned to locate areas in the brain connected with speaking, hearing, and seeing, as well as with logical thinking and control of our body's autonomic processes. Scientists believe that these brain cells are the *source* of thinking. Moreover, it has been proven scientifically that the greater the thinking activity, the greater the number of creases in the brain. Today, researchers can measure the electrical activity of a single neuron and even make a systematic measurement of several neurons. Do these facts prove that human thinking does in fact occur in the brain?

The answer is not obvious, because our example shows a common error we frequently find in Western thinking. Although the brain is needed for thinking activity, it does not generate it. Just as the ground, which is necessary for walking, does not create the prints pressed into it; rather imprints are made by the one who walks on it. Similarly, etheric activity leaves its imprint on the brain, which serves it as solid ground in the shape of gentle creases. The creases should not lead one to deduce that the brain alone generates thinking. We should be able to see that the brain is a reflective implement for human awareness and not the origin of thinking—at least, according to Steiner's view.

Why is it important to make this distinction? Why do we need to ascertain precisely the brain's role in generating thoughts? How can we discover the role that the etheric element plays? The answer has to do with the cultivation of a new and higher kind of thinking that has little to do with brain activity. Our routine thinking, linked to the brain, has many limitations, and it is our exclusive dependence on such thinking that prevents us from seeing those limitations. If we could rise above the limits of abstract thinking for a moment, we could get some idea of its limitations and find the way toward a new, more alive and creative way of thinking activity. The flashes of creative intuition discussed in previous chapters show that such a possibility exists. It is therefore important to understand the nature of intuition and how it is different from normal thinking activity. What prevents these flashes of creation from arriving more often and being more available?

A path of exercise whose roots go back to Vedanta yoga practice can lead to a better understanding of the matter. This exercise is meant to help the student progress along the difficult path of initiation; nevertheless, I chose to present it here with reference to the enhancement of creativity because of the fruit it can cultivate generally in the soul if students will themselves to seriously persevere through its hardships.

The practitioner sits erect, with the body as calm as possible, allowing the inner quietness thus created to expand the inner field of observation gradually. The flow of associations eventually calms down while the practitioner becomes saturated in the peace and calm inspired by sitting motionless. Though mental pictures continue to pass before the mind's eye, one tries to give them no import, and allows them to progressively fade away. Thoughts rise and develop because of the attention we give them, so when we intentionally prevent ourselves from ascribing to them any importance, they naturally melt away and disappear.

Completely silencing thoughts and passing mental images is not an easy task; again and again, one finds oneself facing yet another image, which seems to sneak in by itself in a moment of distraction. The effort required in this exercise is to turn your attention in the direction opposite to the image you're facing. The appearance of the picture naturally entices practitioners to direct their attention to the front and outward; yet now they learn to react quickly and turn their attention away from the image, directing it instead inward, to a plane that they sense is beyond the image.

While practicing, we find ourselves stubbornly fighting against our natural tendency to create imaginative pictures and be attracted to them. Silently, we say to ourselves, *neti, neti* (Sanskrit = "not that, not that") every time we are charmed by an image or an associative spark that appears. As we develop a field of conscious observation, we begin to notice the background behind the associative world. We find that this plane of existence is not empty, but rather is full of inner, living motion, of a hidden life that is not yet revealed to our field of awareness. We tend to develop interest in this inner plane and begin to see details of what is happening there. We feel that the intelligence that lives on this plane is not part of our mental, conceptual world, but rather is an intelligence that is not limited to forms, and is therefore capable of choosing any form.

The sharper the practitioner's sense of observation, the clearer the difference between the associative plane of thinking and this mysterious intelligent activity that displays qualities one has never before seen. Fluid and dynamic, quietly observing, appearing then withdrawing, it begins to play a fascinating role in our field of observation. Our usual, possessive "self" wakes and tries to grab hold of the new discovery: "I want to understand more closely," the personality cries, "I want to hold the newborn baby." Yet doing this chases away free thinking, which has just started to try its first steps outside the practitioner's field of awareness. According to an Indian idiom "the Buddha is shy as a mountain goat"; thus are disciples cautioned to let go of their possessive tendencies and allow the new activity to express itself fearlessly, out of its own power and initiative.

Pure thinking—a suitable name for this activity that is not tainted by selfish considerations and desires of the body or emotions—appears in its full clarity, somewhat transparent, lit by a pale, inner light; it caresses the objects of its inquiry softly and tenderly, yet also with penetrating keenness. If the field of inner observation is developed enough, the practitioner begins to see a sharp thinking movement that at times passes in a flash; it comes from a deep base, still unknown to the practitioner, and ends up as "concept," "image," or what one feels to be "understanding"—something that has taken form in our field of awareness. The practitioner becomes an immediate witness to intelligent movement, which at the end of the process becomes "thinking in forms." One is able to see directly that the conceptual world is fixed, made up of patterns of frozen intelligence—a dynamic flow that has lost its vitality, becoming a two-dimensional projection of a deeper reality.

At the same time, the practitioner sees a current of life forces emerging from an unknown source. While one's conceptual world seems to float in front of the mind's eye as a phantom, flat and unreal, an intelligent current of life forces also emerges from the universal reality in which we take part. This intelligent current is not the form of thinking with which we are familiar, but a living essence, our own essence, in fact, unifying the three basic aspects of thinking, emotion, and will as one whole. As practitioners, we sense that we are not the original source of living thinking, but a human platform enabling its appearance. We sense that living-thinking is a universal force that permeates all reality, and is at the base of all existence.

Once we have experienced this universal truth, we will no longer be able to wrongfully attribute the actions of thinking to ourselves as the origin. We will feel awe at the greatness of universal thinking, and offer the self as a vessel for its expression. The new position will gradually take over the soul and we will learn to understand that it creates an alliance with spiritual reality, which seeks ways of expression on earthly planes. From now on there is no need to bother to look for new intuitions, since divine reality is interested in earthly vessels of expression; it strives to reach the human vessel in order to advance its creative thrust in the world of action. Just as the human vessel has no creative power without divine intelligence, so this spiritual intelligence lacks creative ability on earthly planes when it has no worthy earthly partner.

The great works of science, the greatest breakthroughs, are the results of universal intelligence penetrating the scientist's awareness. Universal intelligence has a way of realizing itself through individuals, according to its choice and the era's readiness to accept new insights. The fruit of individual intuitions is then processed through analytical and synthetic thinking tools; it wears the form of advanced technology, of a medical or scientific discovery, and becomes a tool for the use of human civilization. The foundation of these impulses lies in planes of reality that penetrate the whole world; in these planes humankind is an active participant rather than their originator.

When our soul lacks this kind of insight we tend to crease our brow looking for new solutions. Mechanically, without being aware of it, we turn to the known, dry pool of defined and limited thinking patterns. However, with meditation, practiced according to the right principles, a new inner habit, or new attitude, can open a clearer window for the expression of divine thinking. We learn to trust the activity of pure thinking and find a tolerant, untroubled way to listen to whatever gift may appear out of the unknown. Maintaining a humble attitude, the human creator will allow more fertile intelligent intuitions to appear. One's creative life becomes more bountiful, and the process of creation itself is permeated by inner intimacy, rich with inner life. When the creative process springs from the genuine source, it colors the creator's life with shades of new meaning, since one now has the feeling of creating not from within the limited context of selfish needs, but as a vessel of expression for a deeper, wider movement in which all reality participates. Yes, we are so accustomed to our cold way of thinking that we do not realize that another taste can be found when we are connected to our intimate essence.

Modern artistic creation seems to be very far from expressing this inner attitude. This is probably because, except in rare cases, painters and artists, writers and poets, composers and singers appear to be striving mainly to express their own personalities. Though they may not admit this to themselves, their motives derive primarily from a selfish attitude. Being thus immersed in the subjective aspect of their personality limits their art, which cannot create a genuine resonance in the viewer or listener who is also stuck in a subjective world. A strange norm, with no historic parallel, can be seen in the world of art today: artists can express whatever they like, and viewers are free to receive any impression that arises in their subjective imagination. The demand for an authentic connection between the two is gone and everything is open, everything is legitimate; there are no more inner criteria, and everything is a matter of personal taste.

There are painters, for example, whose paintings tend to describe the world of dreams. Dreams, it is accepted, are general expressions of our unconscious life, and are therefore subjective in nature. There are also, in rare cases, dreams that are figurative expressions of a more profound truth, a vision of a hidden reality living unconsciously in each one of us, therefore giving birth to subtler feelings in the artist's soul. The question now arises: will the painter learn to distinguish between the two different kinds of dreams? Will the painter be sensible enough to touch upon inner truth and evoke a higher, subtler attitude in the observer's soul as well?

Modern artists can cultivate a new attitude that can place their work at the bidding of inner forces that come from the fundaments of their soul existence. This deep basis is not merely subjective, since it permeates all of the human world and more. Stemming from this basis, art unites artist and audience in one reverberation; they share something that creates a common sentiment and common, subtler thoughts.

Human feelings and thoughts that do not roam associatively in the shallow levels of the soul, but rather derive from our inner essence, are connected with the creative forces of universal reality; this is why we feel the unique value of art that comes from this deep, mysterious bond. Nothing else can explain the immortal value of the Bhagavad-Gita, or the awe in our souls when we see a picture by Raphael or listen to music by Mozart. All these share something that is more than a trend or the whim of an age, but has to do with what unites us all as human beings, something that survives the changes in culture and lights them with an eternal light—the essence of our being.

Chapter 22

The Written and Creating Word

"We do not read in order to collect information, but rather to learn and practice reading in every sense. Read on any day as much as you can work through, inwardly, in the time before the next reading. The slower you read the greater will be the possibility that something happens to you during the reading, that something reveals itself. Learn to notice, while reading, that you do not understand: this is the gate through which you can go farther—a secret gate. There are texts written by other than human hands."

—Georg Kühlewind, *From Normal to Healthy*

Written language is usually seen as mostly a way to communicate content and preserve information. Yet written language includes not only the "why" but also the "how." The study of literary, artistic, and scientific works is an important tool of learning in all schools—from the elementary levels through high schools and later in all university programs. Literary works are studied in relevant departments, not only for their content, but also to understand how writers express themselves. In this regard, musical and literary creations are equal; in both, predominance is given to the "how," the way artists express their creation.

In these practices there is some objection to cultivating the student's creativity through learning from the art of others. "Students should express *themselves*," some teachers say. "The process of creation must be completely subjective, otherwise students will be imitating the creations of others rather than making their own!"

Of course, this claim does have some basis in fact. Certainly, any tendency of creators to circulate in known areas usually defeats their attempts to reach the gateway to an inner fount, nor does this approach readily lead to the formation of results. The human soul naturally seeks the easiest path, and the process of creation does not necessarily flow without a certain amout of inner struggle, as we saw in chapter 11, on suffering and creation. However, this is only one side of the coin, and we should delve into and study other side thoroughly before we decide whether it has any value, as we shall see.

People sometimes express the thought, "I've finally connected to the text," meaning that this inner connection and understanding of a given text has suddenly been opened to their own thoughts. What have we actually connected to? What is it that makes us feel disconnected from the text at one moment and connected the next? Creations of thought, and especially art or philosophy, are not just informative texts; they express an inner mood that has been put into shape as written sentences. The essence that starts to live in our soul when we, as readers, say, "I've connected to the text," is the same essence that lived in the writer's soul. When the written work comes from the shallower parts of the writer's soul, the external personality, it is not surprising that what the writer wished to convey may not be what the readers receive. This has become so common in modern culture that it has become a norm; quite a few literary critics believe that what the reader does with the work is one's own business; the work has a life of its own and there is no necessity for the reader to accept what lived in the author's soul. You could argue with this position, but it would be more intelligent and productive to counter it with another well known fact—there are works that touch all readers or listeners in more or less the same way; they evoke a particular shade of emotion, a specific kind of thought. What inner, hidden value do these works have? How is it that they direct the reader or listener to a particular soul experience, rather than to something random and subjective that has more to do with the reader than with the work?

In this respect, esoteric wisdom may clarify something that is not always understood by conventional scientific thinking—something that we can all verify directly for ourselves if only we are attentive to the subtler expressions of our souls. Besides our external personalities, based mostly on the education we received and the physical and social conditions of our childhood, we have another being, more intimate and essential, that exists at a deeper layer of our being. We are accustomed to acting and responding from the external layers and find it hard to listen to something that comes from a deeper layer—a more essential expression seeking a way to the outer circles of life.

There are those who view the inner human essence as being part of one's subjective world and outer personality, as something that goes along with society. Yet deeper research (conducted with the appropriate tools, as discussed in earlier chapters) reveals that, following this line of reasoning, we discover that what we thought of as the subjective aspects of ourselves—the essential parts of our being—are not so much subjective as they are places where we are most connected with others.

Our ability to make deep bonds with others can be realized with no other part of our being. After all, if in our body and our outer personality we are separate from other people, with respect to the essential part of our being, we are parts of the essential All.

In quiet moments of reflection we may feel that we are not so separate from our environment; rather, we are separate parts of one universal being that permeates all reality. Immortal works of art, which survive all changes in fashion and style, are unique because they directly express limitless human depths from which all humanity draws its vitality. When thinkers or creators communicate with a higher level of existence in their own soul they also find the other—their potential audience—and their work thus becomes a connecting thread that enriches all society with the special fruits that have matured in their souls.

Learning the text of such masterpieces does not hinder the reader or student's originality. Quite the contrary; writers express essential motifs in their writing that may energize the reader's soul, waking dormant powers that would have remained asleep without this inspiring touch. Readers' own creativity will not be harmed in this case; they will be able to communicate with the inner fount in their own soul and continue creating in their own way. Their work will not be an imitation but rather a continuation—a new creation.

In esoteric wisdom schools, this principle is taken to a more advanced stage, and is used as an important initiation tool. Esoteric texts are naturally interspersed with descriptions of divine worlds, revelations, and special symbols. Disciples are asked to read the descriptions and do their best to live them. They summon the best of their imaginative powers and try to picture something that's as close as possible to what the writer saw with the soul when connecting with the greater, divine creation. This is an unaccustomed effort for students, since their conceptual world and their pool of imaginative pictures include no suprasensory content from this greater connection. Many disciples err, imagining the divine worlds by using concepts and images from the sensory world. It is not an exaggeration to say that, for them, angels have become winged humans and God an old father or personal guardian—all according to personal desires, fears, and tastes. Of course, this approach is limiting, yet if students allow the images presented to act quietly and patiently on their soul, over time they may find that the images exert a special effect, awakening new abilities in the soul that may develop into tools of spiritual perception in the future.

This process may seem puzzling or even suspect to those who have not experienced it; yet, we must not forget that esoteric students are not satisfied with simply learning the *content* of revelations. Their path of advancement is accompanied by meditation practice and the cultivation of spiritual capacities through experience. Only proper balance between studying texts and meditating will bear worthy fruit.

Experience shows that even people who are not disciples of spiritual science can benefit from reading and studying these special texts. Those who do not strive to develop a higher awareness, yet are interested in cultivating their creative powers, may find that reading esoteric texts is a unique and important tool, since they were not written from the same viewpoint as normal literary works. The most important parts of these texts were written when the writer was at a higher level of awareness. What lived in his soul when he was writing, what he saw and felt in higher planes of existence, is expressed not only in the text's content but also, and to a high degree, in the framing of sentences, choice of words and concepts, and even in the inner rhythm of sentences. For readers to "connect to the text" they must find the same resonance in their own soul as that which was in the author's soul at the time of writing. The connection between author and reader is best when the two are attuned to the same inner resonance. This is not a cliché; it expresses an actual inner alchemy. The disciple's conceptual world is therefore forced to expand into new territory; the new images require one's imagination to rise more intensely; otherwise, the text will cease to speak.

Most readers are probably familiar with the view that our character is formed according to the contents and impressions that we receive and internalize; these impressions enrich and nourish our souls. One who has been gathering only dry information throughout life will find one's soul famished. Those who spend time reading and studying the works of the great teachers will find that this special nourishment fills the soul and provides for its continuing growth. Studying these texts with the necessary devotion, one feels that the soul gradually acquires a special inner flexibility and one is able to grasp the essence of things from several different viewpoints simultaneously. One begins to perceive a vertical dimension of reality where before one saw only superficially. One's thinking becomes clearer and is able to penetrate matters deeply rather than stopping at their surface.

Esoteric texts are not easy to read. An average sentence written by Sri Aurobindo may easily cover ten lines or more. The sentences in Rudolf Steiner's books are not much shorter, and the numerous dependent clauses often add to the difficulty of following the content. The cosmic laws presented in

Gurdjieff's *Beelzebub's Tales to His Grandson* are so complexly phrased that the reader has to go over them many times just to have an understanding of the text. Gurdjieff himself, explaining the process of understanding the inner idea behind a sentence phrased this way, admitted that he intentionally coded the sentences so readers would have to make an effort to understand them. The writings of the great sixteenth-century Kabbalist, the Ari (such as the *Talmud of the Ten Spheres*), are literally constructed like a puzzle. Those who read them without complementary literature, like that of Rabbi Yehuda Lieb Ashlag, may find themselves dealing with descriptions that seem to be taken from the fields of geometry and painting—certainly not texts that stem from the universal, divine reality. The Upanishads and Vedas, the Song of Solomon and Ecclesiastes, John's Apocalypse, and Ezekiel's vision of dry bones—all hide more than they reveal.

As readers, we must indeed stretch our thinking "muscles" when reading and studying such texts. Exalted initiates do not think associatively in the way most people do in normal thinking; rather, they perceive in inspiration the most complex sentence, at times the entire work, complete and assembled, before committing it to writing. Where initiates descend, disciples must ascend, learning the literal meaning, understanding the matter's many connections to the array of general knowledge. Disciples must wait patiently for the picture to live fully in the soul, as closely as possible to the reality that was the writer's point of beginning. An esoteric text, therefore, is a ladder sent from above, which we are invited to climb as best we can—from fragments to a whole experience, from intellectual thinking to thinking that becomes a divine power of observation.

CHAPTER 23

THE MISSION OF THE HUMAN CREATIVE IMPULSE

In the Light-and-Air of Spirit-Land
There grow the roses of the soul.
And their raying red, downpouring
Into the weight of Earth
Fashions the heart of Man.
It rays again in the force of blood—
The rose-red of the Earth—
Forth into the Spirit-fields.

—RUDOLF STEINER, *Verses and Meditations*

The previous chapters discussed the practice and cultivation of our creative powers, yet the most important question is still left in the air—what is the motive for doing so? Why bother with all this effort? What goal does the creative process realize and how can we serve it?

In our modern culture, the answer to this question is rarely connected directly with the essence or quality of creation. The ambition for publicity or for gaining economic advantages is usually considered sufficient and legitimate to justify the creative act; neither those who create nor the business and social cultures in which they live, desire deeper justifications. The sole ruler of the creative act is usually shallow satisfaction, according to which the currents of creation flow and their quality is defined.

In less materialistic circles, greater importance is given to the creator's quality of life and personal satisfaction, as well as to the personal pleasure derived by those who are not themselves creators, yet who sit at creation's table as passive customers. According to this subtler approach, the answer regarding the origin of the creative impetus is answered temporarily when the human creator, whether an artist, musician, thinker, inventor, or developer, feels personally satisfied with the creative process or the realization of one's ideas. Here, too, the disturbing question remains beneath the surface and (in many cases, mostly with people who are extremely sensitive) continues to trouble the creator, finding its way through the hidden cracks in one's protective walls and flowing up to the surface in order to attest to a deep, unsatisfied hunger.

Modern consciousness has a hard time finding the essential connection with its own infrastructure; modern creators have a hard time finding reasonable justification for their actions, efforts, and their mission as creators. Though they sometimes try to fulfill themselves as individuals through the creative act, the search for a meaning that will fill their souls with warmth and vibrant life is not realized in many cases. Such creators may sense that there should be such a meaning under the surface, yet usually fail to discover it within the field of action.

Friedrich Nietzsche in philosophy, Franz Kafka in literature, and Vincent van Gogh in the field of painting are known exemplars of such unfulfilled aspiration; they suffered much through their inability to find an inner truth that they intuitively felt but could not actually realize. For years, I myself tried to find my way as a potential painter, but left painting behind when I could not answer my own question, rising up from within, time and again—"So what?!" Or, in different words, "Is there any importance in drawing or painting, apart from getting paid for it?"

In this chapter, I shall attempt to point to the existence of a broader point of view, which considers human creativity within the wider perspective of a universal one. I shall endeavor to show that the sense and meaning of personal creation can be found only within this broader perspective of the universal process of creating more subtle forms and beings that are finer, and of richer diversity.

Even in the surrounding world of phenomena, human creators today find verification of their sense that the creative act itself is not just something meant to satisfy personal needs but is part of a larger impulse, something that is common both to the self and to overall reality.

A brief aesthetic enquiry into the world of phenomena reveals the special proportions of the Golden Mean, discussed in earlier chapters, that are found in countless natural creations and in ancient art. This evidence shows that there is indeed something in our phenomenal world that is hidden and waits to be discovered. As she gazes over human creations that have accumulated over the ages, the artist sees those that have survived the changes in fashion and have only gained in value, while others left little imprint in historic memory. Naturally, the question arises—what distinguishes one work from the other? What is it that makes one creation so popular in its day, only to sink into oblivion the next, while another creation becomes an ageless monument, steady through the storm of changing fashions?

The search for a valid criterion for the timelessness of a specific creation has encompassed many diverse ideas through the ages, often seeking answers through contradictory ideas. The popularity of the Golden Mean returned to the world of modern architecture with the appearance of Le Corbusier, who tried to connect his buildings to an objective sense of creative continuity by using the principle of the Golden Mean in his work. In another architectural approach, one assumed that correct design, in keeping with the direction of the flow of inner forces within architectural structures, may provide a unique aesthetic and an objective meaning that goes beyond personal taste. This approach was influenced by the harmony found in the world of phenomena, where structural elements are integrated into the aesthetic appearance of nature's creations. For example, the structure of ancient arches in Roman architecture and the complex structures designed and built by Antonio Gaudi (see appendix 2) both express the flow of forces in the structure's constructive elements. In Park Güell (Barcelona) and in other structures built by Gaudi, no two pillars are exactly alike, nor are they vertically oriented. Their structure is the result of a calculation of forces and their direction of flow. The result is more like a live, organic creation than a structure made to serve practical purposes. Yet in Gaudi's creations, the search for inner meaning took further directions. In the structures designed by this unique artist, the shapes flow one out of the other organically, seeming to obey some invisible, inner drive.

A comparable living spirit expressed in solid forms, and the principle of the metamorphoses of shapes and spaces, have been further developed in the works of other designers in all fields of art. The search for meaning does not end with the Golden Mean, aesthetic constructivism, or the principle of organic metamorphosis of forms; spiritual teachers of our time have shed light on this matter from various additional angles, taking the enquiry to further depth. According to Rudolf Steiner, human development is characterized by a change in the structure of consciousness. It was his view that in ancient Atlantis and in the Lemurian period that preceded it, humanity possessed instinctive cognitive faculties that allowed people to directly experience the higher world of the spirit and its inherent laws. Art was considered to be a superior expression of divine creative beings manifested in human creations. The ancients believed that the gods speak through our creations; they think through us and create through us, using the will forces that they instill into our physical bodies. Art was not viewed simply as the independent expression of individuals, which is the current view of the arts.

As Steiner and others have noted, the involution process seems to be aimed at freeing human beings from the divine bosom so that we may have individuality and inner freedom. This liberation had to go through a process of gradual disconnection from the world of spirit, and necessitated a radical change of our suprasensory perception into one that depends on sense impressions. If we look at the continuum of creative works, we see that even though human creations have been directed more and more toward the world of matter and rational thinking, we can still see that the connection with the world of spirit was not severed, and there was a continued interaction. For example, in ancient Greece there was an atmosphere of inner harmony in architecture and sculpture. The main motive of the art was not to glorify a particular individual, but first and foremost to express the perfect, lawful regularity of the human body, a creation of the gods that exists beyond its individual expression in one person or another.

The search for the aesthetic proportions of nature conducted by Pythagoras and other initiates of his time was based primarily on what they experienced in the higher worlds as a "music of the spheres"—a divine harmony expressed in sound. Rudolf Steiner claimed that the original cause for the appearance of human musical instruments was the impulse of the spiritual world, a divine world seeking to express itself on earthly planes through earthly instruments, operated by human hands.

Has the influence of spiritual worlds on human creation come to an end, now that people such as Pythagoras, Plato, Hermes Trismegistus, and others are gone? Is their influence now limited to messages received through spiritual teachers of our time? Spiritual science provides us with a surprising answer; at certain moments when we sleep, we visit higher worlds. This is not a conscious, alert act as it was for unique holy persons down through the ages, but an unconscious visit in the world of higher spheres—a stay that nourishes the soul with fresh vitality to prepare it for a new day, replacing the energies depleted during the previous day. This unconscious dwelling in higher planes of existence, in an atmosphere of harmony and buzzing creativity, is imprinted in the unconscious soul, leaving a deep impression that the soul then carries as a deep imprint into conscious, waking life. Why does the harmonious sound of earthly instruments excite us? Because it awakens reverberations of the impressions we have taken from our unconscious night journey in the higher planes of existence, it is said.

The mission of human creation, according to Anthroposophy, is not a return to past conditions. The structure of human consciousness has changed, logical thinking has taken its rightful place, and the sense of individuality has become an enduring attitude. Modern human creation now needs to reestablish a connection with higher planes of existence, using its new structure of consciousness along with the sense of individuality. According to Steiner, modern art cannot be satisfied with copying objects that the painter finds in nature; nature has its own bountiful ways of expressing its creativity. However, in the spirit of Goethe's teachings, artists can reveal nature's innermost secrets and fully express them in their art. Human artists have an inner experience that is not revealed simply through the senses; they can use their skill so that some of this sensation may be expressed through brush and paint, or through sculpting media. This can be achieved, for example, by expressing higher sentiments that live in the painter's soul, or through colorful expressions of suprasensory reality, such as can be observed in the art of van Gogh, in Zen Buddhist works of art, or in medieval religious paintings.

Human creation is not limited to art. Our thoughts, emotions, and deeds are meaningful creations in themselves, creations meant to serve higher goals—and this is a cosmic role given exclusively to humankind. This important point will be discussed again later.

An original model of this process, paralleling that described in Anthroposophy yet presented from a different perspective, comes from Gurdjieff's Fourth Way. According to this approach, creation takes place between two poles. One is the supreme Absolute, which is spiritual, whole, and fully conscious. The other is at the end of the ray of creation, far from the Absolute's will, a world devoid of consciousness. The two-way flow between these cosmic poles follows a precise regularity, of which the musical octave, running from low to high C , is a perfect example.

The cosmic flow, which contains the worlds in a hierarchical array, follows a universal law that is also demonstrated in the structure of the octave. The passage between different planes of cosmic reality is not consecutive, and includes two problem zones through which the inter-planar flow has trouble crossing without external assistance. The help needed to ensure the continuity of this fertilizing passage between the worlds comes from a complex auxiliary process, a sort of additional octave created out of the main process. In these processes there is an active role for organic life on the planet, and especially for humankind.

Like other animals, human beings process the food we ingest and refine it through inner processes of digestion and breathing. This transformation, combined with other transformative processes shared by all organic life, provides the cosmic process with the assistance it requires to cross the problematic passage. Humankind is unique in this structure in that we have been charged with more subtle, alchemical processes. The functioning process of the cosmic octave requires the contribution of subtler materials than those created through breathing and digesting. By taking in impressions and transforming them through conscious effort, by developing our consciousness and willingly going through experiences of suffering, human beings create new essences, new materials of the finest quality that support the proper fulfillment of cosmic flow. Without this, the flow would come to a halt, and with it the branch stretched forth from the cosmic beam of creation. Here, too, we see that human creation has a universal significance, which provides artists with a more profound and compelling sense of their personal creativity.

Rudolf Steiner describes the process of the worlds' creation and the gradual revelation of the human being using fascinating cosmic pictures. In this process the divine beings work on the human body, giving birth to the forces of life and the world of the soul. Yet our creative process is not unidirectional, but is rather an interactive process in which the creating beings make use of the expressions of the fruit of their creation. Their progress in overall evolution depends on the interaction between them and the created human being. We live in an earthly world and express ourselves in it, yet divine beings dwell in the subtle material of our thinking and emotions, in our visible and hidden intentions, and in our daily activities as well as the activity of our consciousness. This substance of human life provides divine beings with the nourishment they need to progress in the cosmic hierarchy.

Those with the capacity to sense vividly the grandeur of this situation, who can deeply internalize the meaning of this hidden fact of our own soul, cannot help but feel shocked. They will be forced to ask themselves: What kind of nourishment am I presenting to the divine beings that provide me with life? What is the quality of my thoughts? What is the direction of my emotional world, considering this fact?

The superior knowledge that directs our attention to this hidden reality leads us to an inescapable conclusion: the emptying of the human vessel that is full of the "will to receive for itself" enables it to become a vessel that refills itself with an aspiration to serve and bestow pleasure upon the creating Being. This attitude cannot grow when we forget these beings. Inward awareness of this reality, which is embedded in our soul-life, requires us to thoroughly change our inner approach—to decide to refine the quality of expressions that we integrate into the living aura of our planet. It is therefore obvious that human creation will not be able to fulfill its divine calling without a transformation of the human being.

In previous chapters we have discussed human creation from a number of perspectives. We discussed not only artistic creation, but also the whole array of human creativity with its myriad expressions. The exercises for artistic cultivation can be understood, in a narrow sense, to be focused on inventive thinking or art; yet this narrow focus would not attain the broader purpose of those words and lines.

To find the broader, deeper meaning of human creation—our own and everyone else's—we could move toward a gradual change in three related and mutually supporting areas:

1. Expanding our field of awareness
2. Changing our moral attitude
3. Cultivating our skills

The idea of expanding our field of awareness was discussed at some length in previous chapters, so in this chapter we will discuss other, complementary aspects of the subject. The expansion of the field of awareness directs students toward a new inner attitude, one of awe toward the higher world that speaks to us from the depths of the soul. When inner reality becomes an accessible field of research for observing consciousness, a new moral initiative is required. Human creators begin to know two different inner atmospheres that exist within the soul simultaneously. They are different, yet are interlaced in a way that makes them hard to tell apart. We learn to know the different flavor of these inner worlds of feeling that both enhance and fight one another. A new moral attitude gradually crystallizes within the soul; we learn to give in to the creative impulse flowing from the unknown depths of our soul. We develop a willingness to serve this impulse, to provide it with our body, our soul, and our skills, expressing its message through language, music, or matter.

How surprising is it that the human creator develops a new ability to express the creative act in a different way out of this new attitude of self-negation, of giving up our personal abilities? Freeing ourselves of all the illusions we had about our unique talents, throwing away our blind admiration of personal action, our soul is refined, and becomes a worthier instrument for the spirit's actions. The creator gains new powers that stabilize thinking and emotions, providing a better position from which to advance one's creative activities.

Our new abilities are initially revealed as an improved ability to focus, clearer thinking, and refined sensitivity. Yet this is only the humble beginning of a more powerful ability that esoteric knowledge may give the human creator. In his conversation with disciples, Gurdjieff revealed a hidden side of esoteric knowledge that has to do with the vibrating nature of reality. According to him, art could be mathematically exact. One who knows the secret rules of the vibrating world can act in a way calculated to achieve precise results. We know that mathematicians and physicists communicate information to one another in a way that is precise and cannot be modified through personal interpretation. According to Gurdjieff's testimony, the conscious artist can communicate messages of feeling with the same measure of precision, acting to create a defined result.

In view of these brief presentations of various esoteric details we may come back to the initial question: what is the mission of human creation? It seems now that such a question cannot be answered with narrow definitions or clear-cut statements, because it spreads over more than a single dimension.

This creative mission is not limited to art or technology, but encompasses all human activity, including our small, everyday tasks such as rearing children, serving parents, or cultivating a garden. What counts in such activities is not only the content of what we create but also *how* we do it—our inner attitude, our level of awareness, and the orientation of our inner sentiment.

We can feel that the quality of our creative activity is changed when we do not act entirely egoistically, but take our initiatives in service to larger causes, whether for our parents or our country—or for those sensitive enough, service to a higher spiritual cause.

The Earth is evolving; creation of superior forms and beings is endlessly enhanced. Existences, as creations of higher, divine impulses, advance according to presently unknown needs, though we feel an inner urge to cherish and respect them. Nor do we know the nature of tomorrow's evolved, "superior" humanity; nevertheless, we have faith in the divine providence that knows better.

We are called to learn and understand the manifold role of humankind in the entire process of creation and serve it the best we can. This cannot be achieved through abstract, theoretical knowledge; it should touch our innermost feeling. The mission of human creative activities is revealed to us as a great mystery, requiring our best efforts to hear a call that we do not yet hear fully or understand, though we humbly wish to shoulder that creative universal impulse through our limited abilities.

PART THREE

PRACTICAL ASPECTS OF INVENTIONS

Chapter 24

Several Practical Examples

"The intuitive mind is a sacred gift and the rational mind is a faithful servant. We have created a society that honors the servant and has forgotten the gift." —Albert Einstein

How do science and technology advance? On what do they depend? Independent observers ask themselves such questions when they look into the fascinating history of discoveries and inventions. Great geniuses such as Leonardo da Vinci, Nikola Tesla, and Thomas Edison in technology, and Galileo Galilee, Nicolaus Copernicus, Isaac Newton, and Albert Einstein in the sciences, are regarded as revolutionaries whose appearance in society brought about civilization's important breakthroughs. The next question to ask is, if Copernicus hadn't been born, would humanity have continued believing in the old geocentric theory? Had Newton not been born, would differential mathematics and the laws of gravity have remained hidden?

There is something missing from the picture when we regard the breakthroughs of these geniuses simply as personal achievements that would not have materialized without them. I do not wish to take anything away from these amazing people, or from the admiration they inspire, yet can't we regard their personal achievements within a broader perspective?

In considering this, we can look at two interesting and intriguing phenomena within the context of scientific and technological progress. The first is the sudden appearance of a given discovery or invention in several places at the same time by individuals who have not had any previous connection. The second is the failure of inventions or discoveries that appeared on the stage of history before the time was ripe.

For example, geocentric theory— for example, the assertion that our Earth is the center of the universe—did not fall immediately out of favor because of the work of Copernicus as a single person working alone. The determination of Giordano Bruno, Galileo Galilei, and others working along the same lines is testimony that human thinking was already maturing toward a new theory at that time. Had these individuals appeared

1

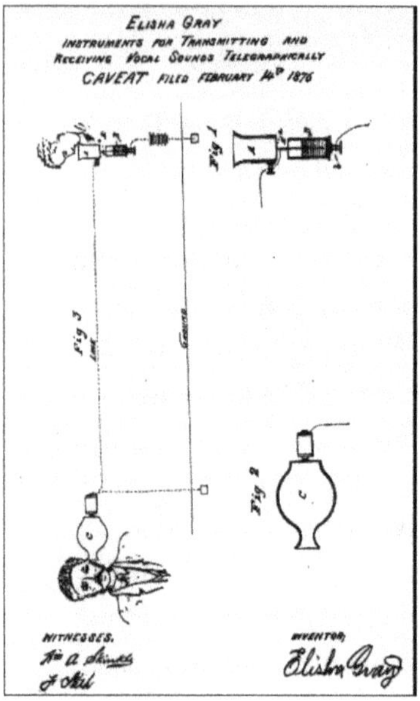

2

3

several centuries earlier, their fight would probably have ended in complete defeat.

Several hours after Alexander Graham Bell filed a patent application for the invention of the telephone (fig. 1), Elisha Grey arrived at the patent registry and filed an almost identical request (fig. 2). The invention of the light bulb is often attributed to Thomas Edison, yet an English inventor named Joseph Swan built a bulb based on the same principle in 1878 and patented it about one year before Edison.

At the time that Johannes Guttenberg printed the Bible with his new press in 1455 (fig. 3), hundreds of manual presses were already being used regularly throughout the huge Chinese empire. In 1476 in England, William Caxton operated a press (fig. 4) similar to Gutenberg's without any knowledge of his German colleague's work.

Other examples are scientific discoveries and mathematical developments like those of Leibniz and Newton, whose work with differential and integral calculations appeared separately at the same time, and Goethe's original botanical ideas (see appendix 2), which inspired a few scientists like Mitchell Feigenboim, Nicholas Metropolis, and Phil Stein in the beginning of the nineteenth century. Their revolutionary theory matured and later gained fame as chaos theory. Is humanity ready to understand Goethe's scientific ideas even now? His unique approach to the color theory and the metamorphosis principle in the plant kingdom do not seem to have many advocates today. Time will tell.

In England in the early nineteenth century, Charles Babbage built what he called a "difference engine" (fig. 5). Using generous governmental support he built the first calculating machine, which was meant to make complex calculations, store data, and perform other actions that

4 

5 

today's computers do easily. Yet nineteenth-century technology was not ready for the new machine, and lacking the necessary apparatus to construct the machine's parts, even Babbage's flawless calculations could not help to realize the construction of the new machine. Government support money ran out, and the project was archived until its reappearance in more modern forms decades later.

There are similar examples in all areas of civilization—not just in science and technology but in law, ethics, religious life, and art as well. Though modern culture cannot perceive it properly, the structure of human consciousness has gradually been changing, and the nature of scientific thinking has followed suit. Expressions from earlier times clearly point to this. For example, in describing thinking activity, biblical language contains such odd expressions as "heart's reflections," "heart's reasoning," or "heart's wisdom." There are those who disregard the relevance of such phrases, seeing them as expressions of the scientific ignorance of the biblical authors, but perhaps this is not so. Mental thinking in our time does, indeed, have to do with the brain's activity, but this appears not to have been the case in ancient times, and people then actually made judgments and intelligent decisions through activity that they felt to be located in their heart area rather than their head. Humankind's soul and mental structure seem to have undergone many changes before assuming their present shape.

Who is responsible for these essential changes in the structure of consciousness? What force works behind the scenes, causing the appearance of the great inventions and revolutionary discoveries that have so changed the face of humanity? We see that changes reach human civilization in waves; the great revolutions come to humanity only when people are ready to receive them. The great geniuses' initiative would have been in vain had humanity not been ready to receive the new ideas. The novelties that appeared through the great revolutionaries in science, technology, and other areas should therefore not be seen as random highlights in the development of humanity, but as expressions of a universal intelligence that chose those talented individuals to fulfill the needs of the time.

What I have said here is commensurate with the nature of creative thinking as described in previous chapters. This thinking is neither deductive nor analytic in nature. It does not reach original insights out of the known data pool, but rather surges powerfully out of the depths of universal thinking, far from the planes of mental thinking, and bursts to the surface as flashes of intuition. Many thinkers and innovators made no attempt to hide their feeling that their sudden insights were a gift from divine grace, and appeared completely by surprise.

Asserting the supremacy of universal intelligence over rational human thinking may offend some of us. We are used to blowing our own horns, believing that we deserve society's admiration. Nobel prizes and honorary degrees granted to scientists and thinkers are only the outer expression of an illusory self-perception. The illusion occurs because the general public sees innovating scientists as the sole creators of their ideas. One of this book's goals is to shed a different light on this matter. The geocentric approach that claimed our planet as the center of the universe has subsided, but the egocentric approach, which sees the individual as the sole source of its own creative works, maintains a persistent grip. Greater changes in science and technology will come when scientists and inventors learn to let go of "creased-brow thinking" in favor of an open awareness, sensitive to the intuitive flows of intelligence that are seeking their way into our inner world. This is not a cliché, but a more balanced presentation of the relations between the inventor or creator and the surrounding reality—an understanding that can be acquired practically.

In this chapter I will illustrate the process that preceded some of my inventions. These are mentioned not only to give readers a glance into the life of someone who makes his living developing new ideas, but also (and especially) to describe some fascinating motifs that are developing behind the scenes—some of them quite mysteriously.

The story of how inventions are born can be divided into three categories:

1. Inventions that are the outcome of a specific mission entrusted to the inventor.
2. Cases where the inventor personally spotted a problem or need and sought the solution.
3. Cases where new means or possibilities were created first, and as a result the question of their possible use arose.

I will mention a representative example from the first category and the story behind it. As we will see, sometimes the process is short and simple, and sometimes it has to do with quite unusual happenings that transpire behind the scenes.

In 1996, a man who had created a new concept in home gardening visited my office. The concept, which he named the PlanTower, was based on five pots, set one above the other around a central pole. At the base of the pole was a large water container from which the water, propelled by a small pump, was supposed to flow to the top pot, and from there drip from one pot to the next below it and return to the container below. In addition to the product's impressive aesthetic aspect, it would cause the plants to grow much more quickly than would systems that use a conventional, passive-watering method, since the water would also contain special fertilizers that continuously enrich the earth in the pots. Moreover, anyone who used these pots for plants could leave them unattended without worrying about watering and feeding, since the pump would work continuously and flawlessly while one is away.

7

When the entrepreneur began preparing the injection molds for the product's plastic parts he was sure that finding the right pump would cause no significant problem. However, his special demands for the pump turned out to be quite complex. It had to conform to four basic standards:

1. Pump water up a 1.2 m (nearly 4 ft.) pole with hardly any effort.
2. Work constantly for two years.
3. Work without clogging, since the water was impregnated with minerals and plant nutrients.
4. Cost less than $2.00 per unit.

It turned out that cheap centrifugal pumps could not push the water up to the height needed. In addition, membrane pumps work only for clean water; anything added to the water would immediately clog the pump. Finally, even if you could find a method of pumping and swirling the water, you would still need a DC motor that could work continuously for two years, and no manufacturer would guarantee a motor for even one year.

The entrepreneur entered my office somewhat despairingly, looking for a creative solution to what at the time seemed to be an impossible mission. After agreeing to do my best, I started looking for an off-the-shelf solution on the market. I soon realized that there was no way to solve the difficult equation posed by the project's demands with existing means.

Rapid thinking in unusual directions disturbed my sleep. I tried to stop searching, yet the thoughts, propelled by their own force, kept swirling in my head like mad hornets. Just before I fell asleep, an image of the human body and its circulatory system flashed through my mind. How, I wondered, can this system pump the blood up to a height of about six feet, making it flow through nearly twenty miles of thin capillaries, and yet function for eighty years or more without being replaced? The wonder of this system seemed inexplicable, considering the limitations of mechanical pumping and condensing. In the morning I started looking for solutions in scientific medical literature.

Among the articles written by medical experts, one by Alexander Mikulin, a Russian engineer, caught my attention. Mikulin changed his vocation to medicine following his own heart problems. He claimed that the heart's pumping power could not possibly satisfy the demands of the blood circulation, which means that the system must have outside help. Whenever a vein sharply changes its shape or direction, a sort of local pump is created, and this helps the blood flow to that place. He believed that it is the vibrations that shake the human body during physical work, walking, and running that provide the needed propulsion. Mikulin developed a therapeutic method based on shaking the body using various means that, according to his testimony, improved his life and the lives of hundreds of patients.

Though I doubted the wisdom of his hypothesis, I took a thin plastic tube and tried to intentionally cause it to deform while shaking it inside a bucket of water. The desired results did not materialize, and I was about to drop the idea when I remembered how I had seen a friend pump gasoline out of his car using only a thin plastic pipe. He held the pipe's top end with one hand and slid it into the fuel tank with the other, shaking it all the while, until fuel started climbing up the pipe. When it had reached the right height, he could turn the top end toward a container and the fuel continued flowing according to the rule of buoyancy of fluids.

"Why not replace the manual closing and opening action with a one-way valve?" I thought. I had a gas mask with such a valve, and I pulled it out and connected it to the immersed end of the pipe. When I vigorously shook it, water easily climbed within the pipe. I kept lifting my hand, holding the top of the pipe as high as I could, and the water kept flowing. "Eureka!" I cried happily, spraying water all over the place like a child experiencing his first water sprinkler.

I now had to find an electromechanical means to shake the immersed end of the pipe in a controlled way, causing water to flow up the pipe. This was accomplished by means of a small electromagnet (fig. 6:*a*) that, powered by the house's alternating current, moved a small magnet (fig. 6:*b*) hanging on the arms of a "spring leaf" (fig. 6:*c*), as seen in the drawing. The hard pipe (fig. 6:*d*) and the tiny valve inserted in the pipe's lower end (fig. 6:*e*) were inside the water, causing the water to rise through another, flexible pipe (fig. 6:*f*) and to the top pot.

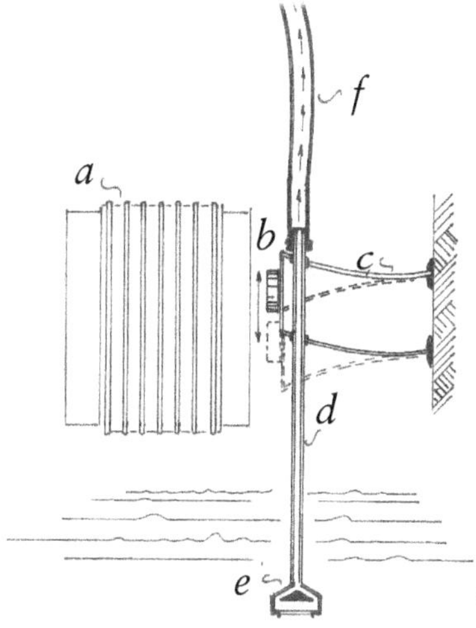

6

The new pump easily made the water rise to 2½ meters (8.2 feet), contained no friction-creating elements, and could be made for $1.20 per unit. The manifestation of this invention in the marketplace was not a simple walk in the park, but I won't go into all the details. What we are concerned with here is the thinking activity that occurred behind the scenes.

Where did the image of the human circulatory system that appeared in my consciousness come from, just as I was about to give up on finding the answer in the realm of mechanical solutions? I was directly aware that once conventional thinking had started to spin around in useless circles, a flash from a completely different plane of existence suddenly appeared; how did this process happen? What relationship should there have been between the two planes for the solution to make its way to the final form? I cannot provide complete answers to these questions; the mystery behind the phenomena only grew with the years. Still, I have learned to note several unusual characteristics behind these occurrences.

When a designer receives a well-defined task, the first step is to review possible solutions. When the possibilities and combinations have reached a high enough number, the designer will be unable to assess all the options mechanically, since it would probably take far too long. Here one needs to transform the problem's data to occupy a "higher thinking plane."[1] Having made this effort in thought, the inventor no longer has to pay attention to each possible solution. Rather, one collectively notes separate categories, rejecting or embracing them as a group. This is a fast and effective process that many go through, though they may not be aware of it. A more thorough investigation will convince us that thinking is intrinsically multilayered. In other words, it is capable of acting on different hierarchic levels.

As children we learn to join one letter to another to form a word. Later we learn to "photograph" the image of the written word and no longer need to join individual letters. As adults, we are capable of reading several words, or even sentences, as a complete photographic pattern. We rise in the hierarchy again when we connect to the writer's chain of thoughts; in such moments, we actually hover over the text with our attention given inwardly to the writer's thought rather than to the form of the words. This is the moment when we guess the writer's idea and are capable of completing it without stopping, even if there's an error in the text. We act in much the same way in other continuous activities without paying much attention. For example, when we drive at night we don't directly look at the marks on the road or the flash of light reflectors; our gaze occasionally floats toward them, and we actually guess the direction of the road ahead. This partially frees our attention to avoid hitting an unexpected object and to talk with our passengers if we want to.

1 A *higher thinking plane:* the process of transformation relates to what I describe as "hierarchical thinking planes." A designer identifies the data as archetypal principles and does not see the sought-for tool as a mechanical system, but as a *virtual* tool capable of providing a certain function. At this stage, it makes no difference to the designer whether the system is constructed of metal or plastic or is built according to a circular or linear principle and so on. Once one is free of the "corporeal attire" of the data, thousands of bothersome details are eliminated that would otherwise have made the search much more difficult. One can look for a solution at the archetypal level. Only at the end of the process will the solution be translated into concrete shapes and be built of materials available to the designer.

Just as we learn to "read" writers' thoughts through their words, similarly the creative designer must work with archetypal principles more than with personal solutions. Working with these archetypal principles, an inventor can move them with lightning speed, causing them to engage with each other; see the results of their interaction; borrow ideas from one field of action and implement them in another; make the principles encounter the problem's data; note the reaction; and so on. This thinking activity does not recognize Einstein's limitation of the speed of light, nor does it even recognize the limits of time and space; such thinking takes place on a completely different plane! This explains why human thinking is able to address so many different possibilities without having to inspect them one by one. Some call this intelligent activity "intuition," since they sense that it does not happen in the normal vessel of our brain. "I'm speaking from my gut!" is a sentence typical of one who feels that the activity of transforming thinking to a higher thinking plane does not occur in the brain.

Anyone who observes this suprasensory process with sufficient sensitivity will find proof of what I said earlier: archetypal principles are not unreal abstractions, but actual entities that cannot be "seen" with our senses, yet that we can grasp with our thinking awareness. Here, thinking realizes its supreme ability to be a tool for perception of ideal essences.

As mentioned, the sought-for idea sometimes arises by surprise; it usually appears only when normal thinking is exhausted and comes to rest. This serves as additional confirmation that the truly surprising solution is not a product of mental ability, but of something else. Furthermore, the mind tends to get in the way, and its activity must therefore retreat for a moment, allowing divine thinking to work without interruption.

Once the idea has sparked, the inventor faces a new difficulty. At times he feels that he already has the answer, but can't quite get it straight; that is, he can't write it down or define it precisely. What is it, then, that hides behind this particular problem? I've already hinted that archetypal intelligence lives on a higher plane of thinking than that of mental activity, where it exists formless, free to assume any shape it desires. As mentioned, it can be expressed in concrete shapes only when it descends to the level of material objects. Passage between the two planes is not always easy, and the archetypal insight sometimes slips away before donning any earthly garment.

This aspect of the inventive process allows an inventor to express professional skill. At times one is required to respond quickly, before the fragile insight dissolves, sometimes leaving no trace; at other times one has to patiently wait for something to "mature," before it can assume a form. It is characteristic of suprasensory inspiration that it cannot be retraced; it is so dynamic that any attempt to fix it is doomed to fail. The inventor, indeed, cannot remember the insight, at least not by the normal standards of memory; yet this does not mean that the insight is not real. Under conditions similar to those in which the first insight arose, an identical insight may rise vividly.

My development of the vibrating pump was accompanied by another experience, relevant to what I have just discussed above. Once the pump's basic principle had been successfully applied, we needed to find the optimal conditions for the moving parts to work smoothly in the finished product. For long hours I tried to balance the factors determining the pump's self-resonance in a way that would maximize its efficiency. When I left the workshop, the impression of the pump's vibration remained in my awareness and I could not rid myself of it the whole evening. I later retired to my evening meditation, with the vibrations still resonating in the background. After about fifteen minutes, when my inner field of consciousness had gotten relatively calm, I experienced something unique. Suddenly, with no prior warning, a vibrating, intensive force burst into my inner field of consciousness; it was lit by a blinding inner light and began to rock my soul, which had been a little sleepy though alert. I experienced vividly how the new, intensive force transferred its vibrating power to my relatively sleepy psychic field, forcing it to resonate with equal frequency. A second or two later, the mysterious force retreated, leaving my soul still resonating for several minutes with the power injected into it.

The experience was not merely surprising; the insights that came with it are still with me to this day. I understood how the forces of the higher worlds imbue more corporeal reality with their intensive vitality using the principle of resonance. The movement between different levels of consciousness, between beings vibrating at different levels of intensity, took place before my inner eyes in a way that made me understand a universal process that seems to dominate all reality, not just my own soul.

When I later tried to describe to my wife the insights I had gained from this experience, I found that, although I tried approaching the matter patiently and from many different angles, I could not effectively communicate the far-reaching knowledge injected into my intelligence in the course of an experience that lasted no more than a second or two. This surely confirms what I have previously said about the uniqueness of spiritual-scientific research; researchers cannot prove their findings to others who have not had the experience themselves. It would not be an exaggeration to say that, once students of spiritual science return to live within the limits of subjective consciousness, they retain some impression of the living insight, yet cannot understand it again in all its grandness, unless they return to those original inner conditions. This principle points to a deep mystery of esoteric initiation, little understood by Western thinking. What one can understand depends on more than just clarity of thinking and accumulation of knowledge; it depends on the inner conditions in the soul, as well—that is, on one's maturity, readiness, and inner attitude.

The next example is from the second category mentioned, and describes an inventive process in which the initiative, from the project's beginning to its end, was in the inventor's hands. Having pursued my studies in the architecture department at the Technion, Israel's institute of technology, I was familiar with the problems related to inventions using natural light. Since the power and angle of the sun's light changes throughout the day and the seasons of the year, it is very difficult to put them to effective use. In summer the radiation provides too much heat, and in winter not enough; in the morning it enters the building directly, and at noon it doesn't enter it at all. Architects often use shading elements to diminish the difficulty, but these solutions are too expensive and do not satisfactorily solve the problem. Coatings of various darkness do filter excess radiation but are themselves heated in the process, thus emitting the radiation into the house in longer, invisible wavelengths; yet they contain plenty of thermal energy. The darkness of the coating also becomes a problem in winter, since the heat and light provided by the Sun's rays are desirable in that season.

This problem attracted my attention from the beginning of my studies at the Technion, but I did not attend to it until later, when I became the owner of a factory that made sheets of transparent fiberglass. If the problem has to do with the Sun's location in the sky, I thought, why not look for an optical configuration that considers these changes in a more complex way than a simple transparent sheet would?[2]

The laws of optics have always fascinated me. When I was a child I used to build telescopes and microscopes, and learned to cut mirrors and focus-

---

2 Utilization of the Sun's rays is a top priority today, as our society searches for new sources of energy. The Israeli companies Luz (now Sollel) and Ormat, which sell and apply solar energy technologies worldwide, have made cutting-edge developments in this field. The Weitzman Institute has also developed, for research purposes, a system made up of thousands of mirrors focused on a single point, where they create a temperature of thousands of degrees Celsius.

7

ing lenses.[3] I remember being very impressed with the story of Archimedes and the use of reflected shields employed in the siege of Syracuse (fig. 7), and it inspired me to build an array of mirrors, each swinging on a separate axis and all connected, so that they could be aimed at a changing focal center using a single lever. I cannot remember now why the project did not work, but the pretty neighbor in the house opposite my parents' home should be grateful for my misfortune, since it was the old wooden closet on her porch that was to be my first target.

I was especially taken by the mysterious principle called "total internal reflection." I therefore started out by defining the need before looking for a practical solution. Since the imaginary plane that includes the trajectory of the sun in the skies changes its inclination throughout the year, the solution needed to include an optical element that receives the sun's rays on one plane and returns them on another. The principle of total internal reflection seemed to maintain exactly this condition—receiving light beams in a given range of angles, and returning them in the complementary range. Yet how could I apply this principle to a fixed, predefined range of angles? I could find no answers in professional literature, and had to look for a solution myself. I started this research by drawing sketches and calculat-

3 In 214 B.C., during the Second Punic War, the famous general Marcellus started a naval siege of Syracuse, Sicily. This city was home to one of the greatest inventors ever, Archimedes. The story is that this unusual genius had hundreds of warriors stand on the beach with their polished shields or other reflective surfaces while aiming the reflected sunlight at a group of battleships besieging the city. Aimed from about a hundred meters, the rays set fire to the wooden ships anchored near the Syracuse walls and led to the end of the siege.

ing the movement of the beams, and later by making transparent prisms out of acrylics.

Long hours of hard work were rewarded with a discovery that enabled me to create a prism that returned the light beams at a predefined angle (unlike a mirror, where the return angle is equal to the incoming angle). I was able to create an optical solution in the shape of a linear prism (fig. 8) for beams hitting a surface at an angle X, so that they would be returned to the same direction—at the same angle X. Since the transparent sheets used for roofing have a wavy curve, I designed an array of delicate linear prisms whose angles change as a function of their geometric location on the wave's curved plane. As seen in the illustrations, the sun's rays hitting the wave at an eighty-degree angle during summer are returned at the same angle, while in winter, when the sun's trajectory is inclined by forty-five degrees,[4] the rays can enter the building.

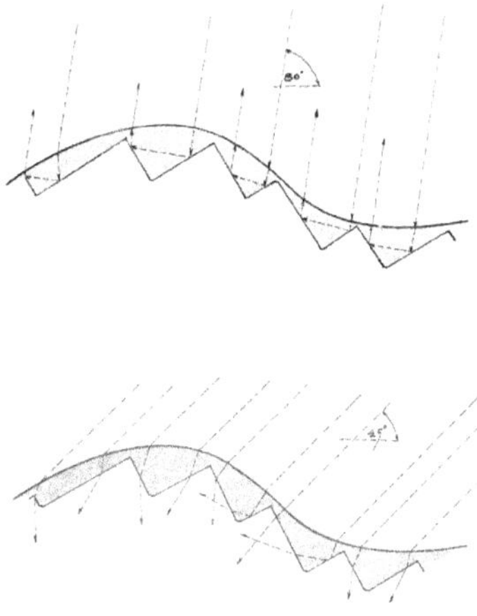

8

The illustration (fig. 9, next page) is taken from the product's publicity brochure. It includes a diagram that shows the amount of radiation entering the building as a function of the different months. Radiation passing through a normal glass sheet reaches its peak in June and July, while the graph representing the Selectogal shows that the level of radiation remains steady throughout the year, despite the great difference in external radiation during summer and winter.

In an age like ours, when technology changes so rapidly, things sometimes happen in an even more surprising way, according to the third category I have previously mentioned: the inventor discovers a new principle or possibility whose

4 The angles are, of course, fixed according to the location where the sheets are installed. At the equator a certain type of sheet using a particular angle will be installed, in subtropical zones another, and so on. Of course, the sheet, commercially named "Selectogal," works only for houses whose roofs lie in an east–west direction.

RFX NGL (NON-GLARE)

RFX NGL EXHIBITS ITS UNIQUE LIGHT DIFFUSING PERFORMANCE.

SUMMER

Reflective performance, which prevents the sun's heat from penetrating while transmitting indirect light into the building.

Summer: direct sunlight is reflected

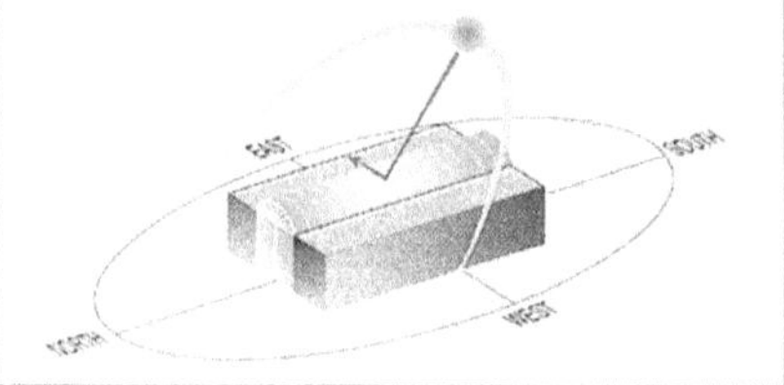

WINTER

Transmissive performance which allows the sun's heat and light to penetrate into the building.

Winter: direct sunlight is transmitted

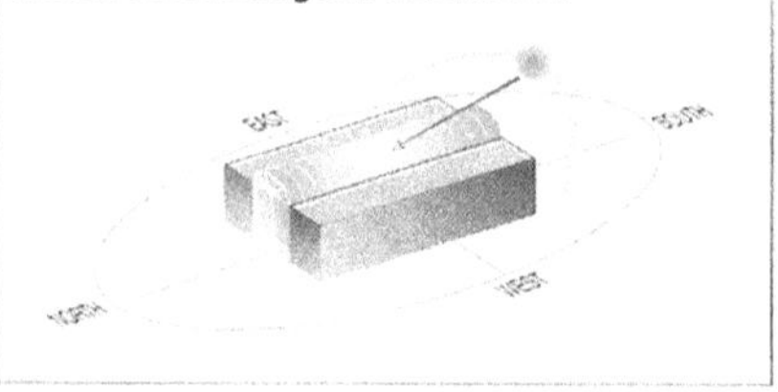

Light transmission: 32%

Reflectivity: above 40%

All year round —

Winter: transmits almost much energy as glass

Summer: transmits far less energy than glass

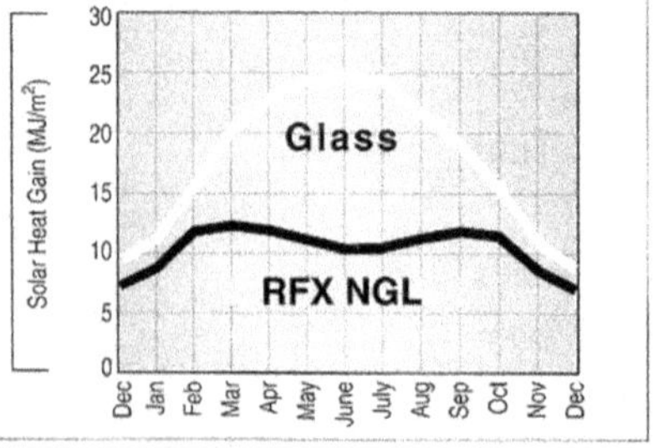

5/8" (16 mm) and 3/8" (10 mm)

USE DIFFUSED SOLAR ENERGY ALL YEAR ROUND

The new and revolutionary conception for diffused light transmission developed by POLYGAL's R&D dept., uses its unique prismatic design together with a coextruded coating, to create the ultimate solar energy selecting, light diffusing PCSS, thus avoiding the characteristic glare of regular Polycarbonate sheets.

ADVANTAGES:

- Energy saving all year round. In summer RFX NGL reflects most of the sun's heat and diffuses the entering light. In winter, the needed sun's energy is transmitted and diffused.
- Virtually unbreakable. No need for safety precautions when installed.
- RFX NGL has beautiful, shiny, high-tech appearance.
- UV protected by its Special Solar Grade weathering surface.
- Lightweight and easy to transport, shape and install.

SPECIFICATIONS:

SHEETS THICKNESS	3/8" (10 mm)	5/8" (16 mm)
Color	Clear outside, opal Non-Glare inside	
Weight	.532 ibs/ft²	.611 ibs/ft²
Rib Spacing	.433"	.787"
Standard Widths	41.45", 47.24"	
Standard Lengths	9'10", 13'1", 19'8"	
U-Factor ASTM C236	.57 Btu/hr×ft²×°F	.53 Btu/hr×ft²×°F
Minimum Radius for Cold Bending	5'9"	9'2"
Thermal Expansion	1/8" per 3'/100°F	
Light Transmission	90° to Surface (ASTM D1003): 32%	
Reflectivity	90° to Surface : more than 40%	

RFX NGL is most effective when installed as roof lights or for east, west and south facing walls.

- *RFX NGL has a limited 10 year warranty.*
- *Use the unique software package, to obtain complete energy information.*

For additional product information, consult the *POLYGAL Polycarbonate Structured Sheet Technical Specifications brochure.*

POLYGAL Inc.
2352 Highway 14 West,
Janesville, WI 53545

The information above relates specifically to PCSS made from a particular polycarbonate resin and is not relevant to any similar generic product. No liability is accepted for any loss or damage from the use of this data which is given in good faith, but without commitment, and no warranty is given or implied.
Polycarbonate is a combustible thermoplastic. Avoid exposure to excessive heat or aromatic solvents. Precautions used to protect other common combustibles should be followed.

01-02-00186 (12/95) CREAM — Advertising & Productions • Advanced Semantics Processing Ltd.

9

proper use is found only later. For example, when the first laser was invented, some mocked its inventors, claiming they had created something that had no use. With the many modern applications found for this technology, who could now ever consider it to be useless? There are, indeed, many new technologies that nowadays await investors who could put them to commercial use. The role of inventors in finding original applications is no less creative than that of those who develop the technology.

Multi Vision Technologies Ltd. was created following an invention whose use was realized only after its discovery, and belongs to the third category of inventions mentioned. In 1997, I was playing around with a ruler that could be tilted to display various changing images. This was a known effect that had begun to make its way into the market in the form of 3-D postcards and other entertaining effects (fig. 10). The illustration shows a scheme that describes how the multi-picture postcard is made. The postcard includes a set of parallel, tiny linear lenses, while below them, at the lenses' focal center; there is a lithographic print, computer-processed using the following method; the print is made by software that divides three or four basic pictures into condensed information slices. These information slices are arranged alternately, so that each segment includes one sample from each basic picture. When the print is located in the linear lenses' focal center, the basic pictures can be seen as whole, continuous pictures, with the particular picture seen depending on the angle of view.

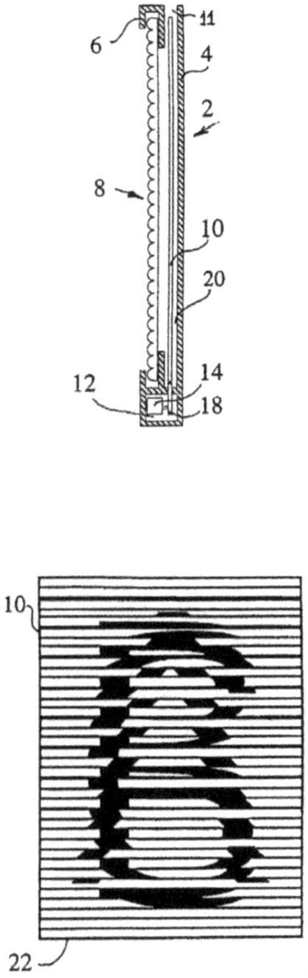

10

Edge view, top; front view, bottom (from the author's 2001 patent document)

Once I understood the principle that allows the multi-picture postcards to function, I had an idea that instead of printing the information on the flat backside of the lens set and tilting it to see the changing pictures, I could print the pictures on a separate film and move the film in relation to the lenses, so that the different pictures would be seen one by one, with no need to tilt the surface. Someone in my office volunteered to create the needed graphic nets using Photoshop software.

Using a chip-processed steel plate, we embedded the needed lenses on an acrylic plate. We gradually learned to create a set of lenses equipped with a transient lithographic film, which could present three different images, according to the different relations between the lenses and the film.

11
Shelf Talker

"Advertisements!" was the first idea voiced during our subsequent brainstorming; this was followed by "changing art images," "children's games," and so on. At a more advanced stage we tried to decide what the most effective application was, among all the different options. Advertising screens to be placed in grocery stores was the most interesting option. We learned that media companies sell advertisements at the point of sale, charging by the month, and changing the commercial messages with each new ad campaign. We obtained a "shelf display" from an American company called Act Media that included a red frame into which we could insert a standard printed ad, hooking it to the shelf wherever the company placed its products. We wanted to know whether the advertising message could be moved using our screens. What could make them move, given that the media company's maintenance crew came once a month, sometimes every other month?

The solution came in the form of an electromechanical system used in clocks that includes a tiny pulse engine that can operate for a year without interruption. Thus, we built the first prototype for a dynamic advertisement screen, the Shelf Talker (fig. 11). It was quite slow, a little clumsy, and had low resolution, yet it worked. Imagine two shy Israelis entering the offices of a giant company that controls 50,000 stores throughout the United States, offering to sell the same product this company sells, yet in a newer, more dynamic form. The company's research and development (R&D) people, who had been working for two years with huge budgets, trying to develop more attractive products, had a hard time swallowing the pill, and so they tried to discredit the product's reliability and sales efficiency (in professional jargon this resistance is called "NIH" (not invented here). The marketing managers, however, saw the product's advertising potential and insisted on giving it a test run in a number of Chicago outlets to examine its effect on sales.[5]

The test's success was followed by commercial-scale orders for thousands of products, which decorate store shelves to this day. The Multi Vision company gradually expanded, with products ranging from tiny shelf screens to huge screens for street advertising. Though the technology and the software developed to process the images were patented worldwide, eventually copies of the company's products made in the Far East began to appear. This is a painful problem, threatening investors' incentive to invest, and thus the general thrust of development in the global economic market. While most of the world has recognized the importance of patent protection as a way to motivate technological novelty, authorities in China, Korea, and Hong Kong (to take some of the most prominent examples) fail to enforce patent laws sufficiently in their countries. Multi Vision Technologies products have been shamelessly reproduced, one by one, with no attempt to change anything in the original design. Because such pirating companies do not invest in developing the product, they can sell such products at lower prices, hurting the company that invented the technology.

The product's success, however, was not a function of originality alone, but also of its placement in a particular advertising niche between the normal, passive screens and the very expensive electronic screens. For the price of one electronic screen you could buy dozens of screens with our technology and spread them all over the store. The advertising effect in this case would be much stronger than that gained from digital monitors, capable of showing entire films. This example shows that creative thinking does not limit itself to the world of material objects, but can spread to many other areas—in this case, marketing and sales.

It is said that necessity is the mother of invention, and the story of the folding shelter and the home filtering system exemplifies a vital, even critical

5 Sales rate: media companies precisely monitor the influence of advertising on sales for a test period of four weeks, and the resulting percentage determines the rate charged for the client interested in the advertising method. In this case they found seventy-one percent improvement in the sale of products from a shelf using the screen, compared to shelves not using any screen.

need that gave birth to two creative solutions. This happened at the time of the beginning of the Iraqi missiles attack during the first Gulf War, back in 1990. The missile threat caught Israelis unprepared. Neighborhood bomb shelters suited an old concept, which relied on reasonable warning time after learning of a bombing threat. The use of missiles, especially missiles with chemical warheads, created a situation in which people could not use the neighborhood shelter, or even the common shelter on the ground floor of apartment buildings. A period of only ninety seconds between spotting the missile and the strike, and the possibility that it might bear a chemical warhead, made the old shelters obsolete.

Not having many options, the authorities propagated the concept of the "safe room." Frightened citizens were asked to seal one room in their home with duct tape and polyethylene sheets. This meant giving up on protection from ballistics in favor of protection from chemicals—and the method was both incomplete and unreliable. Choosing between a shelter and a safe room became a matter of public discourse. The tenuous solutions that the authorities offered the frightened populace were quite ironic. People then took matters into their own hands, turning to professionals considered to be "in the know" to get a reliable indication about which solution to choose against the possibility of an attack.

I was all "sealed up" in a safe room with my family when the first Iraqi missile landed in our area. We sat there with gas masks on our faces and holding atropine syringes in our hands, waiting for radio instructions from the Israeli Defense Forces (IDF). Long minutes of frightened silence passed, until the "national speaker's" voice came over the radio waves. The message was stammered and unclear. Those long minutes we sat awaiting instructions and clarifications left the "man of action" in me stung to the core of my professional pride. I thought, "How can I, who have been involved in developing the active protective suit, bulletproof vests, and 'dry storage' solutions for IDF tanks, sit here completely passive with my family, depending on improvised solutions devised by apparently incompetent authorities? What am I doing here, grasping for amateur solutions like duct tape and nylon?"

Like an active beehive, thoughts swarmed and possible solutions began to arise, one by one. "The short warning time caused by the threat of ballistic missiles entails an in-home solution," I thought. From previous experience, I knew that house walls do not provide good protection, even beyond the lethal radius of a hundred meters, since pieces of bricks and mortar tend to become dislodged from the walls and possibly strike the inhabitants. I didn't even want to think about the polyethylene sheets, since I knew that the chemicals were dispersed using explosives, which would tear away the polyethylene long before the deadly arrival of the chemicals.

The principles behind a new product, which would later be called the "folding in-home shelter" (fig. 12), gradually collected in my thinking. This would be a cube-shaped, six-foot-plus square construction made of metal profiles, which could be installed in one of the rooms of a home. A covering of transparent, chemical-resistant sheets welded at high frequency hung on the inside of the construction (fig. 13), and a miniature pump moved filtered air into the inner space thus created. To protect the sheet and the inhabitants, the whole construction was covered with an external shield, with enormous resistant strength, made of Kevlar, a para-aramid synthetic fiber used to make bullet-resistant vests.

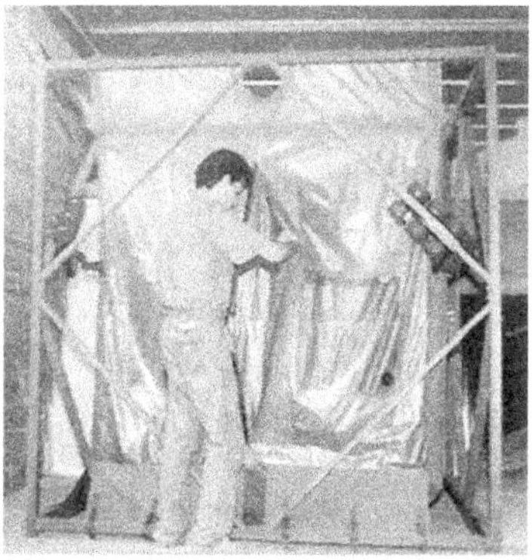

12

13

This solution allowed four to six inhabitants to enter a relatively protected cell in a matter of seconds after the sirens were sounded, and stay there without wearing gas masks. The product could be folded and stored in the basement or even under the bed in times of peace, and reassembled should any possible threat to the populace emerge.

In November 1992, the first prototype of the product was tested by the home-front command inside an improvised room built for an experiment to test the product's efficiency under realistic conditions. The testers created a pressure of about five atmospheres on the building's outer wall, using a 130-pound explosive charge. The following lines are quoted verbatim from the report by the head of the protection unit in the home-front command:

> 2.4 The tent provided the inner space
> with good overall protection,

absorbing a very powerful strike of impact and glass shards, reducing the impact on the inside to a minimal level.

3.1 Conclusions: ballistic cover provides a proper solution to protecting against serious blows of glass shards and the fall of light elements like mortar and roofing tiles.

14

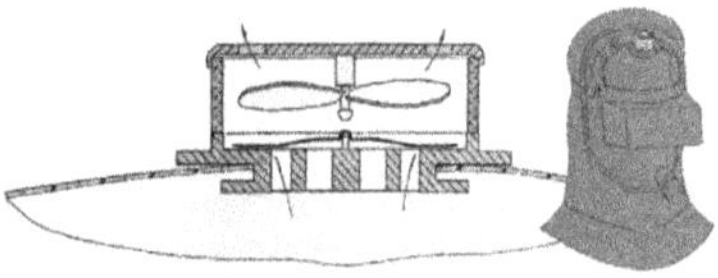
15

In addition to this product, meant to supply combined chemical and ballistic protection, I wanted to create a cheap solution, available to everyone, that would improve the safe room's resistance to penetration by chemical weapons. The safe room isn't really safe, I thought. There are cracks, electricity ducts, gaps under the window seals and the door. These factors do not allow full protection, and no one has the means to test the efficiency of the proofing in a safe room. Moreover, it is not possible to stay in a protected room for long without fresh air, since moisture and carbon dioxide accumulate. A rise in moisture to about ninety-five percent and an over-accumulation of carbon dioxide can be just as lethal as chemical weapons.

The solution I found in this context was a hyper-pressure system for the safe room, intended to pump filtered air into the inner space and maintain an air pressure somewhat higher than on the outside. This creates a constant leak of filtered air to the outside through the small gaps and cracks that have not been properly sealed, making it the perfect sealing solution. The system, composed of a pump (fig. 14) and an active carbon filter, is inserted into a previously prepared opening in a wall or door and using a chargeable battery capable of supplying current for up to twelve hours on a single charge. Another unidirectional valve, with a tiny colorful weather vane that rotates as the filtered air streams out (fig. 15), is set at the other end of the room. The vane's rotation shows that there is a difference in pressure between the inside and the outside of the room; when it does not spin, the protection needs to be examined and improved until a sufficient pressure difference is restored.

The folding shelter never went into commercial use, owing mostly to marketing logistics—the difficulty in funding and producing a sufficient stock in peace time and the problem of supplying it quickly and efficiently enough during times of a likely military threat. The compression system, however, was produced commercially in the Beit-El factory in Zichron-Ya'akov, which bought the patent use rights. Its series of products, known commercially as the "rainbow" series, had decent commercial success, which peaked with thousands of sales of home-protection units during the most recent US attack on Iraq. With these four different inventions—the PlanTower, the Selectogal, the Shelf Talker, and the in-home folding shelter, we can see the practical manifestations of an inventor's creativity and some aspects of his creative process.

Chapter 25

Spirituality and Practical Life

> *"We comprehend the wondrousness of being, but are abashed at the thought, affirming only at rare moments that real possibilities exist. We forget that man was made to be a meeting place of the phenomenal and noumenal worlds. Every man's true nature is one of tranquility, bliss, and happiness. The fact that we do not become what we are destined to be does not diminish this truth."*
>
> —William Charles Segal, *Opening*

These lines were written by a man who for me was a living example of someone whose feet were firmly planted in both a search for spiritual perfection and an active life. William Segal (1905–2000) was a journalist, publisher, and businessperson and, at the same time, a Zen student in Eastern monasteries and a disciple of the Western Fourth Way. When he walked into a group meeting, people felt as if an additional light had been turned on. When he talked, his whole body reverberated like a perfectly resonating instrument. Talking to him, one felt compassion, merged with a sense of endless sadness. Though he maintained contact with Israeli students over many years, he first visited Israel at the age of ninety, making an unforgettable impression on those fortunate enough to know him. This chapter is devoted to that man.

The worlds of technological creation and of spiritual searching are usually seen as two separate, even contradictory worlds. Modern technicians and engineers, considered to be practical, are usually passionate about work in the material world, disparaging those whom they believe float in the hazy planes of imagination. The opposite point of view can be found in a community of apparent "spiritual seekers," motivated by the longing to find something that's beyond the material world, but calls to their souls. For them, occupation with technological reality may seem like a self-centered race to better one's own condition, finding new selfish pleasures and satisfactions—all in the material world. Which of these positions is more appropriate for today's world? What is the most appropriate position for a person in our civilization, where sophisticated technologies dominate, yet where there is also a deep inner yearning of the heart for a meaningful life?

It can be seen immediately that this division results from a somewhat narrow-minded preference for one direction over the other. Although the new conditions created by modern technology allow humankind to re-form our environment with virtually no limitations, we are still in constant dialogue with our environment and cannot completely disconnect from it. In addition to normal food, people need another kind of nourishment—the impressions of the world around us. The external world speaks to us with color and sound and also provides the content for a healthy existence. Yet just as human beings need to take in the impressions of the world around us, we also need to bring our own unique manifestations into this world.

As early as in kindergarten we see in children the vivid need for personal expression through playing and creation. Human dialogue develops into verbal and artistic creation, and it seems that humanity, without even being fully aware of it, realizes an inner calling: once we have taken in the impressions of the outside world—color, sound, and ideal content—we discover an inner need to process what we received and express it, giving back something of our own. If our way of living has not drastically been altered, we will maintain a mutual process of nourishment with our surroundings during our maturity, and, if we should be so blessed, afterward as well.

If the mutual process of nourishment is truly important to the balanced existence of human beings, shouldn't this balance express itself, in its own particular way, in the two communities we have mentioned? Yet what we find in effect is not quite what we might desire. The scientific-technological, materialistic community does take care of the needs of the physical body, supposedly maintaining the biblical edict that humanity was born for toil; yet since physical labor is almost extinct in our Western world, it is replaced with another kind of toil—gyms and bodybuilding machines. This is probably not what was meant in the Bible; fruitless toil does not seem to be the ideal that divinity intended for humankind. Anyone who has ever worked a field, or even a small backyard, or who has practiced carpentry, pottery, or any other craft, knows the feeling of satisfaction that comes with the work process. It appears that the materialistic community, even when it tries to support physical activity, does not do so properly. For example, in the field of sports the cult of the body has become grotesque, with bodybuilding competitions for both sexes, and in science we find a desperate search to stop the human body from aging, a scientific yearning for physical immortality. Modern culture concentrates its creative forces on developing sophisticated new technologies, yet cannot find proper uses for them, since the needs that complement those of the body—spiritual needs—are being neglected; the term *spiritual world* has become a verbal cliché, a polite gesture toward an essence that existed sometime in the far past or in myth.

However, it is not only materialistic society that is unbalanced. Spiritual seekers in some communities disdain anything that has to do with an active life: some Hassidic pupils depend on society to provide for them, and spend all their waking hours studying Torah. Religious monks shut themselves inside their monasteries, protected from contact with the secular world, and true hermits take to the mountains, far from the burdens of human society.

We can see, then, how the proper balance is tilted, on one hand toward the material, on the other toward the spiritual; on either side there is no place for the complete human being. A life that is balanced between spirit and matter is more important for our developing civilization than ever before. Engineers, technicians, and scientists often have no idea what spiritual knowledge can give to their lives, and even to their professional activity. People who limit themselves to the plane of rational thinking find that they dry out; their life forces gradually abandon them.

Modern technology demands mostly mental attention from those who work with it. Analytical activity and logical thinking are at the forefront of technological development. Those in technological professions are often inattentive to the soul, which requires a different kind of nourishment. Their free time—and some today do not even know the meaning of those words—is spent watching sports and other entertainment substitutes. The voices that come from the bottom of the soul yearn for different food, but do not reach one's consciousness, which has learned to narrow its field of attention to life's external aspects. Rather than resting quietly and listening inwardly, people tend to choose an outer life, perhaps attending a flashy concert or premiere in minimal tribute to their bothersome needs before returning to what is generally considered most important today—career and promotion. I cannot say with certainty that this is true of all modern technological communities, but the tendency exists and, according to my impression, as more high-tech components become increasingly involved in human lives, the more such unbalanced modes of life take the lead.

The professional efficiency of the scientific-technological community would not suffer from allowing a deeper spiritual element to enter its life. On the other hand, the work of spiritual seekers would be no shallower if they were to forge their souls in the struggles they can expect in the practical areas of life. Throughout the whole previous chapter, I tried to show that creativity and originality could grow only out of a deep connection with the innermost layers of the soul. At the same time, I tried to emphasize the fact that the soul needs the struggles of an active life in order to bolster its creativity. A proper balance between human needs and our means of expression is a necessary condition for a living, fertile civilization. This civilization will best reach its goals by eliminating the aspect of one-dimensionality from the lives of its individuals.

The question of right balance in life is even wider, since individuals and societies do not live disconnected from the whole of universal existence. Universal evolution in all its grandeur and, especially, the living forces of nature need our human participation. Our creative initiatives are forever interlaced with the everlasting creative impulse of Great Nature. This is why the questions asked in the first chapter—"Who is the real inventor?" and "Is there something really new?"—cannot be answered concisely.

We live in a world that is actually a great riddle; nevertheless, we can sometimes feel that something active is expected from us. My own feeling is that this "something" is not limited to suprasensory worlds—it needs to be implemented here on the terrestrial, material Earth, amid the human condition of life's difficulties and negation. This ignorant, disconnected world needs gradually to be transformed, purified, and penetrated with a more refined, subtle influence.

Jiddu Krishnamurti said it best when he claimed that the many revolutions humankind has experienced changed nothing; the only revolution we are each obligated to carry out is in our own souls. This revolution does not yet seem to be just around the corner, but individuals can take the initiative, meet and support one another, and change something in their lives. Brooks join to form streams, and streams form rivers; we are all responsible.

Appendix 1: Spiritual Science

Rudolf Steiner coined the term *spiritual science*. He considered the body of knowledge he gave humanity to be based on scientific regularity and exactitude no less than that of the natural sciences. G. I. Gurdjieff also brought unique knowledge that was influenced significantly by modern scientific thinking, and this is partially true for other modern initiates of our time.

Humanity's modern teachers assert that, in modern times, divine knowledge is revealed not through mystical ecstasy or through a trance in which normal consciousness disappears. Rather, it is experienced clearly in a conscious, lucid field of observation. New divine consciousness does not aim to abandon thinking in favor of foggy mysticism but wishes to empower thinking so it can recognize facts not perceived through our regular senses. Spiritual science does not rule out the findings of modern materialistic science; it seeks to expand beyond natural science into areas at the foundation of reality, the universal existence of which humanity is a part.

Spiritual science maintains most of the standards to which the natural sciences adhere. However, there are several differences between conventional material science and spiritual science. When conventional scientific inquiry is directed toward an object, researchers are required to separate themselves from the object; the more they succeed in doing so, the more their work is considered objective and, therefore, reliable. This is not the case in spiritual science, in which the researcher, laboratory, and object of inquiry are all united in the researcher's soul. What the spiritual researcher finds in higher worlds is revealed using tools of perception connected directly with the soul, without the medium of the physical body. That such tools of perception exist may surprise some, but there is no doubt that, in order to investigate the planes of the spirit and the soul, physical eyes are useless; more subtle, sensitive tools are needed, tools known as our "soul's eyes," or chakras.

Materialistic science requires that experimental findings should be identical for every scientist conducting an experiment under identical conditions. Spiritual science does not avoid this rule, except that within this science, the conditions are identical only when the spiritual researchers possess the needed tools. What divine consciousness reveals cannot be scientifically verified unless the researcher has personally acquired the proper level of consciousness.

Appendix 2: Short Biographies

Giuseppe Archimbaldo (1527–1593)

This original painter lived in the sixteenth century and served the emperors Ferdinand I and Maximilian II. He became renowned first as the court decorator and costume designer, and then as a painter with a unique approach to human portraits.

He picked the elements of his portraits from the animal and plant kingdoms. For example, in the series called *The Seasons,* he created four figures representing the four seasons of the year—winter, spring, summer, and autumn, the images made up of the typical seasonal fruits (see next page). In the portrait of summer, the character's hair is created from the forms of raspberries, cherries, and plums; the elements that outline the are wild berries; the nose is a zucchini, the mouth a pod of beans; the pink cheek is composed of peaches, the chin is a pear, and the garment is sewn from stalks of grain.

His painting *The librarian* was similarly composed, using images of typical materials in a library. He applied the same technique for other characters, including a gardener, a vegetable vendor, and so on. Archimbaldo's unique art demonstrates what I have previously said about the role of thinking in organizing the impressions of the senses into meaningful images. What the observer sees depends mostly on one's point of view or particular character. Research into human perception has shown that people with an intuitive approach, or those with dominantly visual perception, first spot the human subject, and then the particular details. Those who excel in analytical thinking first recognize the details—fruits and vegetables in one case, books or animals in the other—and only later the whole character.

Archimbaldo's pictures serve as an interesting exercise of visual memory. Look at a picture for a short time, then close your eyes. The experiment can be done in two ways; the first way is to look at the secondary images in detail, trying to remember them one by one; the second is to look at the main character without going into the detail, allowing the whole picture to etch itself

Giuseppe Arcimboldo's portraits of winter, spring, summer and autumn

into your memory. Now, with eyes closed, look at the afterimage before your mind's eye and try to observe its components, one by one. I will not tell you what conclusions you should reach—that task is up to you. It is enough to say that you may find some food for thought about memory and imagination.

Sri Aurobindo (1872–1950) and The Mother—Mirra Alfassa (1878–1973)

Sri Aurobindo was born in India, but received a classical education in Cambridge, England. He later returned to India, and became involved in political activity centered on releasing the Hindu people from the yoke of British colonial rule. As a result of this activity the young Aurobindo was arrested in 1908 and could have been sentenced to death. Miraculously, the only witness the British had who could incriminate him died suddenly a short while before the trial's end, and the authorities had to let Aurobindo go. From then on, Aurobindo withdrew from underground activity and concentrated on activity in the ashram he founded in Pondicherry. This activity continued after his death, under the management of Mirra Alfassa, often called "The Mother."

Sri Aurobindo's mission is commonly considered to be that of an avatar—a divine messenger sent to earthly planes to give humanity a direction of spiritual development that is right for its time. During the course of his spiritual growth he developed a path of initiation known as Integral Yoga. Although this yoga stems from the roots of ancient Hindu culture and the teachings of ancient teachers—the Rishis who wrote the Vedas and Upanishads—Sri Aurobindo's yoga is different from anything that was known until his time.

Whereas ancient yoga systems strove to redeem humankind from suffering through ascension to higher planes of reality and distancing oneself from earthly reality, Sri Aurobindo strove to bring divine reality to earthly planes—to transform the human physical and etheric sheaths so humankind would become the flower of creation, as we were meant to be. Sri Aurobindo wrote philosophy and poetry, and left humanity a precious body of knowledge that provides his followers with divine life-powers. Some of his major works are *The Synthesis of Yoga; The Life Divine; The Supramental Manifestation;* and the immortal poem, *Savitri.*

ERNST CHLADNI (1756–1827)

Ernst Florens Friedrich Chladni was born in Wittenberg, Germany, to an educated family of academics and learned men. Chladni studied law and philosophy in Wittenberg and Leipzig and obtained a law degree in 1782 from the University of Leipzig. When his father died that same year, Chladni began his research in physics in earnest.

One of Chladni's best-known achievements was inventing a technique to show the various modes of vibration on a metallic surface. Chladni repeated the pioneering experiments of Robert Hooke of Oxford University who, on July 8, 1680, had observed the nodal patterns associated with the vibrations of glass plates. Hooke ran a bow along the edge of a plate covered with flour, and saw the nodal patterns emerge. Chladni's technique, first published in 1787, consisted of drawing a bow over a piece of metal whose surface was lightly covered with sand. The plate was bowed until it reached resonance and the sand formed a pattern showing the nodal regions. Since the twentieth century, it has become more common to place a loudspeaker driven by an electronic signal generator over or under the plate to achieve a more accurate adjustable frequency. Variations of this technique are commonly used in the design and construction of acoustic instruments such as violins, guitars, and cellos.

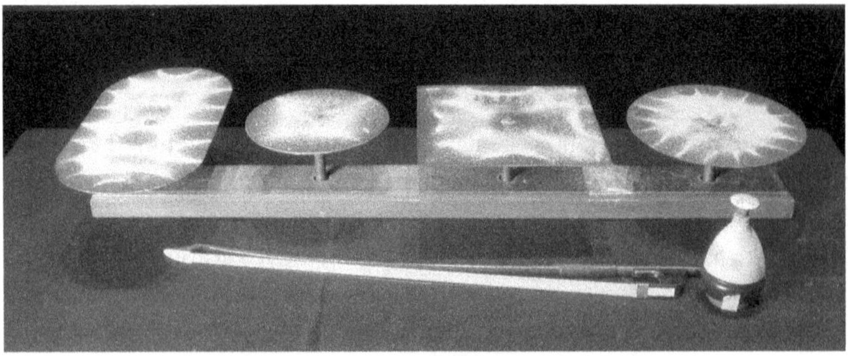

Chladni plates with sand and a bow

Since at least 1738, a musical instrument called a "Glassspiel," or "Verillon," had been popular in Europe. It was created by filling eighteen beer glasses with varying amounts of water, which would be struck with wooden mallets shaped like spoons. Benjamin Franklin was impressed by a verillon performance and created his own instrument, the "armonica" in 1762.

Franklin's armonica inspired several other instruments, including two created by Chladni, one called "Chladni's Euphonium," consisting of glass rods of different pitches. He also improved on the Hooke "musical cylinder" to produce another instrument, the "Clavicylinder," in 1799.

ANTONIO GAUDI (1852–1926)

The brilliant architect, Antonio Gaudi, is directly relevant to our discussion of multidimensional thinking since his architectural design was not based on mental thinking. The forms in his buildings evolve one out of the other in an endless metamorphosis and constant movement. Gaudi's buildings look more like organic limbs created in nature than objects created as a result of human thinking. For example, it is impossible to find two identical pillars in Park Güell, which Gaudi designed in Barcelona; each pillar has an individual role stemming from its unique position in the structure and the direction of forces flowing through it. The unique quality of his buildings demonstrates the sharp difference between the rational thinking of modern architects and the organic approach of this unique genius.

Gaudi is unique not only because of the unusual creative richness of his buildings. Just as he wasn't analytical in the area of form, he also used unique methods in engineering. Engineers use analytical methods to calculate the strength of constructive elements such as beams, pillars, and arches. Because the analytical method is based on simple, basic schemes, it forces a certain pattern of design on the architect. Nature's divine wisdom uses intelligence that does not depend on computers, and therefore is not limited in its selection of forms. In order to calculate the constructive strength of his structures, Gaudi conceived a method that gave his buildings one of their distinctive elements. He built inverted miniature models out of flexible sheets that were arranged according to an inner regularity and that express perfectly the flow of forces through them. After they had hardened, Gaudi inverted them and used them to design the final form of his buildings.

Some of Gaudi's well-known "organic" architecture

Johann Wolfgang von Goethe (1749–1832)

We know Goethe mostly from his immortal work *Faust.* Yet besides writing books and plays, Goethe was a great researcher of nature, who left his mark with his unique color theory and his work in botany. His approach to research was not analytical, as is the norm today, but intuitive—which makes it relevant to this book. Goethe belonged to the Rosicrucian association that was active in Europe during the sixteenth century. For the most part, this was a hidden spiritual group and its members worked in secrecy, away from the prying eyes of the outside world. Rudolf Steiner's development of Anthroposophy is an expansion of Rosicrucian theory adapted to modern times.

As a nature researcher, Goethe developed methods of observation that allowed him to discover the hidden regularity of the plant kingdom and to express this regularity in his descriptions. The most famous of these is his successful concept of an "archetypal plant" from which all the shapes of the species, growing through sprouting, blossoming, and withering, could be described. In 1771 he published his first collection of lyric poems; his novel, *The Sorrows of Young Werther,* in 1774; and in 1795, *Wilhelm Meister's Apprenticeship.* In 1810 his theory of colors and his botanical works were published and in 1830, *Faust.*

GEORGES IVANOVICH GURDJIEFF (1877–1949)

Gurdjieff was born in Alexandropol, Armenia, where he attended a normal school and additionally studied with his personal teacher, Father Borsch. Accompanied by a group of friends, "the truth seekers," he traveled throughout Central Asia, looking for lost knowledge. While traveling, he made contact with spiritual teachers from Sufi and other orders, looking for the meaning of life. His journeys reached their peak when he encountered a secret brotherhood called Sarmoung, whose exact location remains secret. This is where he received most of his instruction in sacred dancing, and apparently was sent back to worldly society to fulfill his destiny as a unique teacher of esoteric knowledge.

Gurdjieff started his life as a teacher in Moscow, and later moved to Essentuki, Constantinople, and Tbilisi, where he gathered small groups of disciples whom he wanted to prepare for their calling as carriers of the esoteric knowledge he brought. After a visit to the United States he finally settled down in France, where he established the Institute for the Harmonious Development of Man. There he developed a complete method of initiation, which he called The Fourth Way. This way, according to his testimony, existed throughout human history. At times it was revealed to the outside world in order to carry out a specific mission, and then disappeared to a hidden plane until its next mission. The Way includes meditative practice, "sacred movements" and dances, music, and learning the ideas that come from inner work. All these practices are meant to develop inner skills and raise pupils to a higher level of consciousness, allowing them to live life more fully and to understand life's inner meaning.

In 1924, following a severe car accident which almost cost him his life, Gurdjieff left his role as an active teacher of his groups of disciples and devoted time to recording his ideas in three volumes: *Beelzebub's Tales to His Grandson; Life Is Real Only Then, When "I Am"*; and *Meetings with Remarkable Men.*

The Fourth Way school continues its activity under the guidance of Gurdjieff's students, and teachers are sent from its headquarters in Paris to establish work groups throughout the world. Such a group began to operate in Israel in the early seventies, and it continues today, following the model of the center in Paris.

Georg Kühlewind (1924–2006)

A writer and a great thinker, Georg Kühlewind was born to Jewish parents in Hungary. He traveled frequently throughout Europe, the United States, and Australia, where he had many students who considered him to be a living teacher of spiritual science. Kühlewind had a doctorate in the natural sciences, and several patents in physical chemistry are registered under his name; yet his activity also spread to the fields of spiritual inquiry, driven by his strong desire to understand the human being, particularly concerning language and epistemology.

At the age of eighteen, Kühlewind first encountered the writings of Rudolf Steiner, and in 1958 he began walking his own independent path of practical knowledge according to the principles of spiritual science. In 1965, he began working with groups of students, integrating into his work additional principles from the worlds of Zen Buddhism and Christian esotericism. In 2004, he came to Israel to conduct a short workshop for students of spiritual science, and especially to lecture to a wide audience of teachers and educators about the subject that became his main interest in his later years—special children, or "star children" (*Sternkinder*). as he called them in his book of the same name.

Many of the ideas in this book are the fruit of our many conversations, empowered by his uncompromising quest to understand the human being and the meaning of existence. The rich materials expressed in his many books are a source of inspiration to students of modern spiritual science, who consider him an authentic representative of the esoteric path of initiation, one who speaks out of personal experience.

Kühlewind's works, translated into English and published by Lindisfarne Books, include: *Stages of Consciousness* (1984); *Becoming Aware of the Logos* (1985); *The Logos Structure of the World* (1986); *From Normal to Healthy* (1988); *The Life of the Soul* (1990); *Star Children* (2004); *Wilt Thou Be Made Whole?* (2008); and *The Light of the "I"* (2008).

BENOIT MANDELBROT (1924–) AND FRACTAL GEOMETRY

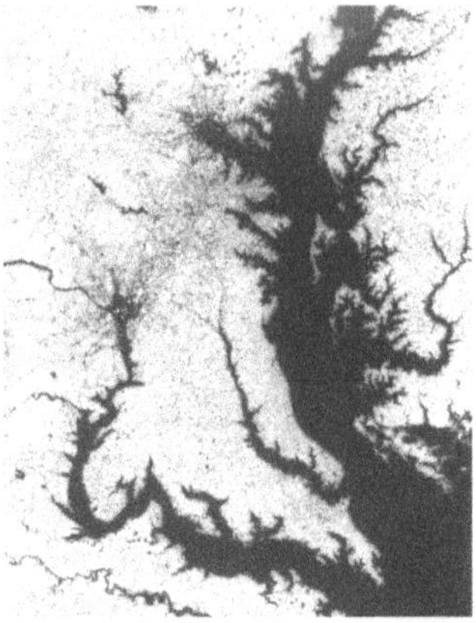

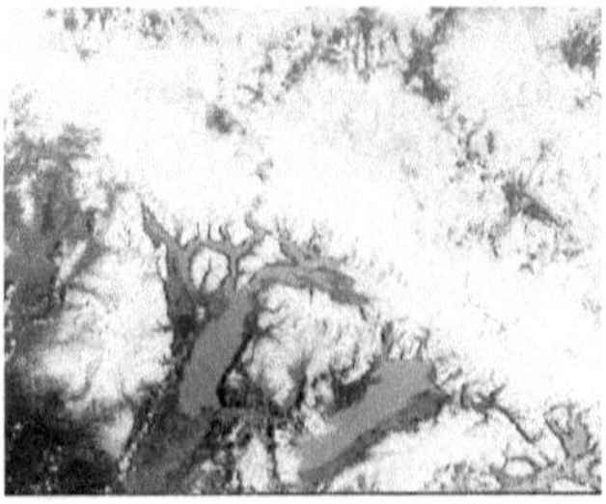

The Euclidean geometry we are familiar with deals with geometric relations in three dimensions; fractal geometry expresses additional qualities of sensory reality. The concepts of line, point, plane, and three-dimensional bodies are objective concepts that do not depend upon an observer. Benoit Mandelbrot, one of the pioneers of fractal geometry, researched qualities of objects in space that depend on the observer's point of view. From a distance, a ball of cotton threads would look like a dot with no dimension. From a shorter distance, it looks like a two-dimensional circle, and from even closer, like a three-dimensional ball. If we come even closer, we will see that this ball is composed of threads; every dot on the thread is defined on a one-dimensional axis. The thread itself is woven of three filaments, which in turn can also be taken apart, and so on. Mandelbrot created a new geometry, opposed to everything our inner logic tends to accept, in which dimensions are counted in fractions rather than whole numbers. This geometry can describe the merging and disintegration of processes; calculate how porous bodies are; and how rough two-dimensional surfaces are, among other things.

Mandelbrot discovered that by using simple manipulation it is possible to create an infinite variety of shapes that never repeat. The shapes are created by taking a certain numerical value, manipulating it in a given way, and using the result as the basic value for the next manipulation, and so on. Though the shapes never repeat, the similarity uniting the family group is evident. Mandelbrot called this property of the group its "self-similarity."

Fractal geometry is the only geometric system able to describe realities that otherwise appear chaotic, imbuing them with striking order.

The three river images (opposite) present similar characteristics despite their differences. Photographs taken from different heights tend to reveal forms so identical in shape that photo analysts sometimes have difficulties determining the height from which such a picture was taken.

The photograph to the right is from James Gleick's fascinating book *Chaos: Making a New Science*, showing computer-processed fractal landscapes. Enlarging any given square in the picture reveals a similar form pattern at every resolution.

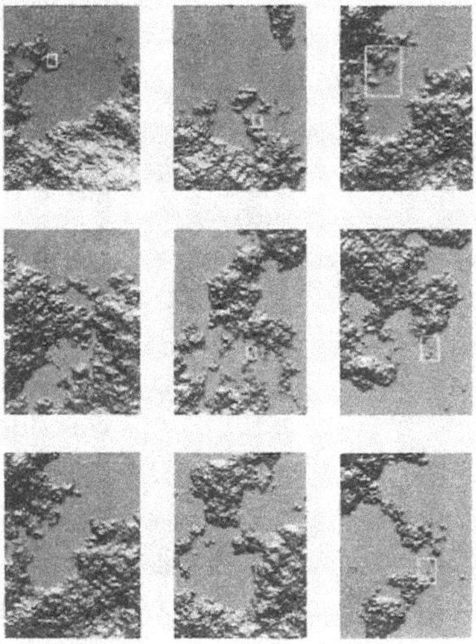

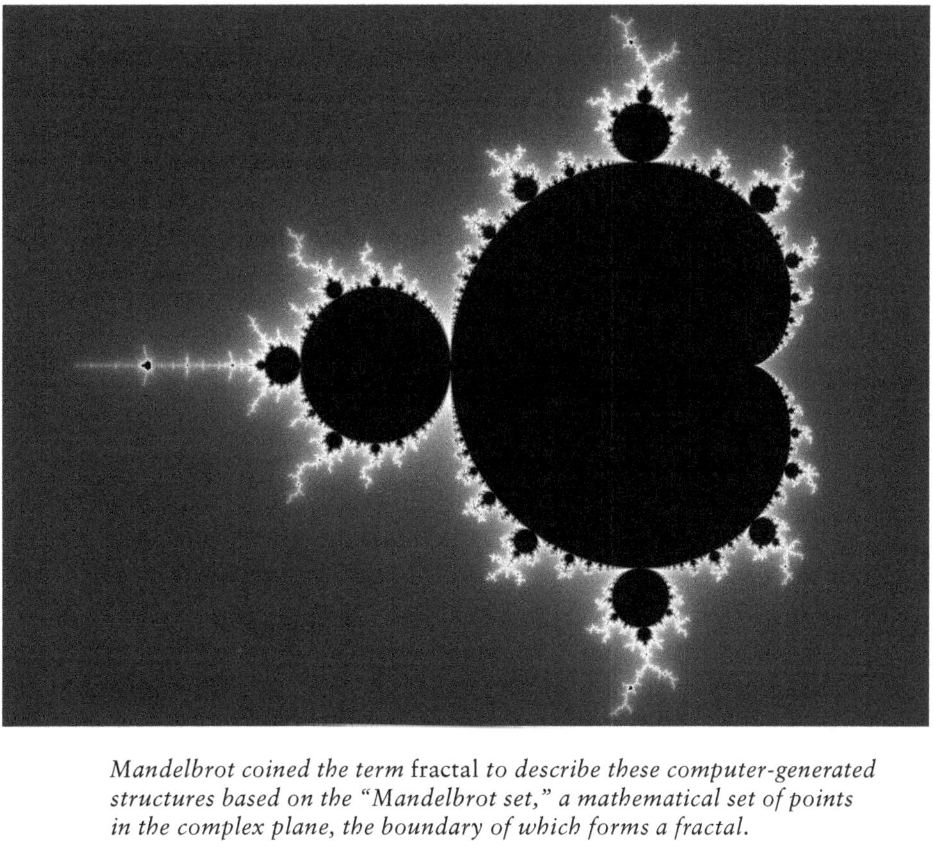

Mandelbrot coined the term fractal *to describe these computer-generated structures based on the "Mandelbrot set," a mathematical set of points in the complex plane, the boundary of which forms a fractal.*

JOHN NASH (1928–)

John Forbes Nash Jr. was born in West Virginia in 1928. At the age of twenty-one, as part of his interest in game-theory strategies, he wrote his first famous work, "Non-cooperative Games," introducing the concept of the "Nash equilibrium." His theory was later applied in economics and won him the Nobel Prize for Economics in 1994. Nash claimed that, of his many theories, this was one of the least important.

In 1948, Nash graduated from Princeton, where he was regarded as an exceptional genius who produced mathematical breakthroughs at a dazzling pace. Despite his arrogant and eccentric behavior, he was popular with teachers and students largely because of his unusual abilities in mathematics. In 1958, he experienced his first attack of schizophrenic paranoia, which lasted about twenty years. During this period, he made strange journeys between the United States and Europe, looking for refuge from his psychological problems. In 1970, his illness subsided after he started taking psychiatric drugs, allowing him to return to teaching.

Although the drug treatment helped him to function reasonably well with his family and friends, Nash was not satisfied. He claimed that his memory had been damaged, and that he could no longer breathe the "thin air of the ultra-logical planes," where he had previously spent many long hours of active thinking.

The Nobel Prize in 1994 brought him the international acclaim he had expected for many years, but he was unable to restore the amazing creative ability he had enjoyed before the disease. His major works are: "Equilibrium Points in n-Person Games" (*Proceedings of the National Academy of Sciences* 36, 1950); "The Bargaining Problem" (*Econometrica* 18, 1950); "A Simple Three-Person Poker Game" (1950); "Non-Cooperative Games" (*Annals of Mathematics* 54, 1951); and "Two-Person Cooperative Games" (*Econometrica* 21, 1953).

Rudolf Steiner (1861–1925)

Rudolf Steiner called his spiritual science "Anthroposophy," meaning wisdom of the human being; or, as he himself put it, "human consciousness." Steiner experienced spiritual visions from early childhood, and when he matured these became an abundant flow of revelations upon which he later drew to talk about the spiritual reality at the foundation of the phenomenal world.

Rudolf Steiner tried to construct his findings scientifically, and on the basis of criteria accessible to normal human understanding. Drawing on the scientific world, Steiner developed new forms of education, agriculture, medicine, mathematics, economy, art, and philosophy. In the course of his life as a teacher of humanity, he wrote about thirty books and delivered more than six thousand lectures to listeners all over Europe.

In 1924 he founded the General Anthroposophical Society, whose center was, and still is, the Goetheanum in Dornach, near Basel, Switzerland. Activity connected with the many branches of Anthroposophy is still managed from this center.

Among his better known books are: *The Philosophy of Spiritual Activity*, his philosophical creed, written in the spirit of late nineteenth-century philosophy; *How to Know Higher Worlds*, a practical guide on the path of anthroposophic initiation, a description of the components of the human being; *An Outline of Esoteric Science*, the development of creation, including the human being; *Cosmic Memory*, readings from the akashic record.

Unlike natural scientists, who consider the brain to be the repository of memory, Steiner points to the etheric sheath, the array of life forces that penetrate the human being, as the place where memory is embedded. By analogy, though on a much larger scale, cosmic memory also exists. In it, the history of universal reality is embedded forever. As a great initiate, Steiner was able to read the details of human and planetary evolution from cosmic memory and provide a rich historical panorama as a central part of anthroposophic spiritual science.

Besides public lectures, Steiner also maintained esoteric initiation activity for a smaller number of disciples. Some impression of what one may find in such courses can be found in books such as: *From the History and Content of the Esoteric School; Guidance in Esoteric Training;* and *A Way of Self Knowledge*, and in various lecture collections.

A common notion in anthroposophic circles nowadays is that the esoteric path of initiation enables anyone who is interested to achieve personal growth without the close attention of a teacher, since the knowledge contained in anthroposophic literature enables individuals to find their own way without personal assistance. The reality we see around us is not compatible with this opinion, and the weaknesses of experienced individuals who have traveled quite a way on the path of initiation by themselves are clearly evident, in my view. The importance of spiritual knowledge that flowed to humanity through this great teacher cannot be measured from the perspective of a few decades. According to Rudolf Steiner's own testimony, humanity will only learn to value this knowledge centuries after he will have left earthly existence.

The first Goetheanum, designed by Rudolf Steiner (above), was destroyed by fire December 31, 1922. Construction of the second Goetheanum (below), also designed by Steiner, began in 1924 and was largely complete by 1928.

Nikola Tesla (1856–1943)

Nikola Tesla was born in Smiljan, Croatia. In 1881, after he completed his studies at the University of Prague, he was working for the Budapest telegraph company and had a vision of an alternative-current motor flying at him from the sky. It was not only the AC motor itself, but the whole electrical system, supplying current to the entire network that appeared next to the motor.

In 1884, Tesla immigrated to the United States and started working for Thomas Edison, who, according to Tesla, exploited his talent and never paid him appropriately. George Westinghouse later hired him and helped the alternative current system he developed become the standard system in the United States and, later, all over the world.

According to his own testimony, Tesla had an unusual photographic memory and an ability to design his complex systems without using models or drawings. Besides this special gift, he was also haunted, until his seventeenth birthday, by nightmares in the form of flashes of light, which terrified him. These flashes of light were later turned to more creative directions, and the quality of his life vastly improved.

In addition to the alternating current system and engine, Tesla also developed wireless radio, and conducted preliminary experiments in radar, roentgen rays, and solar energy, and even conducted some experiments in nuclear fission.

Nikola Tesla's life ended at the age of eighty-seven in his quiet manor house, where he spent his time thinking and feeding the pigeons in his garden. Almost fifty years ago, Thomas Edison was credited as "the greatest inventor," whereas Tesla's genius has been barely recognized. Nevertheless, there are several modern scientists who are determined to realize some of his ideas, claiming that Tesla was far ahead of his time—and that what seemed at the time to be extravagant ideas could be realized today, when modern technologies are more available.

Appendix 3: Patents and Copyright

"At times, when the idea flies birdlike through the mind, one needs wisdom and power to hunt the bird."

"Every discovery comes into the world in its due time, and it does not come from a human source."

—Rabbi Nachman of Breslau

The thinking processes at the base of the creative process are the truly interesting part of this discussion; yet these days it is almost impossible to ignore the commercial aspect of the creative process—patents and copyright. I won't discuss the formal aspect of this issue—this was already done very well by my good friend Dr. Kfir Luzzatto in his book *The World of Patents* and by Danny Kronenberg in *A Guide for Registering and Using Patents*. The following provides a short description of the process of filing a patent application, along with thoughts on the essential principles of copyright protection.

Inventors have the option to edit their own patent requests. The patent registry publishes a manual that clearly sets out the rules. Still, editing the patent, and especially phrasing the claims at the end, is such a delicate matter that the inexperienced writer might find that even after one's beautifully edited request had been granted, the inventor still has no real protection.

Patent request generally includes several necessary chapters:

1. In the first chapter, the inventor defines the state of present knowledge in the field of the invention, pointing to the special need that he believes his invention addresses.
2. The second chapter briefly describes the invention.
3. The third chapter presents a list of the illustrations.
4. The fourth chapter, entailing a detailed description of the invention, accompanied by relevant illustrations.
5. Finally, the application concludes with the fifth chapter, which contains a set of claims that, in the broadest possible, defines

way the degree of protection the inventor wishes to include in the application.

Writing an application is as creative an act as any, and many elements described in previous chapters can be expressed here. The invention's main idea should be expressed in a way that is as archetypal as possible, in the spirit of the criteria mentioned in the chapter about the conceptual world. Though the invention is described using a process or product that is as concrete as possible, the description should express the fact that the request points at the new general principle proposed by the inventor.

The new principle should express the inventive step expressed in the new idea compared with the present state of knowledge. This takes us back to the question asked at the beginning of this book—what is a truly new idea? The term *inventive progress,* which appears in the patent registry's manual, is not defined, and I believe it has never been clearly defined. There are almost as many opinions about this term as there are patent attorneys, and this is not the place to try to settle this delicate matter. The decision about the invention's novelty is eventually left to the examiner's personal judgment.

What, then, is a patent? In the legal, formal sense, it is the right to prevent others from using the knowledge defined in the patent for a limited amount of time. At first this would appear to be selfish, since it seems that it is meant to help the inventor get rich quickly. And, yes, a patent request does hold the promise of unusual profits! Protected by the patent, the producer is immune to the forces of free competition, and can sell products at any price one chooses. Society pays a price for protecting those who wish only to make a fortune for themselves, and the deal may not seem worthwhile.

However, there is another reason for patent protection. The patent is a contractual agreement between the inventor and society; at the heart of it lies the understanding that inventors invest time and money in inventing something that society needs—an essential, declared criterion for granting a patent is "usefulness to society." Inventors are obligated to reveal the secrets of their inventions to the public in such a way that anyone reading the text and illustrations could reproduce the invention. The only reward society offers the inventor is a time-limited protection against free, unlicensed use of this information.

Great artists and inventors in the past never had this kind of protection; then again, they didn't need it. The great patrons of art and science were honored to support the progress of culture, and so inventors like Leonardo and artists like Michelangelo were strongly courted by wealthy and powerful families, the church, and the royal courts. No one at that time even thought of the revolutionary idea of copyright.

There still are vague traces of this approach in modern times. Government funds and philanthropic institutes generously support research facilities, arts, and technology; yet it is hard to imagine how the technological breakthroughs of our age could have materialized without the concept of intellectual property. Creative competition in society is well rewarded by paying royalties to inventors, who repay society with products and processes that promote well-being. It is true that a lot of energy is spent developing products that nobody really needs, but at the same time new means of learning, new medicines, and new recuperation and healing processes are invented, and their value to society is enormous.

Another claim that is sometimes made against the limiting principle of patent law is that the law entrusts "the powerful" with the ability to fortify their position, thereby creating social gaps that would not exist if everyone could use any knowledge freely. By this, people mean powerful corporations like DuPont or General Electric, which invest fortunes in developing new products and give their employees and shareholders a far more generous return than what workers in agriculture or industry make.

The theoretical argument, however, is eventually resolved in practice. Communist regimes have brought industry in the societies under their rule to crises whose dimensions appear only to grow with the years. It seems that society has learned its lesson, and the supposedly egalitarian approach of this failed system will not return.

Human evolution, like all evolution, is a struggle among unequal forces; the strong win at the expense of the weak. Yet the supreme intelligence that directs reality is not the limited, personal intelligence of human society. What seems like sorrow and suffering from a human perspective is decided upon by more intelligent cosmic principles as the chief means of advancing and improving the human species and the living world around us. The human species can find the empathy needed to eradicate ignorance and fight poverty, but the mechanistic approach that demands equality for all, at any price, has already taken a heavy toll in damage to industry and has discouraged personal initiative everywhere it was applied. Armed with the lessons of the past, we must raise our gaze higher and find a better way to handle social injustice than the elimination of free competition.

Giving a reasonable protection—the patent laws—to successful inventors and creators is not really unjust. Social welfare should not be ignored, of course, but at the same time we have to tolerate a certain degree of apparent "injustice" when talking about possessions and material achievements. The genius of nature may also be considered "unjust," encouraging the strongest as the means of developing new species. Justice should not be automatic or mechanical, but should be flexible by broadly considering conflicts, pain, and suffering as necessary means for evolution.

Yet those who oppose free initiative, which allows inventors proper compensation for their work, have not disappeared with the demise of the communist system. A new anarchist approach now appears, disguised as a war against the monopolistic forces of the market. The appearance of the Internet has brought about a gradual turn in modern public opinion, increasing the voices that call for putting all knowledge at the disposal of the public free of charge. Some support copying computer software and breaching the copyrights of musical and visual presentations; others object to protecting industrial companies' logo rights, claiming that the production takes place in weak countries and exploits the poor, local populations. The subject is very complex, and such claims are not groundless; yet society, advancing in rapid steps, must intelligently adapt itself to changing times. The thinking in the responsible institutions does not seem to have extended very far in this area, and is quite tardy in providing solutions to the new conditions that constantly appear before our eyes.

The many lawsuits in the area of copyright at times bring about the collapse of companies that invested their fortune in new products or processes. The cost of development is usually added to the cost of production, with the company expecting a full return. Without effective legal protection, a competitor can produce and sell the product for a lower price, commercially finishing off the developing company. This behavior is unacceptable in the countries united under international treaty, but the biggest pirates are the heads of states that intentionally turn a blind eye to copyright breaches in their jurisdiction. These countries care only about creating new workplaces and advancing their own national economies, and in the meantime hurt research and development initiatives, which rely on proper rewards for their investment. There is no good and evil in economic war; there are only those motivated by narrow, local considerations and those trying to base the global economy on saner principles to prevent it from sinking into complete anarchy.

Bibliography

Alfassa, Mirra (The Mother). *Words of the Mother.* Pondicherry: Sri Aurobindo Ashram Trust, 2004.

——. *The Sunlit Path.* Pondicherry: Sri Aurobindo Ashram Trust, 1989.

Ashlag, Rabbi Yehuda. *Talmud of the Ten Spheres (Sephirot).* Bnei Brak, Israel: M Klarr, *n.d.*

Aurobindo Sri. *The Life Divine.* Pondicherry: Sri Aurobindo Ashram Trust, 1949.

——. *Savitri: A Legend and a Symbol.* Pondicherry: Sri Aurobindo Ashram Trust, 1995.

——. *The Synthesis of Yoga.* Pondicherry: Sri Aurobindo Ashram Trust, 1999.

——. *Sri Aurobindo on Himself.* Pondicherry: Sri Aurobindo Ashram Trust, 1972.

Chernobelsky, Alexander. *Systematic Inventive Thinking and Technical Problem Solving.* Israel: Cronenberg Press (1997).

De Bono, Edward. *Six Thinking Hats.* New York: Little, Brown and Co., 1985.

——. *Teach your Child How to Think.* New York: Penguin, 1992.

Doczi, Gyorgy. *The Power of Limits: Proportional Harmonies in Nature, Art, and Architecture.* Boston: Shambhala, 1981.

Einstein, Albert. *The New Quotable Einstein.* Princeton, NJ: Princeton University Press, 2005.

Gardner, Howard. *Art, Mind, and Brain: A Cognitive Approach to Creativity.* New York: Basic Books, 1982.

Gershon, Michael. *The Second Brain: A Groundbreaking New Understanding of Nervous Disorders of the Stomach and Intestine.* New York: HarperCollins, 1998.

Gibran, Kahlil. *The Wanderer.* New York: Knopf, 1995.

Goleman, Daniel. *Emotional Intelligence: Why It Can Matter More than IQ.* 10th Anniversary Edition. New York: Bantam, 2005.

Gurdjieff, George Ivanovich. *Beelzebub's Tales to His Grandson.* London: Routledge & Kegan Paul, 1950.

——. *Gurdjieff parle à ses élèves.* France: Stock/Monde ouvert, 1973.

——. *In Search of the Miraculous.* London: Routledge & Kegan Paul, 1950.

Kronenberg, Danny. *A Guide for Registering and Using Patents.* Tel Aviv: Professional Literature, 1995.

Kühlewind, Georg, *From Normal to Healthy: Paths to the Liberation of Consciousness.* Great Barrington, MA.: Lindisfarne Press, 1988.

——. *Star Children: Understanding Children Who Set Us Special Tasks and Challenges.* London: Temple Lodge, 2004.

Luzzatto, Rabbi Haim. *The Way of God.* Jerusalem: Feldheim Books, 1966.

Luzzato, Dr. Kfir. *The World of Patents.* Israel: Globes Press, 2002.

Ouspensky, Peter D. *In Search of the Miraculous.* London: Routledge and Kegan Paul, 1950.

Perkins, David. *Archimedes' Bathtub: The Art and Logic of Breakthrough Thinking.* New York: W. W. Norton, 2000.

Rumi, Jalal al-Din, trans. Coleman Barks. *The Essential Rumi.* San Francisco: Harper, 1995.

Scaligero, Massimo. *The Light (La Luce): An Introduction to Creative Imagination.* Great Barrington, MA.: Lindisfarne Books, 2001.

Segal, William C. *Opening: Collected Writings of William Segal, 1985–1997.* New York: Continuum, 1999.

Steiner, Rudolf. *Evolution in the Aspect of Realities.* Blauvelt, NY: Garber Communications, 1989.

——. *How to Know Higher Worlds: A Modern Path of Initiation.* Hudson, NY: Anthroposophic Press, 1994.

——. *Intuitive Thinking as a Spiritual Path: A Philosophy of Freedom.* Hudson, NY: Anthroposophic Press, 1995.

——. *An Outline of Esoteric Science.* Great Barrington, MA: Anthroposophic Press, 1997.

——. *Self-Transformation.* London: Rudolf Steiner Press, 1995.

——. *The Stages of Higher Knowledge: Imagination, Inspiration, Intuition.* Great Barrington, MA: SteinerBooks, 2009.

——. *Start Now! A Book of Soul and Spiritual Exercises.* Great Barrington, MA: SteinerBooks, 2004.

——.*Verses and Meditations.* London: Rudolf Steiner Press, 1993.

Yanai, Zvi. "Living with Uncertainty," *Thoughts.* (Tel Aviv Hebrew periodical).

——. and Yadin Dudai. *The Eternal Search: Conversations with Scientists.* Tel Aviv: Am Oved Press, 2000.

www.ingramcontent.com/pod-product-compliance
Lightning Source LLC
Chambersburg PA
CBHW060129170426
43198CB00010B/1097
* 9 7 8 1 5 8 4 2 0 0 8 1 9 *